A Warrior *of the* People

Also by Joe Starita

"I Am a Man":
Chief Standing Bear's Journey for Justice

The Dull Knifes of Pine Ridge:
A Lakota Odyssey

A Warrior
of the People

∨∨∨

How Susan La Flesche Overcame

Racial and Gender Inequality to Become

America's First Indian Doctor

∧∧∧

Joe Starita

St. Martin's Press ⚇ New York

www.stmartins.com

The Library of Congress Cataloging-in-Publication Data is
available upon request.

ISBN 978-1-250-08534-4 (hardcover)
ISBN 978-1-250-08535-1 (e-book)

Our books may be purchased in bulk for promotional,
educational, or business use. Please contact your local
bookseller or the Macmillan Corporate and Premium Sales
Department at 1-800-221-7945, extension 5442, or by e-mail
at MacmillanSpecialMarkets@macmillan.com.

First Edition: November 2016

10 9 8 7 6 5 4 3 2

For all the women warriors——

past, present, and future

A nation is not conquered

until the hearts of its women are on the ground.

—CHEYENNE PROVERB

Contents

Acknowledgments

In the end, all books are collaborative ventures and this one is no exception. It benefited immensely from a diligent army of people who collectively blended their diverse talents, focus, and energy to make this book possible. My gratitude goes to researchers extraordinaire Kaci Nash, with the University of Nebraska Center for Great Plains Studies; Donzella Maupin and Andreese Scott, with Hampton University Archives; and librarian Steve Rice at the Connecticut State Library. To friends and colleagues Tim Anderson, Kathy Christensen, and Monica Norby, whose good ears, instincts, and common sense kept the narrative on track. To Patricia Lambardi, whose patient listening on cold winter days and incisive comments afterward improved the manuscript in ways both large and small. To Astrid Munn, whose initial research and concise, timely summaries proved invaluable, and John Mangan, for his extensive knowledge of Omaha Reservation geography. To Jane Johnson, Margaret Johnson, Carolyn Johnson, Kathleen Diddock, and Chris Conn—direct La Flesche family descendants whose cooperation and generosity never ended. To Vida Stabler, Lisa Drum, and Taylor Keen—citizens of the Omaha Nation with a vast knowledge of tribal history, culture, and traditions. To Judi gaiashkibos, a special friend whose numerous suggestions and wise counsel were always on the money.

To agent Jonathan Lyons, for his passionate encouragement in the early going, and to editor Daniela Rapp at St. Martin's Press, for her steady hand and superb editorial suggestions in the later stages.

Finally, there are three people whose contributions to this project can hardly be overstated. John Wunder, an eminent historian specializing in the American West, did his part to maintain balance, perspective, and accuracy throughout the narrative. Christine Lesiak, whose documentary on the same subject unfolded at the same time as the book, was—and is—a constant source of inspiration. And without the unflagging energy, sharp eye, day-to-day dedication, and overall talents of Roger Holmes, this story would have been greatly diminished.

Author's Note

Throughout this story, I have tried to capture Susan La Flesche in all her emotional and human complexity—from the innocent joy of childhood, the devotion to her father, and the anxiety of leaving behind a beloved homeland for a New Jersey boarding school to the crushing loss of an early love, the stress of medical school, the fear of dying alone an old maid, the anxiety of searching for a desperately sick girl on the frozen prairie, and the pain of coping with a husband's death.

In a number of instances, her inner thoughts, her point of view, and what she was thinking and feeling at certain moments are all woven into the narrative, often without direct attribution.

These moments when Susan's inner thoughts and private reflections occur in the story are all distilled from an exhaustive examination of the treasure trove of primary source documents she left behind. Specifically, her private thoughts and feelings derive directly from hundreds of pages of her personal diary, scores of richly detailed letters to family and friends, and transcripts from the many editorials she wrote and speeches she gave.

For example, in graduation remarks she gave at Hampton, Virginia, in 1892—a speech entitled "My Work as Physician Among my People"—Susan gave an exceptionally detailed account of her search for and treatment of a fourteen-year-old girl dying of tuberculosis. In the narrative, I borrow heavily from her speech in reconstructing this scene, but I do not cite it in the text so as not to interrupt the narrative flow. It is, however, cited in the end-notes section of this book and in the bibliography, along with all other documents used as the building blocks for this story.

Taken collectively over the arc of her life, these documents provide a rich, intimate, fact-based portrait of a complex woman who often revealed herself in the full light of what it means to be human.

A Warrior *of the* People

1
vvv
The Arrow

It's five A.M. on a midwinter morning, the mercury stuck at twenty below. Overhead, a canopy of constellations spills across the clean winter sky, the quarter moon a slim lantern hanging above the vast, black, desolate prairie.

She's walking to the barn, through the snow, layered in muffs, mittens, and scarves. Still, her ears are numb, her face frozen, her breathing labored.

She steps inside the barn, carefully placing a small black bag on the buggy seat. For a time, if it were less than a mile, she would just walk. Then she took to slinging the black leather bag across her saddle, making house calls on horseback. But bouncing across the rugged terrain took its toll on the glass bottles and instruments, so she eventually bought a buggy, bought her own team.

Inside, her two favorite horses wait impatiently, snorting thick clouds of steam into the ice-locker air. She grabs their harness, hitches them to the buggy, guides them out of the barn. Then she climbs in and gets her chocolate mares, Pat and Pudge, heading in the right direction, their ghostly white vapor trails hanging in the frigid blackness.

It's early January 1892, a month her people call When the Snow Drifts into the Tents. The woman in the buggy, the one lashing her team to move faster, is a small, frail twenty-six-year-old, a devout Christian who also knows her people's traditional songs, dances, customs, and language, a woman who just recently acquired 1,244 patients scattered across 1,350 square miles of open prairie now blanketed in two feet of snow—a homeland of sloping hills, rolling ranch land, gullies, ravines, wooded creek banks, flood-plains, and few roads.

The air crushes her face, stings her ears. She pulls a thick buf-falo robe over her shoulders to buffer the subzero winds, lashing the horses' flanks again and again until the buggy picks up the pace, its wheels moving over one ridge and then another, through deep drifts covering the remote hillsides of northeast Nebraska.

In the darkness they keep moving, keep going, and all the while, over and over, her mind keeps drifting to the same recur-ring thought:

Can I find her?

Will I get there in time?

They were known as the Omaha–*Umo*^{n}*'ho*^{n}. In the language of her people, it meant "against the current" or "upstream," and their Sa-cred Legend, their creation story, said the Omaha had emerged long ago from a region far to the east, a region of dense woods and great bodies of water.

"In the beginning the people were in water. They opened their eyes but they could see nothing. . . . As they came forth from the water they were naked and without shame."

In the beginning, in their eastern homeland near the Ohio River, the Omaha encountered many problems. Having emerged naked from the water, they were cold and wet and hungry, and so— meticulously and methodically—they began to look for solutions, and by and by, they found them: clothing, fire, stone knives, arrows, iron, dogs. Over time, they emerged as a practical people, a people who craved progress, who time and time again looked to conquer hardship and inconvenience with a straightforward determination, with their own ingenuity and technological innovations.

Century after century, perhaps beginning as far east as the Great Lakes, the Omaha followed a mosaic of waterways—first to the west and southwest down the Ohio and then west and northwest up the Missouri. By the middle decades of the eighteenth century, they occupied large swaths of land in northeast Nebraska and northwest Iowa, where they eventually established permanent villages along the banks of America's longest river.

In their Missouri River settlements, the Omaha lived in both igloo-shaped earth lodges and buffalo-hide tipis. Their village was divided into ten clans, and each of the kinship clans had a specific duty when it came to the tribe's most important event: the spring planting ceremonies. Each spring, usually by the middle of May, the women in the village flocked to the fields along the floodplain and began the ritual corn planting, seven kernels to a hill. Soon, varieties of beans, squash, and pumpkins also found their way into the fertile soil.

This was her land, their land, the land of her people, and now she was riding across it in the dark and bitter cold in the month When the Snow Drifts into the Tents. Below the snow lay the prairie, an endless carpet of grass that had nurtured herds of buffalo once estimated at more than forty million. Her people believed the buffalo had been a gift from Wakonda, and the great beasts had helped sustain their way of life for several centuries. But now, as the nineteenth century wound down, the endless wild herds—slaughtered at first for traders, then by railroad mercenaries and sportsmen, and finally as an instrument of government policy—had been reduced to fewer than a thousand, reduced to near extinction.

But her people were still there, still living on their prairie homeland, where many had eventually come to learn a harsh lesson of life on the American Great Plains: Adapt—or perish.

In late June, when the crops had taken root and begun to mature, the entire village broke camp, fanning out across the western plains for the annual buffalo hunt, a critical time to lay in a good supply of winter meat, a plentiful stock of hides. By late August— the month When the Elk Bellow—the Omaha were on the lookout for a sign, for something blossoming on the endless plains outside their tipi village: the prairie goldenrod. Year after year, this had been the signal to tear down the tipis, pack up, and head back to their Missouri River homeland, where abundant fields of ripened corn, beans, squash, and pumpkins were now ready for harvest.

For the women in the village of the Upstream People, their many jobs and tasks had one ultimate objective: to preserve and conserve life. But that life was often hard, a ritualized cycle of physical labor the tribe depended upon to stay in sync. Season after season, year after year, it was women who prepared the fields, planted the seeds, harvested the crops, tanned hides, lugged water, gathered wood, maintained the tipi, collected wild plants and herbs, cut buffalo meat into strips, cooked food, quilted, sewed, bore children, and raised the family.

Omaha women—like many others in tribal encampments scattered across the Great Plains—commanded positions of great respect within the social fabric of the village and held a good deal of power within the tribe. Over time, men and women acquired an equal standing within the delicately balanced rhythm of Omaha tribal life.

In their traditional villages, men did not look down on women or treat them as inferior. If a task proved too difficult physically, the husband would often help out. And before making any important change or doing anything that would affect the family, the husband first consulted his wife.

In 1869, seventeen years after publication of *Uncle Tom's Cabin,* Harriet Beecher Stowe offered a contrasting view of the relationship between men and women, a view she saw as commonplace for traditional wives in nineteenth-century mainstream America. "The position of a married woman," she wrote, ". . . is, in many respects, precisely similar to that of the negro slave. She can make no contract and hold no property; whatever she inherits or earns becomes at that moment the property of her husband. . . . Though he acquired a fortune through her, or though she earn a fortune through her talents, he is sole master of it, and she cannot draw a penny at all. . . . In the English common law a married woman is nothing at all. She passes out of legal existence."

Among the Omaha, it was women who managed all household affairs and who owned the lodge and all its contents. They were free to marry whomever they wished, could reject parental suggestions, and had the power to divorce. If a woman decided to end a marriage, she often placed all of her husband's belongings outside the lodge, an unmistakable sign that their union had ended.

From early on, young girls were never left unprotected. They were not allowed to go far from the lodge unless accompanied by an adult. And in many Indian tribes, a girl's first menstruation often was an important event, something sacred, something to be celebrated—an honor recognizing her passage into womanhood, forever binding her to the fertility of Mother Earth. Some tribes also believed that menstruating women were spiritual beings so powerful they could be called upon for enlightenment, for guidance, for advice. Sometimes they left their homes during the heaviest four days of the cycle and stayed in menstrual huts with other women, engaged in lively discussions across a variety of subjects, often about their children.

Among the Omaha, children were sacred and there were ceremonies celebrating the arrival of a newborn. The people did not believe children were born with original sin or that they were even yet members of the tribe. Instead, they believed babies were living things who had entered the cosmos, joining all other living things. So on the eighth day, a priest conducted a ceremony welcoming the baby into the universe. Soon the baby had a pair of new moccasins, with a small hole cut into the sole of one of them. This was done so if a messenger from the spirit world, where the dead reside, should ever come for the child, the child could simply say: "I cannot go on a journey—my moccasins are worn out!"

The Omaha held a second ceremony once the child could walk, a ceremony that established the child as a distinct person attached to a specific clan with a recognized place in the tribe, a ceremony designed to give the child strength, identity, and self-discipline. In the Turning the Child Ceremony, the mother walked her child to a sacred tent, its entrance facing east, a fire burning in the middle.

"Venerable man!" the mother called out to the priest. "I desire my child to wear moccasins. . . . I desire my child to walk long upon the earth."

Then she dropped her child's hand and the child entered the tent alone. The priest guided the child toward the fireplace, saying: "I speak to you that you may be strong. You shall live long and your eyes shall be satisfied with many good things." The priest then lifted the child by the shoulders and, facing east, turned the child completely around, repeating his words until the child had faced all four directions. The ceremony ended when the priest put the new moccasins on the feet of the child. The priest then made the child take four steps, symbolizing the journey to a long life.

Throughout the long journey of the Omaha people, as far back as anyone could remember—whether encamped in forests, along shorelines, or by riverbanks, in summer or winter, in tipis or earth lodges, hunting or farming—there was often a recurring question, a question that formed part of their identity, a question that seemed to be deeply embedded in the Omaha's cultural lifeblood. It's a question that had sprung from their Sacred Legend, one that had been asked over and over:

What shall we do to help ourselves?
How shall we better ourselves?

The bones in her face and ears ached from knifing through the numbing air. They'd gone three miles but had another three to go, maybe more, the horses pounding up steep, snowy hills, pounding down the back side, snorting heavily, clouds of steam littering the air.

The darkness had started to fade a little now, the snow on the distant hills faintly blossoming in the soft winter light.

She stood up in the buggy, scoured the prairie in the dim dawn, looking for a solitary silhouette, looking for an outline perched on the distant horizon. But she couldn't see it, so she sat back down and whipped her team, yelling at them to go, to keep moving.

She has to make it. She has to find the one-room cabin somewhere on this frozen winter prairie. Though years apart, she and the young girl inside had gone to the same school—the same normal and agricultural college in Virginia, where after the great war they had sent the sons and daughters of black people and the sons and daughters of red people to learn how to become more like white people.

She can't let the girl down. She can't let all the others down, the ones who pushed so hard, all the time, to get her papers filed, her payments made, her books and clothes and housing and train fare taken care of. She can't let them down. But most of all, she can't dishonor his memory.

She cannot let her father down.

Their Virginia school was about 130 miles from Monticello, home of the third president of the United States, a restless, thoughtful, complex philosopher, lawyer, architect, and amateur scientist who had long harbored dreams of expanding the fledgling nation's borders to the Missouri River—and far beyond.

In Jefferson's view of democracy, the lands between the Mississippi and the Rockies, which the Louisiana Purchase had just made available, would become a bedrock of educated citizen-farmers, men and women who would create a new world order, who would become the foundation for a stable, prosperous, industrious, moral America.

So it wasn't long before her people—and many other tribal people long braided into the geographic fabric of the Great Plains—began to see the pool of fur traders, explorers, and adventurers start to expand. And with it came more and more government agents, more soldiers and peace parleys, and more and more treaties gobbling up more and more of the original native lands.

Francis La Flesche, the nation's first Indian ethnographer, would later note a feeling that was beginning to spread among the tribal villages scattered between the great rivers and mountains:

"The white people speak of the country at this period as 'a wilderness,' as though it was an empty tract without human interest or history. To us Indians it was as clearly defined as it is to-day; we knew the boundaries of tribal lands, those of our friends and those of our foes; we were familiar with every stream, the contour of every hill, and each peculiar feature of the landscape had its tradition. It was our home, the scene of our history, and we loved it as our country."

But by and by, the old way of life began to disappear—and in some years, so did the Omaha. The bustling fur trade up and down the Missouri, linking St. Louis with the Upstream People, had introduced something the Omaha could not fight, could not overcome, were helpless against.

By the time Lewis and Clark arrived in the late summer of 1804, wave after wave of epidemics had taken a toll, none more fearsome than the smallpox epidemic of 1800–1801. Sealed inside their earth-lodge homes, often living in three-generational units, the once robust, healthy people had no resistance to, no immunity from, the rapid, fatal spread of the disease, a disease that sometimes claimed entire families in a single week. By the time the disease had run its course, it was believed that more than half of the Omaha Tribe had died of smallpox.

In one form or another, these diseases would continue to stalk the people throughout the nineteenth century and beyond.

For the Omaha and all the others, the opening years and the opening decades of the nineteenth century all seemed to get progressively worse, step by step. For many of those years, the Upstream People were led by Big Elk, a chief of considerable strength, wisdom, courage, and insight. Among his people, Big Elk was revered for his visionary powers, for a unique ability to look down the road and foretell what the future might bring. And more and more as the decades wore on, as he saw more and more of the old way of life disappearing, his frustration and despair began to mount.

"I am like a large prairie wolf," he said, "running about over these barren prairies, in search of something to eat, with his head up, anxiously listening to hear some of his fellows howl, that he may dart off towards them, hoping to find a friend who has a bone to divide."

In 1837, as a guest of the U.S. government, Big Elk visited Washington, D.C.

Like those who had gone before him and the many chiefs who would follow, Big Elk returned from the urban East Coast to the rural plains of Nebraska a profoundly changed man.

With his own eyes, he had seen the flood of whites, in numbers unimaginable. He had seen their cities, their bustling stores and markets, their shops and schools, their government buildings and houses, their neighborhoods and neatly laid-out streets.

When he returned, the shaken chief, who had participated in some of the early treaty sessions, called the Omaha people together and told them of his trip east:

"My chiefs, braves, and young men, I have just returned from a visit to a far-off country toward the rising sun, and I have seen many strange things. I bring to you news which it saddens my heart to think of. There is a coming flood which will soon reach us, and I advise you to prepare for it. Soon the animals which Wakonda has given us for sustenance will disappear beneath this flood to return no more, and it will be very hard for you. Look at me; you see I am advanced in age; I am near the grave. I can no longer think for you and lead you as in my younger days. You must think for yourselves what will be best for your welfare. I tell you this that you may be prepared for the coming change. . . . Speak kindly to one another; do what you can to help each other, even in the troubles with the coming tide."

More and more, Big Elk began to tell his people that the old way of life was doomed, that they could not continue to walk down that road. He told them things many did not want to hear, that they would have to change. That they would have to begin to try to understand the ways of the whites, to embrace them, to integrate some of the new ways into the old ones.

To adapt—or perish.

Before his death in 1853, Big Elk, the third member of his family to lead the tribe, faced a difficult decision: Who would succeed him as chief of the Omaha?

He knew he needed someone whose vision was compatible with his own. He knew he needed someone with strength and integrity. Someone who could begin to assimilate the Omaha into the new world order.

He needed someone like Joseph La Flesche.

Born about 1818 in northeast Nebraska, the son of a French fur trader and an Indian mother, Joseph La Flesche grew up among a new subgroup of mixed-blood children—children who emerged from the bustling trading post culture clustered along the region's rivers, especially the Missouri.

As the nineteenth century unfolded, as more and more outside pressures threatened their shrinking world, the Indians needed weapons—guns—to ward off the threats and to hunt the very animals whose furs could be bartered for those guns. So the fur-trading posts became key centers of commerce linking the white and Indian worlds, as well as white fur traders and Indian women. Over time, their mixed-blood offspring, often with French sur-names, began to populate the trading posts and eventually integrate themselves into business ventures, tribal affairs, and occasionally leadership positions within the tribes.

Even by mixed-blood standards, the young Joseph La Flesche lived a complex life, bouncing from one Indian village to another, observing different tribal traditions and customs, absorbing different cultures and languages. By an early age, he spoke Pawnee, Dakota, Otoe, Ioway, Omaha, and French. He also spent a good deal of time hunting and traveling with his French fur trader father, including several long trips down the Missouri to St. Louis, all of which afforded him a worldview uncommon to many others in that area, in that era. He paid close attention to the two different worlds. And he saw many things he would long remember.

Eventually, Joseph settled down and settled in with his Omaha relatives, and as a young man he took a job working at one of Peter Sarpy's thriving trading posts just south of Omaha. At the height of the fur trade, these posts teemed with all manner of activity and characters. It was here, in the spring of 1833, that the post's workers could have encountered the German explorer Maximilian, Prince of Wied, and his Swiss artist companion, Karl Bodmer, who had embarked on a twenty-five-hundred-mile trek by steam and keelboat up the Missouri to observe, study, and document—with journals and paintings—the colorful American Indians of the Upper Missouri.

And it was also at Sarpy's trading post where Joseph La Flesche met Mary Gale, an engaging mixed-blood daughter of an energetic, strong-willed Ioway Indian and a U.S. Army surgeon, one of the first white doctors west of the Mississippi. Several years after her doctor husband died, Mary's mother married Sarpy, so Mary ended up spending much of her childhood at the trading post where Joseph worked.

A number of years before meeting his wife, Joseph had begun to closely observe the customs of the Omaha, to absorb the age-old traditions, to carefully study the ancient rites and rituals. He also had made a conscious habit of cultivating friendships among the Omaha elders, of listening intently to their accounts of traditional ceremonies, of trying to understand exactly how the fabric of Omaha culture knit together—and what it might take to alter, to rearrange, some of the patterns of the tribe's cultural quilt.

During all of his visits to the other tribes, throughout the long riverboat journeys to St. Louis with his father, in all he had seen and heard around the trading posts, Joseph had come to an increasingly unshakable conclusion: Soon, the overwhelming power and presence of the white man would suffocate his people, kill the old way of life once and for all. So if their people were to survive, a new one must be forged from the scrap heap of buffalo bones, land loss, ambitious settlers, Sioux war parties, devastating disease, and the white man's whiskey. Something must occur, a fundamental shift in cultural values, for the Upstream People to overcome the powerful sense of doom and hopelessness that had begun to settle in and spread through village life.

In 1846, Joseph La Flesche and Mary Gale became husband and wife. By then, Joseph's stock—his thoughtfulness, strength, and respectful commitment to learning tribal culture from the elders— had risen a great deal within the Omaha village, nowhere more so than with the one who mattered most.

Big Elk had taken a liking to Joseph. He trusted him, believed that the younger man had a vision aligned with his own and understood that the flood would sweep them all away if they didn't compromise, if they didn't begin to assimilate. So the powerful, respected chief of the Omaha increasingly took him under his wing and began to signal to others that Joseph would one day succeed him. Although the old chief already had a son, who, based on long-standing Omaha tradition, should succeed his father, the boy was young and sickly.

While the boy was still alive, Big Elk adopted Joseph, suggesting in word and deed that it would be Joseph who succeeded him as the Omaha's new chief. About two years after the wedding of Joseph and Mary, Big Elk performed a traditional Pipe Dance Ceremony honoring Mary. Shortly after, a public crier proclaimed to the village that Joseph was now the chief's eldest son and would succeed him. Not long after, Big Elk arranged to have Joseph placed in his own kinship clan—not his mother's, which was the age-old custom. So step by step, the old chief methodically arranged passage for the younger man to succeed him, to carry out his vision. That younger man, according to the Omaha's 1848 tribal census, was now officially listed as *E-sta-mah-za*—Iron Eye.

One afternoon in 1853, while the people were having a feast, Big Elk went out hunting and killed a deer. A few hours later, he came down with a fever. Big Elk sent for Iron Eye. "My son," Big Elk said, "give me some medicine." Iron Eye sent a runner to Belle-vue for medicine, but it was a three-day journey, too long for the gravely ill chief. Feeling the end was near, the old chief again called for Iron Eye. "My son, I give you all my papers from Washington, and I make you head chief," he told the younger man. "You will occupy my place." Shortly after the old man chief died, *E-sta-mah-za* became one of the Omaha Tribe's two principal chiefs. From that time on, the last recognized chief of the Up-stream People struggled for much of his adult life with the central issues that had first brought him into Big Elk's fold:

How could he, their new chief, find the right balance between who they were then and who they had always been—*and* who they must now become? How could they become white enough to sur-vive in the new world order, but red enough to retain a cultural identity, a strong sense of who the Omaha were? How could they learn to walk the red and white roads simultaneously?

For many years, there was much he had come to admire about white culture, and he was not shy about proclaiming it as the new chief of the tribe.

"The white man looks into the future and sees what is good," he told his people. "That is what the Indian is doing. He looks into the future and sees his only chance is to become as the white man."

That sentiment was not shared by everyone in the tribe, and it eventually led to a bitter division within the Omaha, a conflict over accepting new ways or embracing old ones, a split that pitted the more liberal "Young Men's Party" against the older conservatives.

But not long after becoming chief, Joseph La Flesche wasted little time in leading by example—in showing the tribe the path he believed would lead to the survival of the Omaha, the same one he and Big Elk had often discussed.

In short order, he and members of the Young Men's Party cut hundreds of logs and hauled them to a sawmill. Then their chief hired white carpenters to build him a large, two-story wood-frame house, thought to be the first Indian wood-frame house west of the Missouri. The others in his camp soon followed suit, building smaller wood homes for their families. Next, La Flesche began laying out roads, fencing a one-hundred-acre tract, and dividing it into smaller shares so that each man in the village could have his own plot to farm.

Later, he took a similar approach with his children. He and Mary had four daughters, and Joseph later had three more children with another wife. He saw his children, and all Omaha children, as the tribe's future, and he strongly believed their future was at risk if they remained shackled to the past.

So La Flesche forbade his sons to have their ears pierced and his daughters to participate in the traditional Mark of Honor Ceremony. Among the Omaha, it was customary for fathers who had achieved a certain status for hunting prowess or peacemaking skills to place the mark of honor on their daughters. The mark reflected the father's accomplishments and signified that the girl was the daughter of a chief or of someone of high social standing within the tribe. The mark often consisted of a sunspot image tattooed on the forehead and a four-pointed star on the throat, the points representing the life-giving winds from each of the four directions. Often, the Mark of Honor Ceremony occurred around noon, when the sun was at its highest point in the sky. But La Flesche wanted no such markings, no tattoos of any kind, for his children.

"I was always sure," the chief would later explain, "that my sons and daughters would live to see the time when they would have to mingle with the white people, and I am determined that they should not have any mark put upon them that might be detrimental in their future surroundings."

Yet he was equally insistent that all of his children know all of the Omaha's traditional ceremonies, songs, beliefs, values, and customs—and that they all spoke the Omaha language, the cultural glue that kept their Indian identity intact.

Decade after decade, La Flesche struggled to keep threading an elusive bicultural needle, one that he believed would ensure the success of his children, the survival of his people. And year in and year out, he continually stressed to his children that there was one key value they must all adopt from the white man: education.

Education, he preached, was the key. It could help save their people. It's what could unlock the American Dream.

Education is what we can do to help ourselves—to better ourselves.

Over time, Joseph La Flesche's eldest daughter would become one of America's earliest, most prominent Indian civil rights leaders. His son, the nation's first Indian ethnographer. Another daughter became a teacher. And there was his youngest daughter, Susan. As a small child, she had witnessed the death of one of her people and the indifference of the white doctor to her death. It was something she would never forget.

It's a little lighter now and she thinks she's gone close to five miles, but she still cannot see the one-room home, cannot find it. It's still cold, so cold her face and ears are still numb. It hurts so much she wants to cry, and it makes her feel even more alone, more fragile, more vulnerable. She's scared. There's too much time to think. She feels the prairie closing in, the urge to panic closing in. She wonders if it's her fate to die alone on this prairie, to die an old maid with no husband or children, with no family to comfort her in her final hours.

She's had these thoughts before, many times, and had expressed them in letters to her sisters back home when she was alone and away all those years on the East Coast.

Alone in her buggy, alone on the empty, frozen prairie, alone in her dorm room in Virginia or her rented room in Philadelphia, she often felt out on a limb, isolated. There was no one she could turn to, no one to confide in, no cultural signposts to follow. No one else like her to consult with, to help her on her journey. So she kept going, as she always did, kept moving through the early-morning light, through the snow, looking for a sign of life on the endless sweep of prairie.

Among the tribes of the Great Plains, and throughout much of America, it was not unusual for Indian women to become part of the tribal medical community, to be important healers. The women of the Upstream People knew many of the wild plants and herbs, and so they would take their daughters out on the prairie, along creek banks, or in mountain valleys, teaching them about the various roots, herbs, leaves, and flowers and how they could be used. For winter colds and flu, brewing the leaves of wild sage into a tea. A burning rope of braided sweetgrass for asthma. Boiled yucca plant roots for shampoo. Sweet flag roots for upset stomachs. Cattail roots for dressing burns. The root of the wild rose for rinsing inflamed eyes. The medicine bag of the traditional medicine woman often had cures for a variety of ailments—native cures for poison ivy, constipation, fevers, chills, toothaches, and snakebite.

But the traditional way was not the one her father had chosen for his youngest daughter. He had sent her off in another direction, sent her off on a much different path, an often lonely path with no footprints.

In 1847, Elizabeth Blackwell became the first woman in American history to get accepted to a medical college. It hadn't come easily. Rejected by every institution she applied to, Blackwell eventually gained entry to a small school in rural New York—but for all the wrong reasons. The Geneva College medical faculty assumed it would never happen, so they put her admission up for a vote by the male students. The male students thought it was a faculty prank, so they voted to admit her as a practical joke. When faculty, students, and local townsfolk all realized the magnitude of their misconceptions, that she was serious, they were aghast.

Initially, Blackwell was forbidden to observe or participate in any classroom discussion or demonstration of medical issues. Those demonstrations, it was determined, were unfit for a woman. But Blackwell persevered and worked hard, and in 1849, the twenty-eight-year-old graduated at the top of her Geneva College medical class, becoming the first woman in U.S. history to earn a medical degree.

Yet when the class valedictorian later applied for a job in New York City, she discovered not a single hospital or clinic would allow her to practice.

The reason was simple: She was a woman.

And for half of the American population, that sentiment would remain a major hurdle throughout the nineteenth century—and far beyond.

"In the evolutionary development of the race, women had lagged behind men, much as 'primitive people' lagged behind Europeans . . . ," an American scholar would later note of the prevailing nineteenth-century beliefs. "It followed, therefore, that women could never expect to match the intellectual and artistic achievements of men, nor could they expect an equal share of power and authority. Nature had decreed a secondary role for women. The great principle of division of labor was here brought to bear: men produced, women reproduced."

The Victorian era, spanning the last two-thirds of the nineteenth century, came to embody—most notably within the conservative, religious confines of the eastern establishment—a fixed viewpoint of who women were, what they should become, and where they belonged in the social and moral firmament.

It was a viewpoint championed almost exclusively by an entrenched power structure of white Christian men who dominated every aspect of American life—a power structure that left little to chance when it came to defining a woman's role and declaring its expectations for white women.

To the male establishment, the Victorian woman's place in society and fulfillment in life was to be found in husband, home, children, family, religion, and good works, more or less in that order. Middle- and upper-class women were expected to conform to this ideal. Lower-class and rural women were expected to aspire to it.

And this viewpoint was more than abstract conjecture—it often came with scientific underpinnings, as could easily be found in some of the most popular scientific journals of the era.

"Just, therefore, as higher civilization is heralded, or at least evidenced by increasing bulk of brain; just as the most intelligent and the dominant races surpass their rivals in cranial capacity; and just as in those races the leaders, where in the sphere of thought or of action, are eminently large-brained—so we must naturally expect that man, surpassing woman in volume of brain, must surpass her in at least a proportionate degree in intellectual power," proclaimed the December 1878 issue of *Popular Science Monthly*.

An 1864 issue of the *Journal of the Anthropological Society of London* asserted: During menstruation, women "suffer under a languor and depression which disqualify them from thought or action, and render it extremely doubtful how far they can be considered responsible human beings while the crisis lasts. . . . In intellectual labour, man has surpassed, does now, and always will surpass woman, for the obvious reason that nature does not periodically interrupt his thought and application."

Over time, women came to be viewed as second-class citizens in almost every aspect of nineteenth-century American life: They couldn't vote, seldom held office (in public or private institutions), were given access to few jobs beyond those dealing with the care of children, the sick, or the elderly, and were not taken seriously on virtually any topic of public importance unless their views were ratified by men.

In short, seen through the lens of the white male establishment, a woman's role was sharply focused. She should be pious and pure, remain supportive and subservient, bear and raise his children—and work hard to create a clean, warm, comfortable home, a safe and happy haven for her husband.

After all, what other options were there? What more was there to aspire to? It was clear their emotional makeup rendered them poor candidates for serious occupations, and they lacked the intellectual firepower for professional careers. So no need to spend money educating them. It would be a waste of time.

A white plume curling up into the sky.

The smell of a wood fire.

Squatting atop the next ridge, against the dim horizon, the dark silhouette of a small, crude home frozen against the pale winter sky.

That's the one-room house, the one she's looking for, the one with the sick girl. Late the night before, the sick girl's young husband had made it to her office. He'd begged her to come and see his young wife. He'd given her some directions.

Now the husband greeted her at the door and led her inside. She saw there were three generations of the family living in the one room. She saw a clock sitting on a corner shelf.

And in a far corner of the room, below photographs fastened to the wall, photographs of some of the buildings at Hampton and some of her favorite teachers, she saw a young girl lying on the floor, her weak and elderly mother trying to prop her up so she could breathe. She'd had tuberculosis for more than a year, and now she had the flu and her breathing was soft and shallow, hard to hear except periodically, when she struggled desperately to take a deeper breath and her mother struggled to pull her up a little bit higher.

The young husband brought her a chair and she sat next to the girl.

"She looked up at me, but couldn't speak," Susan would later recall.

The girl was too weak, and their visitor asked the husband why they hadn't come to her sooner.

He couldn't leave her alone, the husband said. There was no one else who could lift her, who could care for her, and the old mother was blind.

It had been a bad winter for many. In the month before, December, she had treated more than 140 patients, the result of a flu epidemic that had swept across the remote reservation. Sometimes it had crippled entire families, families scattered many miles apart, and she had been out making calls every day that month, often in subzero weather, often leaving at eight in the morning and not returning home until after ten at night.

Inside the one-room home, she pulled the chair closer to the girl. She reached down and gently took the girl's hand, and she could feel the girl's fingers faintly trying to squeeze her hand.

"She was too weak to even whisper," Susan remembered.

She reached inside her black leather bag and gave the girl some medicine.

After a while, the stimulants took effect and the girl was able to talk a little. She said she was so tired, so weak and hungry. The girl had not eaten in five days; no one had.

That day, she stayed two hours in the one-room house, as long as she could. She left all the medicine she had and promised she would return soon. Then she got back in the buggy and rode ten miles back across the reservation heading to her office, stopping in to treat other patients along the way, finally arriving home about five P.M.

Her team was exhausted, so she got a new team, found a sled, and stopped by to pick up her older sister and another young woman, both of whom had also gone to Hampton, both of whom were the young girl's friends and wanted to try to comfort the girl. They loaded up the sled with milk and eggs and meat—and they rode all the way back to the one-room house on the frozen prairie.

When they arrived, they unloaded the sled, brought all the food inside, cooked a large meal, and fed the young girl and her family. The food and medicine had given her a little more strength, and she was able to talk to them a little bit.

"It seemed so hard to die without seeing you girls," she told them.

They stayed as long as they could, and then they told the family they had to leave, that the girl's two former classmates were teachers now and had to get back for school the next day.

All three climbed back in the buggy and set off once more for their homes, riding for a long while through the dark and the snow and now it was so cold again.

The next day, and every day for the next two weeks, sometimes twice a day, she hitched up her team and got into her buggy and rode to the one-room house to be with the young girl. Sometimes she would bring food and cook all of them dinner, and sometimes, if the girl was having a bad day, she would spend the night.

Then one day Susan's brother-in-law got very sick, then two more relatives, and then her elderly mother became dangerously ill, so she had to stay and take care of them, and, for three days, she could not make the journey to the one-room house.

But the husband never left the young girl's side.

"He was awake every night and listened for the slightest whisper, ready every moment to lift her to a more comfortable position, seeming to know what she wanted even before she spoke," Susan wrote.

On the fourth day, she got her horses hitched to the buggy and left once again on the long ride through the early evening darkness to see her patient.

The young girl was having a difficult day. She had gotten weaker, her breathing more difficult. All day, lying on a mattress on the floor, in the corner beneath her Hampton photographs, she stared at the door, whispering the same questions over and over.

Is Susan coming today?

Will she see me today?

Yes, her husband told her, she will come today. She will see you.

That evening, while the buggy was still making its way through the snow to her, in the corner of the one-room house, alone on the sprawling, frozen prairie, the young girl died.

It's late evening, early autumn, and the lands she once crisscrossed in her battered buggy and buffalo robe have long ago given way to rich, ripe fields of corn and soybeans unfurling to the horizon.

On a slight rise overlooking the verdant fields, a mile south of where the poet John Neihardt lived before he met the Lakota holy man Black Elk, a feathery row of perfect pines stands at attention, sentinels guarding the southern flank, the only sound in the fading light the song of the meadowlark from a nearby fence post.

Inside the Bancroft Cemetery, fanning out across three acres, lie the remains of more than twenty-two hundred village elders, founders, bankers, schoolteachers, farmers, truck drivers, barbers, bartenders, young children, mayors, sheriffs, hardware owners, meat cutters, pesticide salesmen, families of great-grandparents, grandparents, and grandchildren. A visitor can walk down row after row and see their names: Zuhlke, Barber, Stahl, Hermelbracht, Canarsky, Schoch, Gatzemeyer, Bassinger.

Along the southern edge of the cemetery, toward the stand of pines, near the end of one row, a four-foot-high, simple granite headstone rises from the earth:

Susan La Flesche Picotte
1865–1915

In the language of her grandfather, the French fur trader La Flesche, her name means "the arrow." And between her birth in the waning weeks of the Civil War and her final resting place, the trajectory of her life would encompass a span of experiences and a range of avocations unlike those of any other Indian woman before or since.

As a child born at a time when her people still lived in tipis and earth lodges, alternating between buffalo hunters and corn growers, she could never have known that one day she would deliver babies, suture wounds, cure fevers and colds, treat tuberculosis and influenza, ban communal drinking cups, insist on screen doors, and build a hospital in a remote, isolated corner of the Great Plains.

Back then, in the years after the transcontinental railroad and before the Little Bighorn, she could never have known that she would start a library for her people, translate legal documents, cook and deliver meals to the hungry and destitute, preside at funerals, deliver sermons, sing in the choir, and embrace the Native American Church.

That the day would come when she would attend plays, visit world-class museums, enjoy piano concertos, sit in on poetry readings, dance in summer powwows, sing traditional songs, and convey her people's creation stories and rituals to the next generation.

That she would often go upstream, against the current, taking a train to Washington, D.C., to crusade against the injustice of federal policies that threatened to steal the land from her people, land they legally owned. About the many trips to the state legislature that she would one day make, the impassioned speeches railing against the whiskey peddlers preying on the Omaha, sowing disease and violence and domestic abuse everywhere they went.

About what she would accomplish on March 14, 1889—the day she graduated as valedictorian of her medical school class in Philadelphia, becoming the first American Indian doctor in the 113-year history of her country, thirty-one years before women could vote, thirty-five years before all Indians could become citizens in their own country.

As a young girl growing up on the rich soil of the Missouri River floodplain, Susan La Flesche could never have known that she would come to love her people so much that she would give her life for them. Would come to love her homeland so much that she could never leave it.

And now—resting peacefully near the perfect pines, on a slight rise above the lush, verdant fields, not far from the song of the meadowlark—she never will.

2

vvv

The Village of the Make-Believe White Men

In her mind's eye, the images remained crystal clear, even after many years:

A cluster of white tipis tucked in a thick grove of green trees strung along a peaceful creek. Behind one tent, an Indian man making miniature bows and arrows. Gathered around him, a group of children staring, transfixed.

Boys riding imaginary horses, shooting imaginary arrows at imaginary buffalo. Girls playing house, make-believe mothers making make-believe dishes out of clay and mud.

Crossing the endless prairie on ponies and on foot, up and down rolling hillsides, along the creeks, across open meadows, picking flowers, chasing butterflies. Long summer nights giggling at the awkward courtship rituals of the teenage boys and girls.

The inevitable call for supper. The long winding down, darkness finally descending upon the peaceful village.

Silence.

The distant yap of a lonely dog.

"I have rarely seen such a beautiful sight," she would later write, "as when standing on the top of a high hill, looking down on a field of harvested wheat. We watched the moon rise, flooding the valley with silver light and casting deep shadows around the trees. When November came we husked the almost endless rows of golden corn, and when the cold nipped our fingers we were glad to get back to the warm fire."

Susan La Flesche was born in an animal-hide tipi during her people's annual summer buffalo hunt. It was the seventeenth day of June 1865, the month When the Buffalo Bulls Hunt the Cows. As a small child growing up on the plains and prairies of a remote territory, the fourth and youngest daughter of Joseph La Flesche and Mary Gale enjoyed an idyllic childhood.

But beyond the reach of her childish gaze, the United States of America was emerging from the darkest period in the young nation's eighty-nine-year history. Four brutal years of civil war had left the blood of Union and Confederate soldiers soaking battlefields from Gettysburg to Vicksburg, from Chancellorsville to Chickamauga. By then, the bitterly divided nation of thirty-five million had lost more than seven hundred thousand soldiers, almost 2.5 percent of its population. Soldiers who had often died agonizing deaths—deaths on the battlefield, deaths by accident, deaths from disease, starvation, neglect, and suicide.

As a child living in an isolated corner of Nebraska, Susan knew nothing of the great war that had raged far to the south and east of her Missouri River homeland. She knew nothing of a place called Shiloh, a biblical word for "peace," where in two days of fighting in rural countryside near the Tennessee River, more than twenty-three thousand soldiers died, more than had been killed in all previous U.S. wars. She knew nothing of the terrible sounds the wounded men made on both sides of the river throughout the long night of April 6, 1862. Nothing of the thunder and lightning and wailing that went on that night or of the wild pigs that came out of the woods and feasted on some of the dead—and some of the wounded.

Nor did the young girl know anything about a place far to the west of her tranquil childhood home, a place in a remote corner of southeast Colorado called Sand Creek. A place where the year before her birth a man of the cloth, a Christian minister, led a force of seven hundred Colorado militia and cavalry units against an Indian village sleeping beneath a U.S. flag of peace. How on the morning of November 29, 1864, following a night of heavy drinking, Colonel John Chivington and his men slaughtered 133 Cheyenne and Arapaho, 105 of them unarmed women and their terrified children. How the Methodist minister's men burned the village to the ground, then used their knives to hack off the hair, breasts, and private parts of some of the dead women and children, bringing them home as battle trophies. How, upon their return, the scalps of their victims were displayed to a cheering crowd in the Denver opera house.

The young girl knew nothing of the events to the east and west that ushered in her childhood. She had been born in a tipi—a conical structure with both functional and spiritual value to her Omaha people. The traditional tipi was made of buffalo hides laboriously tanned and stitched together, then stretched tightly across lodgepoles. Cool in summer, warm in winter, it could be taken down and put back up with relative ease, a highly portable home ideally suited for the mobility of summer buffalo hunts. And it also conformed to the shape of the earth, a circle that reflected the people's deeply held beliefs that all living things were connected.

For most of her early years, however, her home was a two-story wood-frame house perched on a low hill slightly above the Missouri floodplain. These square structures of hard corners, right angles, and sharp edges provided white settlers with a practical sense of ownership, safety, and rootedness on the often volatile prairie. The one built in 1857 by her father, with the help of others, was thought to be the first wood-frame house among the Omaha and the other Plains tribes west of the great river. It and others like it, he hoped, would provide footholds for his people in a future likely to be dominated by those settlers.

The two structures, tipi and frame house, symbolized two different cultures, two different ways of looking at life. And in 1860s America, the young Susan La Flesche was one of the very few who learned how to step comfortably from circle to square—and back again.

As a small child growing up in her village, Susan was healthy and happy, incubated in a sturdy home led by two loving, strong-willed parents and three energetic older sisters—Susette, Rosalie, and Marguerite—who sometimes overwhelmed the baby of the family.

Still, over time, visitors and relatives who came to the family home began to notice that the small girl had a sturdy character. Even at an early age, they saw, she seemed to exhibit an unusual sense of self-discipline, intensity, focus, and a strong will, characteristics that in many ways mirrored those of her father.

It was clear to all that her father was firmly focused on two overriding principles: education and hard work. Neither he nor his wife had been educated in the white man's way, and Joseph La Flesche was taking no chances that his children would endure a similar fate. In his home, he required his four daughters to speak to their parents in either Omaha or French. But among themselves, they were to speak English. Only the oldest daughter, Susette, was given an Indian name, *In-shta-the-amba,* "Bright Eyes" in the Omaha language. And Joseph was resolute in forbidding all of his daughters the mark of honor, the tattoos designating them as daughters of importance. Within Joseph's world, visitors clearly observed, nothing was to interfere with the education of his children.

So it wasn't long before Susan, only three years old, joined her three older sisters, taking the road that connected their home with one of the reservation's most visible institutions: the Presbyterian Mission School.

As part of a treaty agreement, the Omaha gave up four quarter sections of reservation land to Presbyterian Church leaders. The leaders, in turn, sold the land and used the money to build a formidable school, an anchor for the church's missionary goals among the Omaha.

Finished in 1857, the mission school was impressive, a hulking limestone building perched on a prominent ridge offering a spectacular view of the Missouri River. It stood three stories high, measured seventy-five feet by thirty-five feet, and included seventeen rooms designed to accommodate about fifty students and staff. The students could not speak in their language, only in English, and a hickory stick was used to make sure they didn't forget. The boys also could not wear traditional clothing, only the white man's clothing. That first year, the school attracted twenty-five boys and four girls and offered classes in reading, geography, writing, arithmetic, and vocal music.

And it also offered something else: It was inside this school that Susan first heard the story of a man who was both a god and a man. At home, she had heard some of her own people's creation stories, some of their Sacred Legends, from her mother and her grandmother Nicomi, but not this new one about the half man, half god, a modest, humble carpenter who promised salvation and an afterlife to his believers. Over time, the young girl would find a way to balance both stories, both viewpoints, in a world that often wanted her to choose one over the other.

In many ways, the Presbyterian school's leadership reflected the Victorian era's goals and values, so there was a unified effort to both Christianize the young Omaha girls and train them in the domestic arts of good housekeeping, proper food service, laundry, sewing, and knitting. And in an atmosphere that embraced everyone as part of the larger Christian family, there were also regular Bible study sessions and religious discussions for both girls and boys.

But in truth, Susan didn't learn much in the mission school. For one thing, her teacher often put a newspaper over his face, leaned back in his chair, and, in the middle of class, disappeared into a fitful slumber. When he did, one of the older boys would grab a book, march to the front of the class, and pretend to take over as headmaster. Susan, too, sometimes got sleepy in class. When she first started, the three-year-old was so tiny that whenever she nodded off, the older boys would pick her up and gently put her inside one of the high, old-fashioned desks, where she, too, enjoyed a good nap.

After just one year, her mission school days ended and a new school system began, the change provoked by an abrupt shift in government policy thirteen hundred miles away. By 1869, beset by a decade of endless Indian wars, corrupt Indian agents, and the shameful specter of Sand Creek and other massacres, the government decided to adopt a new approach to its lingering "Indian Problem." It decided to embrace what became known as the Quaker (or Peace) Policy.

Championed by President Ulysses S. Grant, the new policy was designed to eliminate rampant corruption in the Office of Indian Affairs and elevate the overall moral standing of its employees. Noting the moral swamp created by corrupt whites in Indian country, one agent summed up the problem succinctly: "The progress of advancement, especially in morals, is very much retarded by the

presence of a low class of whites which infest Indian reservations."
Under the new plan, the Quakers and other Christian denomina-
tions would take the lead in using religion as an assimilationist
tool via a network of reservation day schools that would also
promote Victorian social values and a clean, safe, happy Christian home as the ultimate goal of Indian girls.

So in the autumn of 1869, four-year-old Susan and two older
sisters would set off on a three-mile morning walk down a road
connecting their wood-frame house with their new Quaker day
school—a journey that remained in sharp focus for many years.

"The neighbor's children used to wait for us, so 15 or 20 of us,
with our bright tin pails, trooped off, arriving in time for school
at 9 o'clock. . . . When school was out at 4 o'clock we had a gay time
rushing home over the prairies, feeling free to loiter, and sometimes reaching home at sunset."

Although the new way of life for Joseph La Flesche and his
family often meant constant change—from buffalo-hide tipi to
wood-frame house, from marks of honor to unmarked skin, from
Wakonda to Jesus—the old way of life could never be bleached
out, could never disappear, never be forgotten, even among the
youngest members of his family.

Susan and her sisters never forgot the innocent fun of childhood, never forgot walking atop the mud-packed roof of the
dome-shaped earth lodges, picking all the sunflowers and native
grasses that grew there. At sunset, the old men would climb atop
the lodges, sitting alone, lost in thought, lost in prayer. "I remember looking at them reverently as I played around with the other
children," she recalled many years later, "for I regarded them with
a great deal of awe . . . they seemed so wise."

And then it all changed so fast, catching everyone off guard.

"Sometimes I am sorry that the white people ever came to
America," fifteen-year-old Marguerite La Flesche wrote in an 1877

letter to a national children's magazine. "What nice times we used to have before we were old enough to go to school, for then father used to take us on the buffalo hunt. How glad we used to be when the men were bringing in the buffaloes they had killed! I do wish we could go again."

Stand here today, on the rich, verdant floodplain of the Missouri River, and it's easy to see how Susan developed such a deep and lasting love of her homeland. Stand here on a midsummer afternoon and you can still see the thick curtain of hardwoods—oak and maple, hickory and basswood—draped across the high hills and gleaming bluffs. You can still see stands of towering cottonwoods standing guard along the perimeter of the great river. You can see, right here on the edge of the floodplain, a herd of buffalo lolling about in a fenced-in field of native grass, the bright summer sun buffing up the shine on their thin chocolate coats. And in the middle of it all, surrounded by river and bluffs and buffalo, lush rows of corn now cover the ground where she and her family and all the others once lived in their square wood-frame homes.

In 1861, by the time the first cannon exploded over Fort Sumter, the Omaha lived in three main villages about four miles apart on the eastern end of the reservation. The La Flesche reservation homeland was the farthest north, and it already boasted nineteen wood-frame houses, an enclave the more conservative, traditional Omaha had mockingly come to call *To^n Wo^n Gatho^n Waxe Hebe*— "the Village of the Make-Believe White Men."

As one of the leaders of his people, Joseph had been instrumental in acquiring what would eventually become the Omaha Reservation. On March 16, 1854, at a ceremony in Washington, D.C., he was the second of seven chiefs and headmen who signed a treaty that ceded five million acres of the Omaha's traditional hunting grounds north of the Platte River and west of the Missouri to the government, land for which the government paid about eighteen cents an acre. In exchange, the tribe eventually received 302,000 acres in Nebraska hugging the Missouri River about seventy-five miles north of present-day Omaha. But finding a new home didn't come easy.

After the death of Big Elk in 1853, when Joseph became one of the tribe's two principal chiefs, nothing had come easy for him and the Omaha, or for any of the tribes west of the Missouri. Each year, they struggled to find solutions to more and more problems. After giving away almost all of their traditional hunting grounds, the Omaha now faced a new problem: where to live, where to survive, where to find a new reservation to build their villages.

For months, they looked at proposed sites and listened to the suggestions of Indian agents and others. But there was always one problem or another. In late summer 1854, while scouting on the Iowa side of the Missouri for a new homeland, they again found nothing suitable, nothing that met their needs. The land they had looked at, declared the *Nebraska Palladium* newspaper, was "too poor even for Indians to live in."

It was left to their chief to sum up the frustration of having had millions of acres for generations, only to find themselves homeless. "We are strangers in the land where we were born," said Joseph La Flesche.

Finally, by May 1855, the Omaha convinced the government to let them live in their old homeland of Blackbird Hills—a beautiful land of thickly forested bluffs overlooking the river, a land ripe with game, streams, fish, prairie, and plenty of fertile floodplains for corn and wheat, pumpkins and squash.

So they moved in, but the problems never stopped.

A few months later, while out on the summer buffalo hunt, their other mixed-blood chief, Logan Fontenelle, left the main hunting party to pick gooseberries. A Lakota war party spotted him in a ravine and gave chase. They caught him, killed him, and scalped him.

That left Joseph as the principal chief, and the divisions that had been festering for a long time—the animosity between believers of the old ways and advocates of the new—intensified.

Who are we? What have we become? What must we do to remain Omaha? How must we change to survive? If we change too much, will we still be Omaha? If we don't change enough, will we disappear, dying off on the margins?

The questions were always the same, questions that for decades to come would haunt successive waves of immigrants trying to assimilate into the American mainstream. The same questions that haunted the chiefs of many tribes for much of the nineteenth century.

Who gets to choose how you see yourself? Who are you if you lose your language? Who gets to pick the kinds of clothes you wear and the songs you sing? Who will decide if your religion is appropriate?

An eleven-year-old Lakota boy could be George Fast Horse on Monday, walk into his reservation classroom on Tuesday, and be told that he was now George Washington, and the federal census rolls would make it official. The Indian names of Omaha schoolchildren often were too hard to pronounce and considered too heathenish. So overnight, *Wa-pah'-dae* became Ulysses Grant. It happened all the time—the theft of someone's cultural identity. And so the chiefs and the people would ask again and again: *Who are we? Who are any of us without a culture?* The struggle to find that elusive balance between preserving the past and preparing for the future never ended.

Among the Omaha, it wasn't long before Joseph's staunch assimilationist views provoked an increasingly bitter split within the tribe, views that were fiercely opposed by more than half of the Upstream People.

By the mid-1850s, the tribe had divided, physically and culturally, into two distinct camps. The "Chief's Party" favored maintaining cultural traditions and opposed farming and sending their children to school. The "Young Men's Party" wanted to abandon the old Indian mode of life, take up farming full-time, embrace education, and adopt many white customs.

La Flesche, who led the Young Men's Party, had no formal education. He could neither read nor write nor speak English. But it was often said by Indians and whites alike that he was an unusually wise man who possessed an uncommon amount of good sense, clear thinking, sound judgment, and an impressive depth of knowledge on a good many subjects. And he was unwavering in his belief that the vision he shared with Big Elk would save the Omaha. For those who questioned that vision, he often answered with a terse response: "It is either civilization or extermination."

So he began building the two-story wood-frame house, nurturing others in the Village of the Make-Believe White Men, refusing to let his oldest daughter, Susette, bear the mark of honor, readying his plot for vegetables, and asking a good many questions about this thing called Christianity.

It would be another decade before his youngest daughter was born, and in time, he would tell her about his beliefs, about how the Omaha could both retain who they were and prepare for who they must become, how they could succeed in the white man's world by blending the best of both cultures. And he would tell her about the scourge that visited their reservation in 1856, a scourge that Susan La Flesche would deal with for much of her adult life.

As a young clerk at a trading post, Joseph had once witnessed a drunk grab a knife and stab another man in the throat, killing him in front of his small son, an incident he would never forget. Alcohol had long been a feature of the fur-trading culture between whites and Indians, and it had increasingly become a problem among the Omaha. So when public drunkenness reached a flash point in 1856, Joseph got $1,000 of tribal funds and did something that had never been done before: He created a thirty-man Omaha police force, the first of its kind anywhere in Indian country, that was to show no mercy for any drunken tribal member—regardless of rank, position, or status. For punishment, the progressive-minded chief adopted a custom long rooted in traditional Omaha culture.

His son, Francis, later described the traditional punishment meted out to a warrior who jumped the gun during the buffalo hunt, a warrior who decided to seek individual glory and potentially risk spooking the herd, jeopardizing the tribal food supply: "The officers are in charge and woe betide the man who steals away and hunts buffalo all by himself. Many are the hard blows he will receive if caught, and when he has recovered his senses he will find his tent and all its contents reduced to ashes. If he resists the officers, his very life will be in danger."

So under the chief's new rules, borrowing from long-standing Omaha tradition, the penalty for being drunk was a harsh public flogging or, as the missionary R. J. Burtt put it, "a beating severe enough to lay them up for a week." In short order, it became illegal to drink alcohol on the Omaha Reservation.

And it wasn't long before the anti-alcohol policy produced results. After a prominent tribal member, decorated warrior, and personal friend of the chief's submitted to a brutal public whipping, alcohol quickly ceased to be a problem among the Upstream People.

But other problems lingered—hunger, severe hunger, often leading the list. In the spring of 1856, as had happened a number of times before, the government neglected to provide the Omaha with the annuities promised in the treaty. Soon, many of the winter food supplies ran out and many Omaha went days without anything to eat. Seeing the suffering around him, Joseph dipped into cash reserves from his trading business and began buying cattle, then giving away the meat to his hungry people. Meanwhile, he himself began to eat less so there would be more for the old, the young, and the needy.

That problem temporarily solved, the chief moved on to a more personal one. For a number of years, Joseph had been deeply curious about the white man's religion. As was his nature, he wanted to probe, to dig as deeply as he could, so he found interpreters to accompany him or sought missionaries who spoke some Omaha. He asked a lot of questions, and sometimes the stop again–start again conversations would stretch over several days. He also urged those in his village to go to the Sunday church services, to learn more about Christianity, to listen to the words of the preachers, and to find out more about the things in "God's book."

One day in the autumn of 1859, Joseph was walking about when he stepped on a nail. He thought nothing of it and went on about his business. But soon his foot, and then his leg, became severely infected. Just a few weeks later, his leg had to be crudely amputated below the knee. In severe pain long afterward, he sought out one of the reservation's Presbyterian missionaries, Reverend Charles Sturgis. He wanted to know why God didn't like him, why he had caused the accident. For several days, the two men—the Omaha Indian chief and the white Presbyterian minister—struggled to find answers to Joseph's questions, to allay his crisis of faith. One day, Joseph asked if the reverend would pray for him. That if he should die, to pray that God would still be his friend. And if he should live, that God would help him "live in the good road." The accident had focused his mind on trying to resolve a number of religious and spiritual conflicts, so he asked Reverend Sturgis and others a good many questions from that day on.

Meanwhile, the pain in his leg never left, and he continually asked permission to go east and have it treated, a request the reservation agent was reluctant to grant. Finally, in 1861, Joseph was among a delegation of Omaha who went to Washington to finalize some treaty details. Afterward, he traveled on to New York, where his injury was treated and he was fitted for a cork leg. While there, he also got hold of a small electric device, a crude battery.

When he returned home, he gathered all of the chiefs and headmen together for a feast. After they had finished eating, he spoke to them: "You all believe in the power of your medicine men.... Now I will show you something of the power of the white man's medicine."

He told some of the chiefs to join hands and asked others to grab hold of the battery handles. Joseph then turned on the current full force and watched in silence at the wild contortions. While they recovered, he slipped on his new leg and came walking out as though he now had two healthy legs.

Stunned silence.

Joseph sat down on a box, crossed his legs, moved his wooden foot up and down, got up, and walked around. And then he turned to them and said: "The whites were not great and powerful because of any magic power, but because they all worked and sent their children to school."

By the time he finished, most of the leaders and medicine men hated him more than ever.

Susan loved the outdoors. And she loved to work—for the most part, anyway. And growing up in her father's village, she and her three older sisters really had little choice.

Their father was a devout believer in hard work. A believer that hard work provided dignity and a strong sense of self-worth, and in the times they lived, it was also essential to their survival.

When Joseph was a young man, the Omaha had claimed more than five million acres of hunting grounds in northeast Nebraska and northwest Iowa. When he became chief and signatory to the 1854 Treaty with the Omaha, he consented to give away those millions of acres in exchange for a 302,000-acre reservation. And now, in the years after the Civil War, he found himself teaching his daughters how to make the land prosper, how to work his 160-acre farm.

Even decades later, few details of working the family farm escaped his youngest daughter:

> Although we were rather young, still father taught us to work. We planted corn, hoed potatoes, and planted and weeded vegetables. . . . Sometimes some of the men used to laugh at the five young girls who were so glad and eager to help their father and learn all they could from him. . . . Oh! for the delight of those days, as the reaper cut down the golden grain and we went eagerly forward striving to see who could keep nearest the machine. The harvest field held a fascination for us partly, I suppose, because we believed we were helping; but that fascination did not extend as far as carrying *water*, for it was a weary, toilsome walk, clear down to the spring and back again under the hot sun, through the stubble, barefooted, and we were happy little mortals when our dreaded work was done. One of my sisters cut 30 acres of wheat once, and another one could keep up in binding almost as well as any man. Glad we were when the signal to stop was given, and gathering the water pails

we all went home to supper. After the horses were staked out on the hills, the groups of tired men gathered around the camp-fire to talk of coming crops, while the women were interested in their children, and paused only now and then to listen to the talk of the men.

Susan's father was a complicated man, and throughout the last half of the 1860s, whenever Joseph La Flesche stepped out the door of his wood-frame home in the Village of the Make-Believe White Men, the landscape he saw was markedly different from his youngest daughter's landscape of brilliant butterflies, painted flowers, and golden harvests. What he saw was an increasingly complicated world—one in which he increasingly stood at the center.

If he chose to look only at himself, at his own household, he had by almost any standards become a remarkable success, a wealthy man. For years, drawing upon skills he had learned as a young man at Sarpy's Trading Post, La Flesche had been the reservation's principal trader. And he consistently was able to tease about two thousand bushels of corn from his own land, land upon which he also ran fifty head of cattle. Moreover, for years the industrious La Flesche had been the tribe's principal moneylender. In fact, a few years after becoming chief, he loaned one of the Presbyterian missionaries $1,800, a considerable sum for a private loan from an Indian chief living on an 1850s reservation.

But when he looked farther out, beyond his home and corn and cattle, across his own reservation, Joseph La Flesche saw something else. He saw many Omaha who were shattered, their culture shredded by a multitude of forces beyond their control. He saw they were poor and forlorn and dressed in tattered clothing. He saw that many did not have good homes. He saw they were often hungry, starving. As in many other parts of the Great Plains in those years, there was often too little rain and too many grasshoppers, so there was often too little food. Once reduced to a starving, weakened state, many Omaha were also haunted by disease: influenza, tuberculosis, pneumonia, and measles. And he knew from long years of observation that there was little the white agency doctors could, or would, do for his people. He also knew the diseased Omaha didn't trust the white doctors, didn't understand their language, their customs, anything about them. So, most simply died.

Had he been able to lift his eyes beyond his reservation, the chief of the Omaha would have seen that the problems extended far beyond the homeland of the Upstream People. He would have seen the wholesale destruction of the buffalo was in full swing and a transcontinental railroad was under way—steel rails that would bind the American coasts, carve up Indian lands, and create instant white towns and settlements hugging the new rail lines. With the Civil War over, he would have seen that the real flood was now about to begin. He would have seen the swarms of white settlers massing in the East, ready to push in droves across the Mississippi and onto the Plains. Some would even come from foreign countries, drawn by the allure of the 1862 Homestead Act, which promised 160 acres of land to anyone who built a home, lived on the land, and cultivated it for five years, an act that eventually allowed pioneers to claim 270 million acres of the American West.

Closer to home, in the years before his youngest daughter was born, Joseph La Flesche frequently found himself buffeted between two opposing forces: a white government-missionary power structure strongly urging him to lead the assimilation charge and a conservative, traditional Indian base fearing he would sell them out in the name of civilization.

In truth, La Flesche championed assimilation in all its dominant forms—wood-frame homes, individual plots, agricultural skills, white schools, the English language, Christianity. Yet he never mocked or interfered with basic Omaha traditions and customs. To enforce his anti-drinking rules, he had used the tribe's traditional punishment—flogging. He frequently attended the traditional summer buffalo hunt, bringing his family and living in a tipi. He did not ridicule other members who preferred to wear traditional clothing. He did not interfere with courtship rituals, the Pipe Dance Ceremony, customary gift exchanges, the traditional balance of power between men and women, and the chief's privilege to have more than one wife. At one time, he himself had three wives.

And what he also did throughout the first decade of his chieftainship was to cast a scrupulous eye on each and every transaction between his people and the government. With the help of translators, he pored over all the treaty fine print—the cash payments, the annuities, the mandatory protections—and did everything in his power to confront corrupt agents and feckless government appointees. He was steadfast in making sure his people got everything they were owed. In 1860, in what was another reservation first, he had a code of ethics drawn up to ensure that no Indian agent was confused about how business was to be conducted with the Omaha. It was all right there, laid out in black and white.

In his deliberate, thoughtful, and probing way, he also began to dig deeper into the Christian world—into biblical references, Christian values and history, the relevance of Christianity to everyday life. He would often corner Reverend William Hamilton, another Omaha Presbyterian missionary, to divine deeper meanings from the word of God, meanings and references that Joseph didn't fully grasp. Reverend Hamilton responded by digging up a number of scriptural texts and references, reading and discussing them with his curious Omaha Indian friend.

One day, the reverend read Joseph a singular passage: "My

kingdom is not of this world; if my kingdom were of this world, then would my servants fight." Joseph froze, sat still for a long time, saying nothing. Then he said he could hear no more, that he must go away and think about what he had just heard.

A few days later, Joseph returned. He was alive and animated in a way the reverend had not seen before. "My friend," Joseph told the reverend, "you have often read to me out of God's book, and I thought I understood the meaning of it, but I did not." Joseph said he had thought long and hard about the "my kingdom is not of this world" passage and had arrived at a profound conclusion.

"I cannot make a man good by issuing an order," he told Reverend Hamilton. "I can say to a man, 'You build a house and live in it, and no longer live in a tent.' He will go and do it. But I cannot say to a man, 'Your heart is bad, have a good heart hereafter.' There is a something over which no man, however great his authority— even if it is as great as that of the Great Father at Washington—can have control. Over that God alone can rule."

For many years, the struggle to walk a cultural tightrope between his evolving Christian beliefs and the ways of his Omaha people never seemed to end. Joseph once tried to explain that struggle to his brother, White Swan, who had long lived among their close friends and relatives the Ponca.

"I will speak on another subject," Joseph told his brother. "It is the subject about which I told you from time to time, when you lived here. I did not say, 'Abandon your Indian life.' I did not say, 'Live as a white man.' Nor did I say, 'Live as an Indian.' But I say again: Depend upon God. Remember Him. For if, instead of remembering God, you love this world alone, you shall be sad—you shall surely be sad in the future. God is ahead of us. We will go to Him."

With his children, he increasingly used specific examples, often drawn from the natural world around him, to illustrate the interplay between traditional Omaha and Christian values.

One summer, when his oldest daughter was a small girl, the tribe was on its annual buffalo hunt. It was evening, the tents pitched, the campfires glowing, the women busy cooking. Susette was playing near her father when a small boy came up and gave her a tiny bird he had found. She tried to feed it and make it drink and played with it for a while. Then Joseph told his daughter to bring the bird to him. He held it in his hand, gently smoothed its feathers, and offered her a suggestion:

"Take it carefully in your hand, out yonder where there are no tents, where the grass is, put it softly on the ground, and say as you put it down: 'God, I give you back your little bird. Have pity on me as I have pity on your bird.'"

"Does it belong to God?" Susette asked.

"Yes, and he will be pleased if you do not hurt it, but give it back to him to take care of."

At other times, Joseph would make it a point to tell his children and others in their village: "When you see a boy barefooted and lame, take off your moccasins and give them to him. When you see a boy hungry, bring him to your house and give him food."

His youngest daughter, Susan, never forgot the scolding she once heard her father give someone who violated his ethical code. "He who is present at a wrongdoing and lifts not a hand to prevent it," Joseph La Flesche told the offender, "is as guilty as the wrong-doers."

And there was another thing his youngest daughter would never forget. She was but a young girl at the time and had gone to help care for a sick, elderly Omaha woman. She stayed with the woman, and as the night grew longer, the woman grew weaker. Four times that night, a messenger was sent to the white agency doctor. Each time he promised he would soon be there. But he never came. Shortly before morning, Susan watched as the elderly woman died an agonizing death.

"It was only an Indian, and it [did] not matter," she would later recount. The white agency doctor preferred "hunting for prairie chickens" instead of "visiting poor, suffering humanity." It was an incident that would have a powerful impact on the trajectory of the life of Joseph La Flesche's youngest daughter.

Beginning in early childhood and continuing throughout her life, it was not unusual for Susan La Flesche to be surrounded by a succession of strong, disciplined, inspirational women, perhaps none more so than her oldest sister.

Susette was eleven years older than her youngest sister and had become a prominent example of Joseph's unflinching belief that education was the key to unlocking the American Dream—both for his own children and for all the Upstream People. And it didn't take long for the older sister to show her younger ones the combination of focus, effort, and determination, qualities they had often seen growing up, that they would need to succeed in the new world order.

All along, the older sister's childhood dream had been to teach Omaha children in their own school on their own reservation. So she spent six long years—from fall 1869 to summer 1875—at the Elizabeth Institute for Young Ladies in Elizabeth, New Jersey, working hard, getting good grades, devouring Shakespeare, teaching part-time to help pay for her education. After graduating from the boarding school in June 1875, she returned home and was told she could not teach on the reservation. But one day at the agency office, she found a copy of the "Rules and Regulations" governing reservation employment. In one section, she noticed it said Indians should be the preferred teachers, so she dashed off a letter to Commissioner of Indian Affairs John Q. Smith, saying she was qualified and would like to apply for a teaching position at her reservation school. The commissioner told her she could not teach without a certificate, so she asked the Omaha agent for permission to leave the reservation to take the exam for her teaching certificate. The agent refused to give her permission, so she got one of her father's best horses and rode twenty-eight miles to Tekamah, where she asked the superintendent of schools to give her the exam. He gave her the hardest reading and arithmetic sections, but she passed anyway, got the certificate, and rode back home. She sent the certificate to the Indian commissioner, who told her she couldn't teach without a certificate of good moral character. So she wrote Miss Nettie Read, one of her teachers at the New Jersey girls' school, who sent a number of letters attesting to her good moral character. She sent the letters to the commissioner and heard nothing for several months. So she wrote him again, saying she would take her story to the newspapers if he didn't respond. Not long after, the commissioner approved her position and she became the first Indian teacher on the Omaha Reservation. The government gave her a small, dilapidated building and $20 a month. She gathered some children, scrimped and saved, and eventually bought a small organ to teach them music, then started a Sunday school for her students.

The government's official census rolls back then identified the twenty-one-year-old teacher as Susette La Flesche. But in a few years, she would be known to many whites, from Chicago to Boston, New York to Washington, simply as Bright Eyes.

So by the fall of 1875—the year Mark Twain published *The Adventures of Tom Sawyer*—Bright Eyes was living her dream on her reservation homeland. She was teaching her people, young Omaha boys and girls, what they would need to know to survive in the world beyond the Village of the Make-Believe White Men. She had her own little house, a small classroom, a small government paycheck, a used organ for music lessons, and her Sunday school classes every week.

And she had something else: That fall, her three younger sisters all moved in with her. They were all going to the same school where Bright Eyes taught, so their father thought it best his daughters all live together, near their school, and help one another out, with Bright Eyes acting as head of the household.

By age ten, Joseph's youngest daughter already had long benefited from similar arrangements, benefited from the many branches of the La Flesche family tree, from the extended kinship lines in which she often found herself immersed. Relatives and kinfolk and clan members who would come by on warm summer nights during the buffalo hunt or cold winter nights back in the village and tell the stories of her people—the Sacred Legend, the Omaha creation story, stories of animal spirits and supernatural creatures and magical characters. Stories that gave Susan a strong sense of ancient beliefs, of her cultural heritage, of who she was.

A frequent visitor was her grandmother Nicomi, a bold, powerful woman who had never been confused about her identity. The daughter of an Ioway chief, she spoke only Omaha to her family and had once hidden her infant daughter from her army-doctor husband when he wanted to take them all to St. Louis. The grandmother often drew upon her native heritage for the stories her young granddaughter loved, stories that reflected a rich sense of Indian culture.

In the winter of 1875–1876, when all four sisters were living in a small brown house at the Omaha Agency in Macy, it was not unusual for Nicomi to occasionally stop by and tell a story to help pass the long, cold nights. Or for Bright Eyes to pass along some of the stories she had heard from her grandmother. For Susan and generations of Omaha children, these stories often had a character like the Rabbit or the Coyote or Ictinike embedded in their cultural fabric. They were "tricksters"—mythological spirits and cultural icons, characters frequently known for their deceit and treachery and cleverness, tricksters who were often trouble-makers and prolific liars not to be trusted. There was frequently a moral to the story, and the story often involved adventures in the wild, a story like the one Bright Eyes was fond of telling her younger sisters. It was called "How Rabbit Captured the Turkeys."

> Once there was a young man named Rabbit, who lived with his grandmother. And she told him to get some-thing to eat.
>
> "Well, I will get some food, Grandmother," he said, "if you will have the fire ready." So he took his bow and arrows, and also a bag filled with grass. By and by he saw some turkeys.
>
> "Ho! Rabbit, what do you have in your bag?" they asked.
>
> "I have songs."
>
> "Sing us some," the turkeys said.
>
> "Come dance for me and I will sing for you," he said. "But while you are dancing, you must keep your eyes closed, for if any of you open your eyes, all of you will have red eyes."
>
> The turkeys danced while he sang . . . and as they danced he grabbed first one and then another, putting them into his game bag. But one turkey, suspecting something wrong, opened one eye and cried out, "He is killing us all." Then the surviving turkeys flew away. . . . And from that time on, turkeys have had red eyes.

And so it continued almost every night that winter: When the chores were done and the little house cleaned, the three youngest sisters would all gather around the bright wood fire, cutting and sewing their dresses. And while they cut and sewed, Bright Eyes would read aloud to her younger siblings—sustaining an oral tradition that began with Grandmother Nicomi, then went to the mother, Mary Gale, and continued now with the oldest sister, Bright Eyes. In two generations, the youngest daughters of the La Flesche family had gone from hearing the Sacred Legend to hearing Shakespeare, from learning about the toils and troubles of Ictinike to learning about the toils and troubles of King Lear.

Susan loved learning, studying, doing well in school. She loved her family and her reservation village homeland. And she adored her oldest sister.

"I am a little Indian girl twelve years old," Susan La Flesche wrote in a letter to a popular children's magazine. "I go to school at the Omaha Agency. I study geography, history, grammar, arithmetic and spelling. I read in the Fifth Reader. . . . Some Senators and Congressmen came to see the Omahas. They all came to our house and sang 'Hold the Fort' with us. My oldest sister played backgammon with one of the Congressmen and beat him."

So the sisters' first full school year together ended and the summer of 1876 began. That year, the great shaggy beasts that had long roamed the Great Plains by the millions, the ones that had been a gift from Wakonda, were so scarce, so thinned out, that the Omaha were forced to travel all the way to western Kansas to find a meager winter meat supply. It was the last organized buffalo hunt the Upstream People would ever have.

Another incident also occurred that summer, an incident many people initially did not believe, were unable to comprehend. But when it proved true, its consequences were soon felt throughout the American West, in every tribe and every reservation, on the lands of the Omaha, in the Village of the Make-Believe White Men, and eventually inside the two-story wood-frame home of Joseph La Flesche and his family.

That summer, the nation was poised to celebrate its centennial. From Philadelphia to Washington, New York to Boston, the great cities of the East were flexing their patriotic muscle, unfurling flags, hanging bunting, building bleachers, warehousing confetti, lining up marching bands. And then in late June, there was some news that began to spread like wildfire, news about an incident that had happened along the banks of a remote river in the southeast corner of Montana Territory. About how George Armstrong Custer, the Civil War's impetuous boy-general, a national hero with presidential ambitions, had ridden out at dawn on June 25, heading toward the river. And how later that day, a group of half-naked savages armed with bows and arrows had taken on the world's finest cavalry, armed with the most modern weapons— and wiped out their glamorous commander and his five companies to the last man.

The army generals were furious, and in short order one thing crystallized in the minds of the nation's leaders: The western territories could never be settled into a safe, productive network of family farms and ranches until the likes of Sitting Bull and Crazy Horse and all of the Lakota and their allies were crushed, broken, and confined to reservations. So the army began an all-out assault on the hostile tribes, started rounding up and relocating other tribes to the Indian Territory, lands that would later become Oklahoma, and served notice that they would now be calling the shots when it came to reservation policy.

After this policy had been in effect a number of months, the Omaha Indian agent filed his annual report with superiors in Washington. "The uncertain attitude of the Government toward the Indians does much to retard their improvement," wrote

Agent T. T. Gillingham. "The prospect during the past year, that they might at any time be turned over to the Military Department, has had a very depressing effect upon the Omahas, and if perchance it may not be out of place here, I will suggest that because a few bands or tribes are hostile and require the presence of troops to keep them in subjection, I can see no more reason for putting the whole Indian population under military control than there would be to place a city or State under martial law because a certain ward or county was over-run by rioters or outlaws."

Not long after the agent filed his report, Joseph La Flesche, his oldest daughter, and many of the Omaha got a jolt of news that both angered and scared the Upstream People. The Ponca, their longtime tribal relatives, friends, and neighbors, had been told that the government wanted their reservation. They were ordered to pack up immediately and move to a strange place called the Indian Territory.

But Standing Bear, one of the Ponca chiefs, said no. They would not go. His people had two treaties ratified by the U.S. Senate, he said, treaties that showed they legally occupied their reservation homeland near the confluence of the Niobrara and Missouri Rivers. He said they would not go to this new place they knew nothing about. So the government put him in leg irons, threw him in a military stockade, and eventually began to cut off water and food to the seven hundred peaceful Ponca camped in their winter village. Hearing that some of the old and some of the young were near death, Standing Bear relented, and in May 1877 a cavalry detachment began the long forced march of the Ponca to Indian Territory—something Joseph La Flesche and many other Omaha feared could now happen to them as well.

Standing Bear and the Ponca, including Joseph's brother, White Swan, all arrived on the scorching Oklahoma plains in July 1877. Within a year, more than one-third of the tribe had died, many from malaria. On Christmas week 1878, the chief's only son, a fourteen-year-old boy named Bear Shield, lay curled on the bottom of a canvas army tent, dying of malaria. But before his eyes closed in death, the boy extracted a promise from his father: Upon his death, the chief would take his son's remains and bury them in their beloved Nebraska homeland.

So on January 2, 1879, Standing Bear and twenty-nine others—with little food, little money, and few winter clothes—began walking five hundred miles into the teeth of a severe blizzard to fulfill his pledge to the dying boy. In early March, after a journey of sixty-two days, Joseph La Flesche got word the Ponca were camped near his home. He and his oldest daughter went to see them, and they were shocked at what they saw: faces gaunt from hunger, skin blackened from frostbite, hollow-eyed children, ragged clothes, emaciated horses, and so many so sick. Not long after, Bright Eyes recalled, "One of my sisters looked out of the window and said that some soldiers had come."

The soldiers marched Standing Bear and his starving followers to the military stockade at Fort Omaha, where Brigadier General George Crook was in command. Crook was sympathetic to the Ponca's plight and tipped off a local newspaperman. The newsman began to write a series of stories about a middle-aged Indian father who simply wanted to bury his son, but the government wouldn't let him, and before long a good swath of the public began to rally around Standing Bear's cause. Soon, two prominent lawyers agreed to sue the government on Standing Bear's behalf, and in short order the weary Ponca chief found himself in a federal courtroom—in the crosshairs of one of the nation's earliest civil rights cases. A landmark legal case that would determine whether the government had the right to imprison him and whether the protective cover of the U.S. Constitution extended to people who looked like him.

On the morning of May 1, 1879, on the third floor of a lime-stone federal courthouse in downtown Omaha, U.S. district judge Elmer Dundy's gavel smacked against a wooden bench and the trial of *Ma-chu-nah-zha v. George Crook* began. The government prosecutor pressed forward on a singular argument: Since Standing Bear and all other Indians were not citizens of the United States, he could not sue the government. So the judge, he argued, had erred by ever allowing the case to reach court. To bolster his main argument—that only U.S. citizens had access to U.S. courts—the government prosecutor relied heavily on a decision the nation's highest court had made twenty-two years earlier, a case involving a black man who, like Standing Bear, had also come to federal court to seek his freedom.

Dred Scott, born a slave in Virginia, had gotten nowhere in asking the federal courts to set him free. In a 7 to 2 vote on March 6, 1857, the United States Supreme Court ruled that anyone of African ancestry—both slaves and those set free by masters—could never become a U.S. citizen and so they could not sue in federal court. Slaves were the private property of their owners, and the court could not legally deprive owners of their property. Writing for the majority, Chief Justice Roger B. Taney declared that a Negro had "no rights which any white man was bound to respect."

And in the spring of 1879, in Omaha, Nebraska, the federal prosecutor did not want the present court to forget its past. Chief Justice Taney's 1857 majority opinion in the black man's case, he argued, must also remain the guiding legal principle in the red man's case. If a Negro did not have legal access to a federal court-room, he said, then surely an Indian didn't either.

Before the trial ended, Judge Dundy agreed to do something he said had most likely never been done before. He agreed to let one last speaker address the packed courthouse.

They all saw him rise slowly from his seat, the eagle feather in the braided hair, the bold blue shirt trimmed in red cloth, the blue flannel leggings, the Thomas Jefferson medallion, the necklace of bear claws. Accompanying him as he walked to the front of the courtroom was a young, dark-haired Indian woman who had been sitting near Standing Bear all along. As he held out his hand and began to speak, Bright Eyes translated:

"That hand is not the color of yours, but if I pierce it, I shall feel pain," Standing Bear told the judge. "If you pierce your hand, you also feel pain. The blood that will flow from mine will be of the same color as yours. I am a man. The same God made us both."

On May 12, Judge Dundy delivered his judgment in a lengthy written decision, a legal opinion that chartered new ground. An Indian, the judge declared for the first time in U.S. history, "is a person within the meaning of the law," with the "same inalienable right to life, liberty and the pursuit of happiness as the more fortunate white race." The U.S. government, he ruled, had no legal right to imprison Standing Bear or forcibly return him to the hated Oklahoma Reservation. Therefore, the judge concluded, the chief was free to continue his journey to bury his son in one of the tribe's sacred burial sites near the Nebraska–South Dakota border, near the confluence of the Missouri and Niobrara Rivers where the Ponca had lived for many generations.

The trial of Chief Standing Bear—and its groundbreaking legal ruling—had generated much publicity throughout much of the country. Prominent East Coast newspapers had displayed running updates in their news columns and sympathetic editorials on their opinion pages. Prominent citizens, many of whom had once been seized with an abolitionist fervor, had been looking for a new cause and now they had found it: the plight of Chief Standing Bear specifically and that of the American Indian in general.

Besides Standing Bear, readers of some of the nation's largest newspapers had also become more aware of the slight, articulate Indian woman who had translated Standing Bear's words from Ponca to English. Increasingly, Bright Eyes had become identified with the Ponca chief's struggle, and during the next several years, she would travel far from home, up and down the East Coast, speaking passionately on all the political, legal, and social issues swirling about the status of the American Indian in the last quarter of the nineteenth century.

Back in the Village of the Make-Believe White Men, Susan La Flesche had heard a good deal about Chief Standing Bear, about the trial, and about her older sister's role in lobbying for greater civil and political rights for the Indian people. The wider world seemed to be a part of their lives now, expanding far beyond the cluster of white tipis, the rolling hillsides carpeted in vibrant flowers, the little house filled with warm fires and colorful stories, the quiet, peaceful village on the edge of night.

In the autumn of 1879, two different trains left a corner of the American Great Plains, bound for the East Coast. One carried a crusading newspaperman and a weary Indian chief who had lost much of his family to disease and his homeland to government incompetence. That same train also carried Francis La Flesche, a nineteen-year-old Omaha Indian who would one day become the nation's first native ethnographer. His father had insisted that Bright Eyes could go on an extended speaking tour only if her half brother escorted her to the faraway cities in the East.

In the other train was a thin, scared, fourteen-year-old Omaha Indian girl. She and one of her other sisters were both headed to Elizabeth, New Jersey, to the same school where Bright Eyes had spent six years and fallen in love with Shakespeare.

Susan La Flesche had a lot to think about as the long train wound its way across half of America. She could have thought about how much she already missed her father and her mother and her sisters. How much she missed her home and her horse and riding bareback across her beloved prairie homeland. And she could have thought about something else.

Every time she got a little scared, every time she felt the railcar closing in on her, when she wondered what such a young girl was doing on a train taking her so far away from all the people and places she loved, she could have thought back on something her father had said to her years earlier.

She could think about that time when she was only six years old, how he had pulled her and her sisters aside and asked them a question when they all lived together in the Village of the Make-Believe White Men.

"My dear young daughters," the father had said, "do you always want to be simply called those Indians or do you want to go to school and be somebody in the world?"

3

vvv

An Indian Schoolgirl and
the Harvard Scholar

For so many summers, she had gazed across the silent, endless sweep of her prairie homeland and seen the same tableau: clouds squatting on the horizon like milkweed pods. A buffalo herd grazing in the lush, greasy grass of a distant valley. A big buckskin romping across the rolling hillside. A circle of white tipis and the orange glow of the evening campfires.

But Susan La Flesche had never seen anything like this, had never before imagined anything like it.

In the early fall of 1879, she and her sister Marguerite, three years older, stepped off a train and onto the streets of Elizabeth, New Jersey. In her fourteen years, Susan had never left the reservation, had never set foot off its 1,350 square miles tucked away in an isolated corner of the central Great Plains. She and Marguerite had grown up there, had grown up in the security and safety of the Village of the Make-Believe White Men, and then their father had decided they needed to leave their village and their reservation and go to a place called New Jersey, to a private girls' school to continue their education. So here they were in early September— without preparation, without guidelines, without a context: two

Omaha Indian teenage girls standing on a street corner, looking out not at a village, but at a small, noisy, urban industrial center carved from America's East Coast, a city overflowing with white men and women.

They saw that all these white men and women seemed to be in constant motion, a frenetic, restless, bustling collection of horse-drawn carriages clopping across the cobblestone in all directions. Soon they found themselves walking down streets lined with glass storefronts, blocks brimming with tailor shops, grocery stores, restaurants, banks, haberdasheries, fruit and vegetable markets, fresh-fish stands, newspaper offices, shoe stores, bars and taverns, and lawyers' and doctors' offices. They saw apartment buildings and homes and schools and libraries and enormous churches. They saw fine suits and work clothes, top hats and, on some of the women, high, pointy-toed, leather lace-up shoes.

And like their father and Big Elk before them, they saw in those first few weeks the one thing they could never quite come to grips with, the one thing that was always the same: They could not comprehend the sheer number of white people.

By the fall of 1879, Elizabeth had become an energetic community of about twenty-eight thousand residents, a rapidly growing and increasingly important industrial and commercial center sparked, in large part, by its access to a number of ports and harbors and its proximity to New York City, just a stone's throw across the Hudson River. And by then, Elizabeth had also gotten an economic boost from another direction.

Six years before Susan and Marguerite arrived, Isaac Singer had bought thirty-two acres of Elizabeth real estate and in short order built an enormous factory that began to mass-produce sewing machines. By the time the young La Flesche sisters stepped off the train, the Singer Sewing Machine Company in Elizabeth, New Jersey, employed about six thousand people—at the time, the largest single workforce in the world. For Susan and Marguerite, it was a number impossible to comprehend. It meant that their entire tribe, a reservation of about twelve hundred Omaha Indians, could be put to work on a single floor of the Singer factory.

It meant that this one factory employed almost two and a half times more people than the twenty-seven hundred non-Indians who, according to federal census figures, officially lived in Nebraska Territory in 1854—the year their oldest sister, Bright Eyes, was born.

In the fall of 1869, ten years before her two younger sisters arrived, Bright Eyes had come to study at the same private girls' school in Elizabeth, the first of her tribe to do so. And now their father had three daughters who had all come to enhance their education at the New Jersey boarding school, who were establishing a different mark of honor. The school was initially established in 1861 as the Union School for Girls and Young Ladies, and its two main teachers were Nettie Read and Susan Higgins. In 1870, Read became principal and the school's name was changed to the Elizabeth Institute for Young Ladies, located at 521 North Broad Street, the bustling main thoroughfare in the rapidly growing community.

One of the teachers back at the Presbyterian Mission School on the Omaha Reservation had a contact at the Elizabeth school and had arranged for Bright Eyes to be admitted. That same Presbyterian connection also got Susan and Marguerite into the Elizabeth school, and it was friends of the Institute for Young Ladies who ultimately paid for the education of the two La Flesche sisters, just as they had done for Bright Eyes.

During her six years at the Elizabeth Institute, Bright Eyes had excelled at all of her studies, developing a particular passion for literature and writing, for poetry and drawing. By the time her two younger sisters arrived in the fall of 1879, the twenty-five-year-old

Omaha Indian woman, who had gained national prominence during the Standing Bear trial earlier that spring, was on the verge of significantly raising her profile, of becoming one of the school's most illustrious graduates.

Throughout the summer and early fall of 1879, a group called the Omaha Ponca Relief Committee had been brainstorming different ways to take advantage of the momentum the trial had created, different ways to capture that energy and transform it into a national platform for expanding Indian rights. How could they cash in on this momentum? How could they raise both money and awareness of the increasingly complex political, legal, and social issues American Indians faced?

By early September, the committee had decided on a plan: It would launch a full-blown East Coast speaking tour designed to expand Indian civil rights in U.S. courtrooms and to restore the Ponca homeland in northeast Nebraska. The crusading newsman Thomas Tibbles would be one of the key speakers. Standing Bear would be another. And so would Bright Eyes, who had lived in the East, knew white ways and customs, and spoke both English and Ponca fluently. It also wouldn't hurt the cause that she was articulate, modest, dignified, and beautiful.

So that fall and into the winter of 1879, Bright Eyes began to appear regularly before larger and larger crowds in Chicago, Boston, and eventually New York City, just across the Hudson River from where Susan and Marguerite were now starting their lessons at the private all-girls school. Although sympathetic to the cause, Bright Eyes initially was reluctant to participate in the long, three-month tour. All in all, she much preferred getting lost in her books, her poetry, and her artist's sketch pad—or discussing the value of a good education with her youngest sisters.

But for Standing Bear's message to resonate with East Coast audiences, it was critical his words reach them through a good interpreter. So in the end, Bright Eyes agreed to become, in effect, the first Indian woman to enter the nation's public-speaking arena.

On the evening of October 19, 1879, Standing Bear, Bright Eyes, Thomas Tibbles, and Francis La Flesche made their first appearance of the speaking tour. The Ponca chief walked across the stage at Chicago's Second Presbyterian Church in moccasins, deerskin leggings, blanket, and bear-claw necklace, an eagle feather in his straight black hair. Bright Eyes stood beside him in a plain dark dress with a white lace scarf at the throat, interpreting his remarks to the large crowd. Ten days later, the mayor of Boston introduced the young Indian poet to a packed house at Horticultural Hall. Bright Eyes spoke slowly and carefully, in precise English, her voice rising and falling to make her points.

There was a time not long ago, she said, when she had given up hope, had lost all faith in the future of her people. But it was nights like this, she told the crowd, that kept her away from the edge. "I come to you with gladness in my heart and to try and thank you, for here, after a hundred years of oppression, my people have for the first time found public sympathy, and as soon as the truth of their story was known help was given them."

Although Standing Bear and Bright Eyes had gone east to assert their freedom, to declare their independence from the old way of doing things, to build a future for their people, they often felt shackled by the past—by the simplicity, the sentimentality, and all the shopworn stereotypes they encountered. Many Americans, they discovered, preferred to see Indians as relics of the past, not as they were in the present or wanted to be in the future. It was easier that way.

Throughout the speaking tour, some newspapers began referring to Bright Eyes as the "Indian princess," a phrase she disliked intensely. So some mornings in their hotel, over breakfast, she would read aloud to Standing Bear, translating stories in that day's newspaper from English to Ponca, stories about the "noble chief," the "Indian princess," the "dignified warrior," the "three fine species of the aboriginal race," the "Indian maiden." The year after she was born, Henry Wadsworth Longfellow, one of Boston's renowned poets, had written *The Song of Hiawatha,* an epic tale about native life by the shores of a great lake, about a Victorian Indian hero of the forest and his loyal Indian wife.

One evening in Boston, the four visitors were all invited to the home of a wealthy publisher. One guest who had arrived early stood in the middle of the doorway, eagerly awaiting the appearance of the young Omaha Indian woman, a woman who spoke five languages, had graduated from a private East Coast girls' boarding school, could discuss the fine points of *King Lear,* had an essay published in the *New York Times,* and who routinely dressed in fashionable modern clothing. When Bright Eyes finally stepped through the door, Longfellow stepped forward, clasped her hand, and, looking intently in her eyes, exclaimed: "*This* is Minnehaha!"

In early December, the group made its first public appearance in New York City, sharing a stage with Peter Cooper and other prominent citizens at Steinway Hall. Professor Roswell Hitchcock was among the first to speak. On Indian matters, he said, the nation's pendulum had swung maddeningly back and forth—between romantic forest dweller and bloodthirsty savage. But the Indian, he noted, is also human. "Take away the accident of savage costume," he told the cheering crowd, "dress us just alike, and there might not be much difference between Manhattan and Omaha."

The next morning, after she had accompanied Standing Bear onstage and translated his remarks, Bright Eyes could read that Standing Bear, with his long black hair, linen shirt, rough sack coat, and black pants, looked like "an athletic savage—if such a term may be applied to a very docile Indian—clad after the conventional style of the pale-faces."

Over time, Bright Eyes would travel up and down the East Coast, take her message of Indian rights to foreign countries, and write frequently about citizenship and land issues, becoming the first Indian woman to actively and openly crusade on behalf of all native people. That fall, her name was often in the New York papers, and she had impressed a good many powerful people in the nation's most powerful city.

And just across the Hudson, Susan was now following in her famous older sister's footsteps, fulfilling their father's dream, a long way from the Village of the Make-Believe White Men.

That dream included a rigorous academic grounding at the Elizabeth Institute, a grounding that initially focused on what were often referred to as the "common branches": arithmetic, reading, writing, spelling, and composition. In time, their Elizabeth education was expanded to include courses in philosophy, literature, and physiology, a course that likely nurtured some budding interests that Susan would later explore in much greater depth.

But the education of Susan and Marguerite included many lessons and instructions far removed from the classrooms at 521 North Broad Street. Throughout their school years at the institute, there was never enough money for the sisters to return to their reservation during the long Christmas and summer breaks. As a result, they ended up spending almost thirty-six consecutive months in their temporary East Coast home.

So by the time the two young graduates of the Elizabeth Institute finally arrived back on the Omaha Reservation, their education had included something else: an extended immersion in the ways of whites and a thorough exposure to all aspects of white culture. One goal of the institute, like that of many other eastern schools of the time, was assimilation—to prepare its nonwhite students to succeed in the dominant culture.

And by almost any measure, the two Indian sisters bouncing along in a buckboard back across the Nebraska prairie in late summer 1882, sisters who switched effortlessly from Omaha to flawless English and back again, were a major success story.

When Susan looked out across the familiar prairie those first few weeks back home, it seemed different somehow, the people seemed different. A lot had changed in the nearly three years she'd been gone.

For one thing, her two oldest sisters now had white husbands. About a year earlier, Bright Eyes had married the newsman Thomas Tibbles, and now they were both off stumping on behalf of Indian rights. Her sister Rosalie, meanwhile, had married Ed Farley, a hardworking son of Irish immigrants. Unlike her three sisters, Rosalie had decided to stay put, to become a mother and raise her children on the ancestral lands of the Omaha. She and Ed now had two young sons and a stable household, one that often served as the gathering spot for reservation guests, a kind of social crossroads where everyone was welcome and one that Susan often visited to see her beloved older sister and her two little nephews. The household, the children, the family, and the land they lived on made her feel grounded in a way nothing else really did.

For another thing, the old Presbyterian Mission School was back in business. In 1869, when Susan was only four years old, the mission school had closed its doors, making way for the Quaker day schools. But ten years later, not long after she and Marguerite left for New Jersey, the old school had reopened. So Susan applied for a teaching position and soon got a job at the revamped mission school, where she taught for about two years, including a six-month stint working with a group of young children.

And there were other changes almost everywhere she looked. After she'd been back a while, it seemed to Susan that both the physical and cultural landscape of her reservation had begun to tilt more heavily toward her father's long-held vision of how the Omaha were to survive. It was an observation by others as well. In an 1882 report to his superiors, Omaha Reservation agent George Wilkinson noted that the reservation now boasted 119 wood-frame homes and that 250 of the tribe's 1,193 members routinely spoke English in most of their daily affairs. Furthermore, he wrote, a good many others could read English but lacked the confidence to speak it.

For weeks Susan also heard stories from her mother and grandmother, from Rosalie and Bright Eyes, getting caught up on all the family gossip, on all the reservation news that had happened while she was away. And she also heard many more stories from her father. She heard him talk about the continuing friction between the two tribal divisions, the dire need for bigger and better crops, the accomplishments of her half brother, Francis. And she likely heard him and others who were still talking about an incident that occurred while she and Marguerite were away, an incident that had shocked the nation and many Omaha as well, including her father.

On July 2, 1881, Charles Guiteau, a disgruntled office seeker, shot President James Garfield at a Washington train station. In the long aftermath, doctors probed Garfield's wounds with filthy hands and dirty instruments, looking for the bullet lodged in the badly wounded president. While Garfield held on for seventy-nine days, much of the nation ultimately blamed the unsanitary medical care for his death—a sentiment also reflected among some of the Omaha. The newsman Tibbles later recalled an evening when he, Bright Eyes, her father (whom he referred to by his Indian name of Iron Eye), and a number of other Omaha sat around a prairie campfire discussing the wounded president, then in his ninth week of fighting for his life. Wrote Tibbles:

"The doctors," asserted Iron Eye, "will finish Guiteau's work."

"If they had sent him out to us," said Kaga Amba, a chief who had just returned from Washington, "we should have cured him."

"I know an Indian who was shot in the back, and the ball went almost through him, and he got well," Wajapa, one of the leading men, volunteered. "Sticking that tube into the president every day is what is killing him."

Iron Eye chimed in again.

"If a man lives until the fourth day after he has received a dangerous wound, we think he is sure to get well, and we call that fourth day by a special name which means 'the walking day' because an Indian doctor makes his patient get up then and walk at least a step or two."

But in those first few weeks, and for a long time afterward, what Susan mostly heard from her father was news of a significant change that would soon come to their reservation—a change that would dramatically impact many of the western tribes, starting first with the Omaha. A change, unbeknownst to the seventeen-year-old Susan, that would have profound consequences for her people, consequences she would have to deal with for much of her adult life.

On August 7, 1882, a few weeks before Susan and Marguerite returned from New Jersey, shortly after Congress gave its approval, President Chester Arthur signed into law what was known as the Omaha Allotment Act. The act allowed the heads of each Omaha family to receive 160 acres of their own land, land that would be carved from the communally owned tribal land base. If everything went as planned, individual Omaha tribal members would soon become the private owners of those parcels, which the government then would hold in trust for twenty-five years.

This idea, that the vast tribal land bases west of the Missouri should now be cut up into 160-acre, privately owned plots, reflected a complex and controversial government policy, one that would cast a wide shadow over Indian country throughout the 1880s and well beyond. Powerful advocates of this policy—including Secretary of the Interior Carl Schurz, Senator Henry Dawes, Brigadier General George Crook, journalist Thomas Tibbles, and a wide swath of energized East Coast reformers—passionately believed that individual ownership would greatly accelerate civilization of the Indian, that it was a surefire way to eventually integrate America's native people into the nation's political, cultural, and social mainstream.

They all believed that the twenty-five-year trust period would buy enough time for individual Indian families to learn the true value of private ownership, how to nurture and take care of their own land, how to make a profit from it. In effect, it would force them to become self-sufficient farmers and ranchers, motivated by the principles of a competitive, free market economy. Ultimately, a taste for money and possessions would take hold, allowing many to achieve the same status as the white farmers and ranchers who increasingly had begun to crowd their lands. Meanwhile, any surplus land—reservation land left over after all the individual plots had been awarded—could be sold to the many whites who coveted Indian lands.

But not everyone viewed the allotment policy as such a charitable enterprise. The concept of private ownership, of an individual holding a piece of paper declaring he alone owned a specific section of land with precise borders, was a difficult one for many Indian people to comprehend. For centuries, many had lived on lands whose boundaries were fluid, lands that tribes often claimed as their own, but not in a legal sense, and not as individuals. For generations, the need of the individual had always been subordinate to the needs of the tribe. They had hunted buffalo, raised corn, picked chokecherries, harvested wild turnips, gathered wood, shared pastures, and pooled resources for protection against enemies—all for the common good, for the collective benefit of the whole, not the individual. It was how they had always survived. And when the reservation system came about, it was the tribe that owned the reservation lands, never its individual members.

This reluctance to break up tribally owned land into individual plots had confused and confounded successive waves of Washington bureaucrats. To them, not wanting to own your own land, your own home, your own crops, your own stock, made no sense. Among Indians, frustrated Senator Dawes once remarked, "there is no selfishness, which is at the bottom of civilization."

And there were also others who worried, and warned, that over time the vast tracts of western indigenous lands would simply become too tempting. That ultimately the sparsely populated, underdeveloped reservations would be seen as a waste of valuable land—land that more ambitious, productive white settlers could put to far better use.

Francis La Flesche, who one day would become a noted anthropologist with the Smithsonian Institution, was among those who urged caution. After all of the allotments had been made, he argued, there would still be a good amount of reservation land left over. And Susan's half brother worried openly that leasing this surplus land would open the door to white farmers and ranchers, who eventually would take control of reservation lands. Fresh off the long East Coast speaking tour on behalf of Indian rights, Francis strongly urged his influential father to enlist the support of their Boston friends and allies. He wanted those reformers to help slam the door on the whole notion of whites being able to lease—

and eventually buy—surplus Indian lands. But his fears fell on deaf ears.

The idea of allotting lands was not a new one. It had been with the Omaha for many years. Although the treaties of 1854 and 1865 both specified providing 160 acres to each family head, nothing had ever come of it. But for Susan, her family, and all the other Omaha, that indifference began to change in the spring of 1877— the spring that the Ponca were forcibly removed from their Niobrara River homeland.

When they saw how easily the government could herd their close friends, allies, and relatives from their Nebraska reservation to the scorching plains of the Indian Territory, where so many had died that first year, many Omaha were fearful the same fate awaited them. If it happened to the Ponca, they asked, then why couldn't it happen to us?

So by 1882, an influential number of Omaha had increasingly come to see private ownership as a hedge against the government forcibly removing them from their ancestral lands. If they had title to their own land, if they legally owned their 160-acre plots, then how could the government force them off that land?

Not surprisingly, Joseph La Flesche helped lead the push that ultimately resulted in the Omaha Allotment Act—five years before Congress approved the more expansive Dawes Act of 1887 that impacted many of the nation's Indian tribes. Among other things, Joseph saw remaking the Omaha Reservation into a patchwork of privately owned, 160-acre plots as another significant step toward assimilating his people into the American mainstream. But getting there didn't happen overnight.

First, La Flesche enlisted the help of powerful allies to lobby Congress on behalf of the Omaha. Later, they sent a tribal petition to Congress and held tribal council meetings and discussions, public and private, throughout the reservation. Finally, there was widespread agreement among both progressive and traditional factions that allotments were the best weapon the Omaha had to maintain their lands and preserve their culture.

All in all, it took about two years for some of the large tribal land base to be whittled down to 160-acre plots. By 1884, Omaha agent Wilkinson neatly summed up the results of the Omaha allotment process to Washington superiors: 954 parcels of land totaling 75,931 acres disbursed to 1,194 individuals. For many, the numbers were cause for celebration, proof of the Omaha's determined march toward assimilation.

All along, the overarching goal of the allotment process had been a fundamental one: to preserve the Indian land base, to keep these ancestral homelands in the hands of the native people, to help ensure they were not forcibly removed and dispossessed of the very lands that gave them their culture, their spiritual beliefs, their identity. And along the way, by owning their individual plots, by turning profits on their private farms, the allotment acts would greatly enhance their journey toward citizenship, would greatly accelerate the overall civilization of the American Indian.

But in the end, the Omaha and Dawes allotment acts did something else, something quite different: They greatly accelerated the amount of Indian lands that eventually passed from red to white hands. Ultimately, despite all the warnings from Francis La Flesche and others, despite all the pronouncements of well-intentioned reformers, white settlers gobbled up surplus reservation lands, and desperately poor Indians prematurely sold off their allotments, dramatically reducing a once robust native land base almost overnight.

The Omaha had done everything right, had believed in the allotment process, yet by the opening years of the twentieth century, they had lost almost fifty thousand acres of their reservation. By the middle of that century, the Upstream People had lost more than one hundred thousand acres, leaving fewer than thirty thousand acres of their own land still in their possession.

Nationwide, the same forces reduced an overall Indian land base of some 150 million acres before the 1887 Dawes Act to about 48 million acres by the time it was repealed in 1934, an overall loss of 102 million acres—an area about the size of California and Maine combined.

Not long before his death, a prominent, half-blind Lakota chief likely spoke for many of his countrymen: "They made us many promises, more than I can remember," said Red Cloud, "but they never kept but one; they promised to take our land and they took it."

In the summer of 1883, Susan La Flesche was still in her teens, yet she had seen and experienced far more than her Indian counterparts both at home and on other reservations scattered throughout the American West. As a child, she had gone on the summer buffalo hunts with her family, lived in a tipi on the western plains of Nebraska, walked across the rolling prairies of eastern Nebraska, and grown up in a rectangular wood-frame house in a progressive village not far from the Missouri River.

She had attended Presbyterian and Quaker schools, done well in both, learned about a savior who promised eternal salvation, heard her father talk about the Good Book, and watched a woman die an agonizing death when no doctor came to help her. She had an older sister who had already become famous for her Indian rights campaigns and a half brother who would soon become famous for his detailed studies of Indian culture. She had ridden a train, gone thirteen hundred miles from her tribal homeland, spent almost three years in a private East Coast girls' school, and had already heard of William Shakespeare and pulmonary arteries.

She had worn pointy, high-laced leather shoes and soft, deer-skin moccasins. She had lived in cities laid out in rectangular quadrants and in tipi villages arranged in circles. She had ridden bareback across sunflower-covered hillsides and in horse-drawn carriages atop cobblestone streets. She was comfortable at formal poetry readings and at summer powwows. She knew about symphonies and tribal drum groups. And she could switch effortlessly from perfect Omaha to perfect English.

That summer, she had grown into an attractive young woman with long dark hair and dark features. Although she had seen a lot of white civilization in a faraway eastern city and had noticed all the changes occurring right around her, on her own reservation, she wasn't quite sure what to make of it all, didn't really know what to do with her life. What direction to take next.

For now, her job teaching at the Presbyterian Mission School gave her stability, a purpose.

And then one damp and gloomy afternoon in early July, her half brother, Francis, arrived at the mission school in a buckboard wagon. Lying on a cot in the back was a middle-aged white woman, soaked, shivering, in a great deal of pain.

Back then, Susan could not have known that the afternoon of July 3, 1883, marked the beginning of an invaluable relationship between a precocious eighteen-year-old Omaha schoolgirl and a groundbreaking forty-five-year-old Harvard scholar.

Alice Cunningham Fletcher was born on March 15, 1838, in Havana, Cuba, where her father had gone to help quell a serious illness. But plenty of Cuban air and sunshine didn't do the trick, so the family moved back to the East Coast, where her father died when Fletcher was not yet two. Her mother soon moved the family to Brooklyn, and Alice began her education in a private girls' school. She spent much of the next three decades in New York, eventually becoming an active member in a number of women's clubs, including the Association for the Advancement of Women and the Woman's Congress. By the late 1870s, as she entered her early forties, Fletcher began to carefully shape a long-held interest in history into an increasingly popular series of public lectures, initially along the East Coast and later in the Midwest. Her "Lectures on Ancient America" struck a responsive chord in many audiences, and her persistence in trying to dig out more scientific information hit a rich vein in the fall of 1879.

That fall, in response to her request for some documents, the director of Harvard University's Peabody Museum of American Archaeology and Ethnology in Cambridge, Massachusetts, invited Fletcher to study at the museum to help hone her growing interest in archaeology—a field then bereft of women. A little intimidated by his offer, she initially resisted. But Frederic Putnam persisted. Soon, he helped her join the fledgling Archaeological Institute of America and arranged for her to have work space inside the museum.

That same fall, Fletcher happened to be visiting her mother's hometown when she got wind of an event that had much of Boston buzzing, an event that would fundamentally alter the direction of her life. After one of their rousing public appearances in Boston, Bright Eyes and Tibbles suddenly found themselves face-to-face with an energetic, articulate, forty-one-year-old woman. While twenty-two-year-old Francis La Flesche stood discreetly off to the side, the woman eventually posed a question: Would they be willing to help her go out west and live with Indians?

After their talks, Bright Eyes and Tibbles were not typically besieged by white, middle-aged, East Coast female intellectuals desperate to head to the Dakotas, pitch a tent, and live among Indians. So they didn't really respond. They didn't really know if she was serious, or how serious.

But Fletcher was serious. About eighteen months later, she again met up with the two Indian rights crusaders in Boston. This time, she gave them a tour of the Peabody Museum and emphasized once again how badly she wanted to cross the Missouri and stay on Indian lands. So by midsummer of 1881, convinced she meant what she said, Bright Eyes and Tibbles sent her word: If she could make it to Omaha in the fall, they would escort her into Sioux country. Once there, they could all camp for a while and then she would be on her own.

And so it came to pass: In September, Fletcher took a train to Omaha, where Bright Eyes and Tibbles met up with her and took her on horseback and buckboard first to the Omaha Reservation, then to see Standing Bear and the Ponca, and finally on to Sioux country in South Dakota. Fletcher had come west to do a serious, up-close study of Indian people, to immerse herself in their camps, document their customs and social structures, note the cultural significance of their songs and dances, ask a lot of questions, and take a lot of notes—and she soon got an eyeful.

All along, the plan was for her to convey in detailed letters to both herself and her Peabody colleagues the facts she had gathered, all the firsthand observations and cultural interpretations she had made. By late fall 1881, there were very few American observers who had endured the physical and emotional rigors of living among the Indians, who had taken seriously the effort to record their customs and cultural traits. And none of them were women.

While on the ancestral lands of the Sioux and Omaha, Fletcher also became keenly interested in their religious ceremonies, an intense interest that eventually sparked the publication of her first significant article: "Five Indian Ceremonies." The fifth—and by far the most detailed account—was about the Omaha's Pipe Dance Ceremony. To get the telling detail, the religious and cultural significance of this dance, she had relied a great deal on another member of the La Flesche family. Her collaboration with Francis La Flesche on the Pipe Dance Ceremony marked the beginning of an intense, intimate, and complex relationship that would span three decades.

More than three decades earlier, back in the traditional village of the Omaha, Chief Big Elk had used this same ceremony—the Pipe Dance—to honor both Joseph La Flesche and his wife, Mary. To honor and direct such kindness toward women was not unusual for the Omaha or many other native tribes. Women were held in high esteem by the Upstream People, and their opinions, thoughts, and wishes were greatly valued, as were their overall physical health and emotional well-being. And within her dwelling, within her own family, she almost always was the center of attention. If a husband became abusive, the wife left him and she had the support of her family and the tribe. The children stayed with the mother, and the abusive husband became homeless.

Throughout much of the last quarter of the nineteenth century—when Fletcher herself was bumping up against rigid gender barriers—potent social forces often reduced American women to simple stereotypes, framing them as a class of people whose value did not extend much beyond their predetermined roles as loving wives, nurturing mothers, and conscientious Christian homemakers. Those women who wanted to break out, who wanted intellectual challenges and a hand on the ballot box, who sought to free themselves from the bondage of Victorian expectations, often found themselves swimming against a powerful current seeking to maintain the status quo at all costs. The arguments to do so came from many different quarters, including the scientific one. For one thing, theorized a number of important Victorian-era scientists, white American women were not biologically equipped to balance the rigors of intellectual and mental exertion with their more important reproductive responsibilities. Women, they believed, not only jeopardized their own health, but threatened the very existence of the species by pursuing mental and physical activities equal to those of men.

Herbert Spencer, an influential British philosopher, sociologist, and biologist of the era, went so far as to suggest that a woman's reproductive makeup prevented her from evolving to the same levels as a man. When eight-year-old Susan La Flesche was taking her classes at the Quaker day school on the Omaha Reservation, Spencer set forth his theories in black and white. Women's minds lack "those two faculties, intellectual and emotional, which are the latest products of human evolution—the power of abstract reasoning and that most abstract of emotions, the sentiment of justice," he wrote in *Popular Science Monthly*.

By November 1881, Alice Fletcher had returned from her outings with the Sioux, where she had gathered a substantial amount of valuable firsthand accounts of native life, including striking gender differences between tribal and mainstream cultures. That fall, she had moved in with the Omaha to begin what she hoped would be an intense ethnographic study of the tribe. But by the time she arrived, the allotment issue had cast a large shadow across the reservation and Fletcher soon found herself at the center of it.

When she had first arrived on the Omaha Reservation earlier that fall, she was immediately taken to the home of Susan's older sister Rosalie. The strong-willed East Coast ethnologist and the twenty-year-old Omaha Indian mother hit it off from the start, developing a deep and loving friendship that lasted for many years. Soon after, Bright Eyes brought her parents to meet Fletcher. Joseph left that initial meeting impressed with the intelligence, passion, and sincerity of their visitor from the East. Over time, Fletcher's relationship with the La Flesche family expanded and deepened to include almost all of its members.

Within a few days of moving in with the Omaha, Fletcher and Joseph La Flesche began meeting regularly to devise a plan to get the stalled allotment process rolling again. Before long, Fletcher had become an inexhaustible advocate, championing the policy as an invaluable tool for the Omaha's future. To that end, she met regularly with both tribal leaders and the rank and file. By December 1881, Fletcher had crafted a petition to Congress, asking that the signatories be given title to their land. There were fifty-three signatures—including Joseph La Flesche's and those of a dozen others from the Village of the Make-Believe White Men.

Her petition soon triggered a congressional bill for the allotment of Omaha lands. But then months went by and the increasingly impatient La Flesche and others heard nothing from Congress about the bill's fate. So Fletcher packed up, hopped a train, and went to the nation's capital. In Washington, she spent three months in the spring of 1882 lobbying aggressively on behalf of the Omaha and the bill. By summer it had been passed and signed into law by President Chester A. Arthur. In the spring of 1883, the government assigned Fletcher to oversee the allotment of all lands on the Omaha Reservation. And the job came with her own designated assistant and interpreter: Francis La Flesche.

Fletcher and her young assistant arrived from Washington in May. She immediately went to work, lobbying aggressively once again, this time to persuade the Omaha to stake their claims in the reservation's far western regions. And she succeeded. Before long, Joseph La Flesche and fifty families, some from the Village of the

Make-Believe White Men, opted to settle in the Logan Creek area on the western end, an area where Susan once rode her horse, where she had fond memories of summer campsites along the creek.

Unlike the hills and bluffs and heavily timbered regions on the eastern part, the creek valley on the western end offered a good deal of fertile land. It also boasted a railroad that followed the creek, providing Omaha farmers with potential access to markets. Then, too, the new settlement of Bancroft had cropped up just across the reservation line, a community of white farmers who some believed would be good role models for the Omaha.

In the end, the petition sent to Congress, the bill it spawned, and the reality of privately owning 160 acres went a long way toward calming the Omaha's intense anxiety and fear that they would be the next ones shipped to Indian Territory. More than a year later, after all the land had been allotted, after the tribe had progressed a good deal further on the road to assimilation, their agent was prompted to remark that the Omaha were "a determined and progressive people, and in a very hopeful condition."

And at the time, some Omaha were willing to lay a good deal of the credit for that at Fletcher's doorstep. In the end, she had used her intellect, her fierce drive, her physical and emotional strength, her strong connections among both the Omaha and the congressional crowd, to become a powerful, influential force on the reservation. "No one," remarked Rosalie La Flesche, "had more influence than [Fletcher]."

But her forceful advocacy also created ill will among other members of the tribe, ill will that lasted many years. And later, many Omaha believed it was Fletcher—either directly or indirectly—who was behind the disappearance of a number of the tribe's most sacred objects, objects that eventually ended up in prestigious East Coast museums where she had strong connections. The resentment among a good number of Omaha at the disappearance of those objects never diminished.

In 1883, however, Fletcher was generally well thought of by the Omaha and was at the beginning of a close and lasting relationship with the La Flesche family. By early summer, she was also living in a white tent on the far western edge of the Omaha homeland—a long way from Havana and Brooklyn, from Boston and the Peabody Museum.

About a century later, another Peabody Museum scholar would describe in detail the living arrangement her famous predecessor had carved from the vast Nebraska prairie. Fletcher had gotten her own tent from the Omaha and set up her base camp on the banks of Logan Creek. Inside the tent, noted her biographer, Joan Mark, was a sturdy table and chairs in the middle, buffalo robes lying about, and portable cupboards where Fletcher kept her dishes and cups. There was also a cot in the back where she slept. And because the Omaha were well aware of how much she loved wildflowers, the table was seldom without a colorful floral arrangement. So this became her office, her work space—a bustling headquarters for the painstaking task of overseeing the transformation from tribally owned lands to privately owned lands.

And in typical fashion, Fletcher threw herself into the job with a relentless zeal, working all hours of the day and night, working through hot and humid days often followed by relentless torrential downpours come evening. On July 3, yet another cloudburst swept in, soaking her to the bone. She ignored it, didn't change out of her soaked clothing, just kept working feverishly on the allotments. A few hours later, she had severe chills. Soon, she was in so much pain that she couldn't walk, couldn't move. So she sent for her trusted assistant. Francis gently put her on a cot, placed her in a buckboard, and set off for the Presbyterian mission about thirty miles away.

For the next three weeks, Fletcher was so sick, so racked with pain, that she couldn't be moved; even her bedding could not be changed. She didn't see much hope. "My life dwindled away," she would later write. "All thought it more than likely I would die."

But she didn't. Gradually, she got a little stronger, a little better, each day. It was five weeks before she was finally strong enough to be placed on a mattress, put in a buckboard, and driven another ten miles to the Winnebago Reservation.

At the Winnebago government headquarters, Fletcher came under the care of the agency doctor, who told her what she was suffering from: inflammatory rheumatism. For five long months—from the Fourth of July to Thanksgiving—Fletcher remained bedridden, unable to work with her customary energy and aggressiveness.

And almost every day during those long, bedridden five months, Fletcher was tended to by an attentive, diligent, upbeat young girl. Week after week, Susan La Flesche took care of the East Coast scholar who had come west to study the Indian people. Day after day, she stayed with Fletcher, helping to slowly nurse her back to health, often observing what the agency doctor did and said to his patient whenever he came to visit.

Eventually, after almost eight months of being unable to leave her bed for long, Fletcher began to recover, began to get back to the task at hand.

But no matter how busy she got, no matter how hard she worked, she often thought of the eighteen-year-old Omaha girl back at the mission who had worked so hard to nurse her back to health. During those five months together, the Harvard anthropologist had seen what a number of others had already observed in the teenager: intelligence, focus, discipline, maturity, a good heart, and spirit.

And then one day, Alice Cunningham Fletcher had an idea.

4
⌄ ⌄ ⌄
Can Black Children and Red Children Become White Citizens?

It's five thirty A.M.

Depending on the day of the week, nineteen-year-old Susan La Flesche could be on her hands and knees, bucket and brush by her side, scrubbing down the dormitory hallway.

Or—dust cap on her head, broom and dustpan in hand—she could be sweeping her dorm room or an assembly hall or one of the classrooms. She might also be in the laundry room, heaving heavy piles of wet clothing from one place to another. Or she could even be in uniform, drilling on a school parade ground.

Samuel Chapman Armstrong, a onetime U.S. Army general in charge of the Hampton Normal and Agricultural Institute, ran it with the discipline and military precision of a basic training camp. "I venture to say," the general frequently observed, "few students anywhere have their time more fully occupied than the Hampton student."

It had taken the connections of Alice Fletcher and the persistence of several other strong women to get her in the door, but once inside the institute, Susan got right to work.

That meant she, like all of the school's black and Indian students, rose each morning at five fifteen A.M., 365 days a year, often seeing the sun creeping up over her Virginia campus. Here, the young Omaha Indian girl was now in charge of taking fastidious care of herself, her clothing, and her room, so she would awaken early, clean herself, get dressed, and begin her early-morning chores, which also included making, mending, washing, and ironing all of her own clothes. After an hour or so of cleaning and tidying up, all the girls went to breakfast and then reassembled at precisely eight A.M., when her room—and every hall and corridor in Winona Lodge—underwent official inspection. After the inspection, Susan, like the other girls, changed into a uniform of dark calico and muslin and joined the boys for classes starting promptly at eight forty A.M. By three forty-five P.M. Monday through Friday, the students had finished the seventh and last class of the day. After classes ended, all boys performed a series of military drills twice each week. And each girl received a mandatory two-hour cooking lesson one day each week as well as occasional sewing lessons.

Often, the sheer amount of work the students did to offset tuition was impressive. As recorded in the 1885 year-end report, the school's Tailoring Department, which consisted of a dozen girls and two boys, produced "160 uniform coats, 236 pair of trousers, and 92 vests, of Middlesex blue flannel; also 50 work suits of Kentucky jeans, 226 linens, 174 Percales, with 348 collars, and 233 'hickory,' and gray flannel shirts, besides 363 pair of drawers, and 375 night shirts for the use of students. Making, with about 500 other garments, a total of 2,522 pieces so far this year." Susan herself took $6.70 of her hard-earned money and bought enough muslin to make three suits with trimming, a lawn dress, and several smaller items.

But like many of the other young women, Susan also had a few hours of free time most afternoons until the dinner bell sounded at precisely six P.M., when all students filed into the cavernous dining room on the first floor of Virginia Hall. After dinner, everyone went to the third floor for prayer meetings, where the general often gave inspirational talks on the values he was trying to instill in the students and how those values would pay off down the road. Then it was time to study, a mandatory two-hour session each weekday from seven to nine P.M. At precisely nine twenty P.M., a bell rang, signaling the end of the day.

Sixteen years before Susan and her sister Marguerite arrived in August 1884, the Hampton Normal and Agricultural Institute first opened its doors to former slaves, free blacks, and their children. A new concept in American education, Hampton's goal was to help transform these students—many of whom had never been in a school—into teachers, farmers, carpenters, blacksmiths, tailors, seamstresses, and homemakers. In exchange for learning how to read and write, for learning a marketable skill, the students would pay for their education by doing manual labor, by working off the debt in the school's farm fields, barns, kitchens, and laundry rooms. And from the beginning, the institute's founder and its first principal made it clear that work—hard, steady work—had a moral value that helped build self-sufficiency and strong character.

Armstrong was born in Hawaii to parents who were prominent missionaries. Hopscotching across a cluster of islands throughout his youth, he eventually learned a set of bedrock principles: the moral value of hard work, commitment to a cause, and the sanctity of helping others help themselves. Those principles stuck with him after his father's sudden death in 1860, during his undergraduate years at Williams College in Massachusetts, and when he volunteered to serve in the Union army. They stayed with him while he rose through the officer ranks, when he was captured at Harpers Ferry, and throughout the bloody siege to repel Pickett's Charge at Gettysburg.

And they were with him midway through the Civil War when Lieutenant Colonel Armstrong became commander of the Eighth U.S. Colored Troops—a regiment of mostly ex-slaves, a group of people he'd had little contact with, black soldiers who would soon trigger a deep personal concern and many questions. What would become of them? What could be done for them? What could they do for themselves? How could they ever acquire the knowledge, skills, and education to become self-sufficient? To become a functioning part integrated into the whole?

So not long after taking charge of the regiment, the sixth of ten children of devoted missionary parents oversaw a school created for the benefit of his colored troops. He wanted to see if he could find answers to his questions, if the core principles he had acquired in Maui could be applied to a makeshift school at a Maryland military camp filled with colored soldiers fighting for their freedom. Armstrong was initially shocked, surprised at how little his men knew, bewildered by their basic ignorance. At Williams College, hundreds of miles to the north, they hadn't taught him about Nat Turner's 1831 slave revolt. He didn't know that soon after the rebellion the Virginia General Assembly—like other state legislatures in the Confederate South—passed a law making it illegal to teach slaves, free blacks, and mulattos how to read and write.

Although the Civil War ended a few years after the Maryland military school began, Armstrong's concern for his soldiers—and the overall welfare of black men, women, and children—did not. Laws that outlawed teaching people of color to read and write eventually were wiped from the books, but by then the damage had been done. By the end of the Civil War, illiteracy and poverty had become deeply entrenched, part of a culture that had no educational underpinnings. A culture of widespread illiteracy, wrenching poverty, and joblessness that had developed over many generations and would endure for many more.

W. E. B. Du Bois, a celebrated journalist, author, and civil-rights activist, would later sum up the irony of being free, poor, and illiterate in a land of plenty. A black person, noted Du Bois, "felt his poverty; without a cent, without a home, without land, tools, or savings, he had entered into competition with rich, landed, skilled neighbors. To be a poor man is hard, but to be a poor race in a land of dollars is the very bottom of hardships."

So in post–Civil War America, as the Reconstruction era gained momentum, many of the nation's staunch abolitionists, devoted East Coast reformers, and energized clergy confronted a similar question: How could black Americans—all of the country's recently freed slaves and their children—learn the skills to get a job that would enable them to become stakeholders in the economic, educational, and political fabric of their country?

On April 1, 1868, Hampton opened its first classrooms on the banks of Virginia's Chesapeake Bay, classrooms that General Armstrong believed would go a long way toward providing the answer. "The thing to be done," the general declared, "was clear: to train selected Negro youth who should go out and teach and lead their people first by example, by getting land and homes; to give them not a dollar that they could earn for themselves; to teach respect for labor, to replace stupid drudgery with skilled hands, and in this way to build up an industrial system for the sake not only of self-support and intelligent labor, but also for the sake of character."

In Armstrong's vision, modeled in part after his father's school in Hawaii, Hampton would become a working laboratory, a place to mold a new generation of black teachers who would then fan out and plant the school's self-help seed and up-by-the-bootstraps philosophy throughout the land—specifically in the Deep South. This, Armstrong and his allies at the American Missionary Association believed, provided the best and swiftest way to assimilate impoverished, illiterate blacks into the dominant white mainstream.

So to carry out that vision, one of the school's early requirements was declaring the intent to become a teacher. And of the 723 graduates in Hampton's first twenty classes, about 84 percent became teachers.

One day in 1872, one of those teachers-to-be wandered in looking dirty, disheveled, and destitute from his long journey to get to the Virginia institute. He asked the assistant principal if they would admit him. The assistant principal looked at the ragged sixteen-year-old boy, thinking he would reject his request on the spot. Instead, the assistant principal asked the boy to sweep the recitation room. Energized by his prospects, the boy swept the floor three times—then, for good measure, dusted the room a fourth time. Having passed a vigorous "white glove" inspection, the assistant principal pulled the boy aside. "I guess," he told the boy softly, "you will do to enter this institution."

Booker T. Washington would become Hampton's most celebrated graduate. From the beginning, he embraced the institute's philosophy and came to revere its principal, whom he described as "the most perfect specimen of man, physically, mentally, and spiritually." Nine years later, in 1881, with Armstrong's glowing recommendation, Washington helped found Alabama's Tuskegee Institute.

Three years earlier, in 1878, a development occurred that would substantially alter the school's makeup, opening the door to a whole new group of students whom Hampton's educational architects would diligently try also to prepare for assimilation into white culture. After the Red River War between the U.S. military and Plains Indians in Oklahoma and Texas wound down in 1875, the army rounded up seventy-two suspected ringleaders—mostly Arapaho, Kiowa, Cheyenne, and Comanche. All seventy-two were imprisoned without charges, without a trial, at Florida's Fort Marion.

There, they came under the supervision of Captain Richard Henry Pratt, who would later found the Carlisle Indian Industrial School in Pennsylvania. At Fort Marion, Pratt became interested in initiating remedial English-language and American culture classes for young Indian warriors, mostly from the Great Plains. After they had all served their time, Pratt convinced seventeen to continue their education.

So on the night of April 18, 1878, at the request of General Armstrong, those seventeen, plus another fifty-three that included both men and women, all arrived at Hampton, becoming the first American Indian students to attend the agricultural and vocational school. For these Indian students, Hampton was envisioned as a kind of "reeducation camp," a place where they could be coaxed into letting go of their Indian ways and customs, trading the bow and arrow for the plow, the scalping knife for a handsaw. The goal for the Indians was the same as for the black students: to build strong character, create a new wave of teachers, learn to work at a skilled job, and become a leader. In the end, it was also hoped that the new group of Indian students could help inspire local whites to be more accepting of the school's black students and that the black students could help civilize and assimilate the Indian students. And it wouldn't hurt if the two groups could find a few strong, inspirational student leaders.

Alice Fletcher was certain she knew one such student and was equally certain that Hampton would provide an ideal setting to continue the education of Susan La Flesche. And the Harvard scholar wasn't shy about using her connections and influence to make it happen.

When Susan and Marguerite arrived at Hampton by train in late summer 1884, it was the second time in five years that the two Omaha Indian sisters had had the topographical rug pulled out from under them. Once again, their new surroundings looked nothing like their prairie homeland. And it certainly looked nothing like Elizabeth, New Jersey. Nestled on the verdant Virginia coast, Hampton offered views of the massive expanse of Chesapeake Bay. Unlike any body of water they had ever seen, the bay looked like an ocean to them. Wherever they went, they could smell the heavy salt air, and in the distance they could see the smoke coming from the nearby city of Norfolk. In their new home, there were boats and barges and sailboats filled with oysters, crabs, and fish of all kind and other watercraft loaded with coal, wood, and livestock. Dolphins exploded out of the water, and fish flew through the air. The rich soil in the nearby fields nurtured bountiful orchards of lush apples, pears, grapes, and figs. And it seemed there were fields of potatoes everywhere, fields where barefoot children wore big straw hats as they dug deep into the ground.

Not long after Susan and Marguerite arrived, they moved into their new rooms at the spacious Winona Lodge. Sixteen years after opening its doors, Hampton had experienced impressive growth— so much so that new dorms had to be built. The school's Indian population had risen from the initial seventeen to more than a hundred by the early 1880s, when both the Indian and black girls were housed in increasingly cramped quarters at Virginia Hall. So it wasn't long before a fund-raising drive began to get the Indian girls a dormitory of their own. To reach the fund-raising goal, Hampton administrators eventually turned to an Indian woman who was now well-known up and down the East Coast. Yes, said Bright Eyes—she would help them raise the money. After they reached their $30,000 goal, a sparkling four-story brick building rose up just south of Virginia Hall a year before the two younger sisters of Bright Eyes arrived on campus.

The year the two sisters arrived, Hampton boasted 659 students—384 boys and 275 girls. Of the total enrollment, 127, or about one-sixth, were Indian students from nineteen different tribes, including more than half from the Sioux Nation. And of the 127 Indian students, 52 were girls, all of whom stayed at Winona Lodge. The architects went out of their way to keep the lodge from reflecting the cold, hard-edged institutional look of many boarding schools—long, lifeless corridors, physical separation, little communal give-and-take. By contrast, Winona was a place where "each room is a little castle for the two or three girls who occupy it," said Josephine Richards, who oversaw the lodge. "Here in leisure hours they can read, write, sew and receive their friends, while the little ones have many a nice play with their beloved dolls." She also noted other benefits of the living arrangement. "In this way too they learn that putting a room in order in the morning, and keeping it in order amid all of the vicissitudes of the day, are two quite distinct things."

As with many boarding schools and dormitories, Winona's dining room offered a challenging atmosphere, a place where it was often complicated to draw a line between chaos and community. Hampton wanted the feel of the latter, so it developed a philosophy of how to achieve its dining room goals. Miss Richards explained: "In the Winona Dining Room . . . rules of absolute silence are not enforced; the aim is to put down anything rude or boisterous, but to make the room a bright, cheerful, home-like spot. To preserve a happy mean between restraint and lawlessness, to thaw out the true Indian shyness and silence of new-comers, yet at the same time to bridle the little tongues of the over vivacious, is not always easy, but the success already attained is cheering."

Inside both Winona Lodge and Wigwam Lodge, where the Indian boys stayed, it was against the rules to speak any Indian language—against the rules to speak anything other than English, remembered Josephine Waggoner, a Sioux Indian from Sitting Bull's tribe who attended Hampton the same time as Susan and would later write about her experiences. And those rules were strictly enforced. To help promote the English-only policy, students from the same tribe were not allowed to room together, forcing them to communicate in English no matter how primitively, Waggoner recalled. A point system also helped enforce the policy. Students caught speaking their native language would get a demerit, wrote Waggoner, admitting that she herself frequently violated the policy. If they accumulated five such marks, which many initially did, they were forced to work all day Saturday—a coveted time of relaxation, carefree fun, and competitive games of lawn tennis, croquet, and the relatively new American sport of baseball, which often pitted all-black teams against all-Indian teams.

English-language skills were never an issue for Susan and Marguerite, both of whom had come to Hampton on scholarship. In fact, Susan's superb command of English and her previous educational experience quickly landed her on the school's academic fast track—called "the Normal course." This level of course work was reserved only for those who could speak, write, and read English with a high degree of efficiency. So during the first of her two years at Hampton, Susan studied physiology, physical geography, arithmetic, literature, and the Bible. Additionally, she excelled at reading, English composition and grammar, and elocution.

Susan loved to read, and she had plenty of opportunities in

literature classes throughout her two years at Hampton. In one class, which dipped deeply into contemporary literature, the students all got a good dose of Henry Wadsworth Longfellow, John Greenleaf Whittier, Washington Irving, Oliver Wendell Holmes, and Julia Ward Howe. Although Irving's "The Legend of Sleepy Hollow" got the favorite nod, they also took a particular liking to William Cullen Bryant and "Thanatopsis"—so much so that most of the class copied the entire poem into their notebooks. Then they shifted gears and plunged into classical literature, including a six-week romp deep into the heart of the *Iliad*.

Just a generation earlier, the parents of some of these students were charging across the western prairies, bow and arrows in hand, trying to get the drop on free-roaming herds of wild buffalo, while others staggered stoop shouldered through stifling Georgia cotton fields, whipped by day, chained in their sleeping quarters by night. And now their children were clustered in a classroom perched on the banks of Chesapeake Bay, engaged in robust arguments over Agamemnon and Achilles, Helen and Hector.

Susan got exemplary grades in all her classes during her first year at Hampton. And the same held true throughout her second year, her senior year, when she studied biology, physics, civil government, political economy, and history, as well as another round of literature, reading, English composition, and elocution. By the start of her second year, rather than material for new dresses, Susan had decided to invest her meager Hampton wages in music. "Miss Richards, how much more would it cost to take lessons on the piano?" she wrote one of her teachers. "Couldn't I pay the extra myself because I want to know how to play the piano so much." She also had done the same for art lessons and eventually spent a fair amount of her free time practicing at the keyboard and on the sketch pad. And Susan, like all of her classmates, also had many opportunities to regularly meet and enjoy the company of boys and girlfriends in a variety of settings.

When Susan and Marguerite weren't in class, in the laundry room, or doing homework, they also helped tutor some of the other Indian girls with weaker English skills.

The range of Hampton's students—in their English skills, age, educational background, and ability—was broad. In some of the night classes, several of the students were thirty and forty years old. Many were former slaves who now hungered for an education, for some Christian instruction. They were so motivated to learn, to make something of themselves, that they worked hard, physical jobs all day, some in the school's sawmill, and then went to night school from seven to nine P.M.

In the school's first-year preparatory classes, classes frequently filled with students who had a poor command of English and limited educational ability, there was often a jarring initial collision between the younger black and Indian students.

Many years later, Waggoner, the young Sioux girl from North Dakota, vividly recalled the influence the black children from the South had on the Indian children from the Plains when they first encountered one another in a Virginia classroom.

"Most of us studied because we had to, not because we wanted to learn," Waggoner wrote in her book, *Witness*. "None of our parents encouraged us to study. Education was a small item to them. Later on, when we sat in the same classroom as the colored children, we saw how they studied and worked over hard problems, sometimes crying in despair. One girl said, 'Oh, Josephine, help me. If I don't get good marks they'll send me out of here and I never can finish my education. My folks are paying hard-earned money to put me through school; I must make my grades. I must. Oh! Let us pray. Josephine, you pray for me. . . .'

"The colored children were an inspiration to us. We began to sit up and take notice. Education must mean to them more than just reading and writing. It meant thinking and doing, it meant character and self-support, it meant an occupation for life."

After a number of years, this unique American experiment in biracial education produced a robust report card from its principal. "This mingling of the black and red races in the past seven years has worked well," General Armstrong wrote. "With many different characteristics, [both races] . . . need the same lessons; of the dignity of labor because the one has never had it to do, and the other did it under compulsion; of manual skill, because they must either work or starve; from books, because both need a modicum of education to do their duty as citizens; and the most capable of either should be taught to become teachers and leaders of their people. Each race has learned much from and been helpful to the other. There is no friction and no nonsense about race superiority. This is a school for civilization rather than for any one class. . . ."

And class wasn't the only arena where black and red students got an opportunity to mingle. Although Hampton's workweek could be long and exhausting, weekends offered a change of pace. On Sunday, with the school's heavy emphasis on a Christian-based education, there were prayer service options in the morning, piano-induced sing-alongs later, and Sunday school and traditional church services in the afternoon. Susan, meanwhile, had taken an interest in some of the small black churches in the rural areas outside of Hampton, where she often taught Sunday school. Come Sunday afternoon, it also was not unusual to find her sitting among a group of elderly black men and women, reading aloud to them.

Hampton students also had the opportunity to help develop and nurture a social conscience. One year, a tornado tore through the Omaha Reservation, destroying a home. A group of mostly Lakota Sioux boys donated some of their own money to help pay for the damage. The home belonged to an Omaha, a tribe long considered a traditional enemy of the Sioux. Another year, members of the Lend A Hand Club heard about a poor black couple suffering from old age and rheumatism. Every time it rained, their dilapidated shanty leaked all over. So the club emptied its treasury—all $15—and used the money to buy a set of new shingles. Then they got a wagon team, loaded up the shingles, drove to the elderly couple's house, and with the help of some neighbors, the black and Indian work crew soon replaced old with new. Problem solved.

By exposing Indian students to the larger world, by educating them in classrooms, farm fields, carpentry shops, and sewing rooms, by introducing strong Christian beliefs and the values of hard work, self-sufficiency, and responsibility, Hampton was, in theory, creating a new army of Indian soldiers who eventually would march back to their reservation homelands and reshape them in the image of white men and women and their civilization. The kinds of soldiers General Armstrong believed would attack the old ways of "life in the blanket," ushering in the new world order—new schools, new churches, new farm implements and farming techniques. Soldiers who would blow up the outmoded concept of tribal community life, replacing it with sturdy individuals who grew attached to private property, free enterprise, and the notion of becoming citizens.

On one level, the overarching goal was disarmingly simple: to drive a wedge between who these Indian students once were and who they should become, to separate them from their cultural past while preparing them for their cultural future. Apparently, it had never occurred to anyone if this was really possible—or whether it was even the right thing to do.

But the general never doubted those goals, and to achieve them, no group was more important to his overall battle plan than

Indian women. It was they, he believed, who would be critical in winning the war against the backward, primitive, "savage" ways of the past. They were on the front line, the ones most likely to embrace Christianity, to adapt and mold their homes in the Victorian image. The ones who would nudge their husbands from the forests to the fields and impart the values they had learned on the banks of Chesapeake Bay to their children back on the distant prairies. It was Indian women, like women in virtually all indigenous cultures, who were, he believed, the primary agents of social change. The Northern Cheyenne, prairie and mountain dwellers far to the west of the Omaha, had long summed up this belief in their own way, in their own tribal proverb. "A nation is not conquered," the Northern Cheyenne believed, "until the hearts of its women are on the ground."

And General Armstrong would not have disagreed. "On the Indian girl, as upon women everywhere," he believed, "depends the virtue, the true value of the red or of any race."

In numerous ways, Susan La Flesche was the ideal student for General Armstrong's Hampton experiment. For the most part, she already embodied many of the traits, values, characteristics, and beliefs he and his staff were working hard to instill in her classmates. She already had accumulated life experiences that few other Indians—and even fewer whites—could match. She was fluent in native languages and in English. She was an increasingly devout Christian who had grown up in a unique village on a Great Plains reservation among her Omaha Indian people. She'd spent three years observing and absorbing cultural and educational values in a bustling East Coast city of white men and women. And now she was sitting in classes, going to social events, and attending church services with the sons and daughters of former slaves. She had also joined a Hampton temperance group, was a member of the Christian Endeavor Society, and was involved in the Lend A

Hand Club. She spent time visiting the sick and the poor and made a serious effort to begin building friendships with some of the white teachers she had come to admire. She was inspired. She was hungry. And, only nineteen, she was primed to absorb all that this social experiment in biracial education had to offer.

During Susan's two years at Hampton, there was a young oak tree not far from Winona Lodge. In 1861, not long after the Civil War began, a Union officer at Hampton's Fort Monroe made a startling announcement: Should any slaves make it to Union lines, he said, they would be safe, they would not be returned. They would be free. Soon, hundreds of slaves began pouring into the fort, seeking their freedom. A camp to house them was built outside the fort. Then came a push to offer some kind of schooling, although it was against Virginia's 1831 law to educate slaves.

Nevertheless, Mary Smith Peake, the mulatto daughter of a free black mother and a French father, was invited to begin teaching the recently arrived former slaves. So on September 17, 1861, she conducted her first class of about twenty students under the shade of the young oak tree. One day a few years later, in 1863, members of the area's black community once again gathered beneath the tree. They had all come to hear something they couldn't quite believe: the first reading on southern soil of President Abraham Lincoln's Emancipation Proclamation. Some wept openly at the words. Over time, the tree became known as the Emancipation Oak.

It still stands today—near the entrance to the Hampton University campus.

Within the traditional culture of the Upstream People, a firm set of well-defined customs and rules dictated the proper etiquette young girls were to observe at all times. Young Omaha girls never went to the spring to fetch water unless accompanied by an older woman—a mother, an aunt, or some other relative. Young married women seldom, if ever, went anywhere alone. And Omaha custom forbade young men to visit young women in their homes.

At an early age, mothers even taught their young daughters the correct way to sit and to stand up. Proper etiquette, Alice Fletcher and Francis La Flesche noted in their book on the Omaha Tribe, required a woman to sit sideways on the left, "her legs drawn round closely to the right. No other posture was good form for a woman. . . . Concerning this point of etiquette mothers were rigid in the training of their daughters. To rise well, one should spring up lightly, not with the help of both hands; one hand might be placed on the ground for the first movement, to get a purchase. A girl was taught to move about noiselessly as she passed in and out of the lodge. All her errands must be done silently. She must keep her hair neatly braided and her garments in order."

At Hampton, young boys and girls were openly encouraged to mix. Although rigorous classes and hard physical labor were key elements of the school experience, Saturday evenings and Sunday afternoons often gave way to a variety of events that socially engaged boys and girls, Indians and blacks, teachers and students. Saturday nights frequently offered a range of choices to fit the needs of the school's many different students. They could choose to play tenpins, checkers, or dominoes. They could attend temperance meetings, join the glee clubs, sit in on guest speakers, and listen to recitations. There were marches, parades, concerts, and literary events of all kinds to pick from—events in which teachers doubled as chaperones.

The Hampton philosophy of a coeducational experience, of boys coming to Winona Lodge for regular Saturday evening dinners, Sunday meals, and weekend socializing between the sexes, profoundly shocked the Indian parents of the Indian girls. In Susan's own family, her father had steadfastly refused to let Bright Eyes go east on the Standing Bear speaking tour unless chaperoned by her half brother, Francis. Other parents refused to let their young daughters go so far from home for such a long time to a school that openly encouraged young boys to socialize with young girls. It was a situation they could not comprehend, a world dramatically removed from traditional tribal customs, beliefs, and rituals.

But the architect of Hampton's educational philosophy was resolute in his belief that the old molds had to be shattered and new ones formed. General Armstrong thought the best way to break down deeply entrenched social restrictions was simply to offer Hampton's young Indian girls and boys ample opportunities to meet, to get together, to openly discuss their experiences, their thoughts, their goals, their feelings. In time, Armstrong believed, the social interchange would prepare both sexes for a smoother entry into mainstream American society.

In his annual report on Hampton's 1885–1886 school year, Armstrong summed it up this way: "The intermarriage of graduates and the resulting home life are among the happiest effects of this work; 171 have married. The family is the unit of Christian civilization. The mingling of sexes in school has proved most satisfactory."

So opportunities for Indian boys and girls to meet happened all the time. And sometimes the boys and girls ended up falling in love. And sometimes that love became complicated, pulling in a wide range of others who had strong advice for the young lovers, who sometimes had agendas, who wanted them to see the bigger picture when the nineteen-year-olds just wanted to see what nineteen-year-olds see when they're in love.

His name was Thomas Ikinicapi and he was a Sioux full-blood from Dakota Territory. He had arrived three years before her, and during their two years together at Hampton, Susan was never confused at what she saw. She saw the thick mop of coal-black hair, the dark eyes and straight nose, the prominent cheekbones and smooth copper skin. And when he was in full dress uniform, when he was marching in formation on the school parade grounds, she saw it all come together.

He was, Susan said, "without exception the handsomest Indian I ever saw." Weak and often in fragile health, the Sioux boy came from a prominent family who had sent him to Hampton to sharpen his educational skills. But "T.I.," as she called him, did not have a lot of academic ability. After four years at Hampton, he still struggled to write and speak basic, fundamental English. But what he did have was a sweetness about him, a kind, gentle, compassionate personality.

And he had fallen deeply, madly, head-over-heels in love with his English tutor—a striking nineteen-year-old Omaha mixed-blood with long, luxuriant dark hair and a sophisticated air.

In most ways, the Sioux full-blood and the Omaha mixed-blood inhabited two different worlds. One was soft and sickly, the other hearty and healthy. He was from the country, she had lived in the city. He struggled with basic English, she quoted Shakespeare. He was in remedial classes, she excelled in elite classes. He most likely would return to his reservation and lead an ordinary life. She might one day write her own ticket, breaking through barriers in ways none of her people ever had. So it was a mismatch—socially, academically, intellectually.

And Susan didn't care. She couldn't get him out of her mind. She sometimes dreamed about him. She had fallen for the kind, handsome, soft-spoken Sioux boy from Dakota. It felt good, and for now she didn't care about mismatches or career opportunities or big pictures. She was nineteen and in love for the first time, and so she saw what nineteen-year-olds in love see.

Although T.I. was often on her mind, she also was preoccupied with a good many other thoughts by the early spring of her senior year. They weren't new thoughts. Through it all, in love or not, she never lost sight of why she was at Hampton, of the need to excel, of how she needed to use all of her energy and discipline and focus to get to the next level. By now, a growing number of people were counting on her, the kind of people she could never imagine letting down—starting with herself. Ever since seeing the sick Indian woman die and the white doctor's indifference, ever since hearing her father ask if his daughters wanted to be "simply called those Indians," ever since helping nurse the Harvard anthropologist back to health, those thoughts had been building, growing, maturing.

And now, in the waning months of her senior year at Hampton, she had decided to do it, to do something no Indian woman had done before: to try to get into medical school, to become a doctor, to one day return home and take care of her sick and destitute people for the rest of her life.

She'd revealed her ambitious plans to Alice Fletcher and shared them with a few other teachers, particularly Dr. Martha Waldron, Hampton's resident physician. Together, they had all begun to focus on Dr. Waldron's alma mater, the Woman's Medical College of Pennsylvania, gathering information, evaluating references, slowly trying to piece together Susan's prospects for admission.

For now, however, with graduation just a few months down the road, Susan had to keep her focus on Hampton and her classes.

On the morning of May 20, 1886, about 135 miles southeast of where the third president of the United States had long dreamed of carving a new world order from the American West, a twenty-year-old Omaha Indian girl from Nebraska stood motionless on a Virginia stage, looking out at the more than one thousand guests who had gathered for the eighteenth commencement ceremony at the Hampton Normal and Agricultural Institute.

It was a fine late spring day—a tableau of rich sunshine and fleecy clouds, soft breezes and a gentle rippling of the nearby waters on Chesapeake Bay, as described in the the the *Hartford Courant*. In the crowd were hundreds of black students and some of their mothers and fathers, some of whom had once worked the surrounding fields in bondage. There were Indians from a dozen different tribes and some of their parents, some of whom had once been at war with the U.S. government. There were also some northern whites and southern whites, as well as representatives from both the U.S. Senate and House of Representatives Indian committees. Dr. Waldron was in the crowd, as was Alice Fletcher, who had come down by train from Washington, D.C. Soon, all of them were focused on the young girl in the pretty striped dress, waiting for her to begin her speech.

First there was an opening prayer and several stirring Negro spirituals, and then Susan La Flesche approached the podium. By tradition, she was to give the first speech at graduation because she was the salutatorian—number two in her class of fourteen, eleven black students and three Indian students. Although the graduation ceremony itself offered a clear view of the present and a peek at the future, Susan's speech—"My Childhood and Womanhood"—romanticized at length about the past, about an idyllic childhood roaming across a prairie homeland rife with mythic characters and pleasant memories.

In elegant, graceful words, she told the large gathering about beautiful villages of gleaming tipis lined along fast-flowing creeks and dark green woods back in her native Great Plains homeland.

How as a little girl she remembered summer evenings in her village when muscular young men would play traditional games and indulge in all the courtship rituals geared toward the young maidens. She told them about how lovely her homeland was, the magical beauty of June sunsets and July moonrises and the thrill of the autumn harvest, when the village came alive and everyone, even small children, had to pitch in and do their share.

Then she shifted gears, talking about the present, about the individual responsibility that came with her education, and how both Indians and whites now must work together to achieve their mutual goals. "We who are educated have to be pioneers of Indian civilization," she told the crowd. "We have to prepare our people to live in the white man's way, to use the white man's books, and to use his laws if you will only give them to us. The white people have reached a high standard of civilization, but how many years has it taken them? We are only beginning; so do not try to put us down, but help us to climb *higher*. Give us a chance."

She assured the crowd she was prepared to do her share, to climb as high as she could, to bring as many of her people as possible with her. And it would all begin with her ardent desire to become a doctor. Then she could care for them physically, teach the Omaha the importance of hygiene and cleanliness to ward off disease, how to care for their bodies as well as their souls. "I know I have a long, hard struggle before me, but the shores of success can only be reached by crossing the bridge of faith, and I shall try hard. . . . I can only rejoice that the Lord has given me such a great privilege and . . . I look forward to the coming years with a great deal of pleasure."

Standing alone on the large stage, she ended her speech by couching her emerging philosophy of life in a series of maritime metaphors: "As you look out on this beautiful water you see the ships go sailing down the bay, some with new, white sails, strong but untried as yet, others with torn sails which show their struggles with the wind and storms (and are they not as beautiful showing work that has been done?). All are going forth to work. We do not know the storms and struggles with which they will have to meet. It is even so with us; but with our faith firm in God we know that whatever shall befall us, He will bring us unto the 'desired haven.'"

The applause was thunderous. Susan stood still. General Byron M. Cutcheon approached the podium. His footprints had been all over the Civil War—Vicksburg, Fredericksburg, Knoxville, Jackson—and there was a Medal of Honor to show for it. He was now a Michigan Republican in the U.S. House of Representatives, and he had been called to the stage for a specific purpose: to present Hampton's salutatorian with the Demorest Prize, a gold medal awarded annually to the student who got the highest examination scores during the junior year.

As the guests and other students looked on, General Cutcheon stepped forward to present the medal to Susan. Then he spoke to her and to the assembled crowd. "It is a great thing to be one of the first women of your race to lay this foundation," the general said. "I charge you to regard it as your duty to live for your people. To devote yourself to them."

When it was all over, Alice Fletcher wasted little time conveying the achievements of the day—the spectacle, the significance, and the sentiments—to the graduate's family back on their Great Plains reservation. It was a day that saw Hampton's valedictorian, a black man from Philadelphia, standing on a stage in what was once the Confederacy, next to the school's salutatorian, an Indian girl from Nebraska. It was a day in which parts seemed to pass, Susan would later say, "as in a dream."

All of it was captured the next day, May 21, when Fletcher dashed off a long letter to the new graduate's sister Rosalie. Her youngest sister, Fletcher noted in the letter, had put a jolt in the crowd. Susan had looked beautiful in her simple striped dress. Her face "was very lovely," and she "spoke clearly and every one was delighted with her," the anthropologist wrote.

Rosalie read the letter, then set off up the road, taking it to the home of Joseph La Flesche. Back in the Village of the Make-Believe White Men, the old man listened carefully as the words of the Harvard scholar described how his youngest daughter had graduated from a Virginia school. How she had received a big award for exceptional academic skills. How she now wanted to become a doctor, then return home to care for her people.

"I am so glad that she is to go forward in her grand career," Alice Fletcher wrote. "She is I think the first Indian girl to advance so far."

5

∨∨∨

The Sisterhood
of Second Mothers

Much to the surprise of Susan and everyone else, the Woman's Medical College of Pennsylvania rejected her scholarship application. There would be no scholarship for Susan because there was no money left. It had all been doled out months earlier.

But Alfred Jones, secretary of the medical college's executive committee, left the door slightly ajar. If Susan wanted to apply, if she still wanted to take a shot at going to the medical college, she needed to submit a tedious, time-consuming, handwritten application. In it, she would have to spell out in detail her educational qualifications as well as an accounting of her health and character in the form of testimonials from others. And now, casting a much larger, darker shadow over the process, lay the obvious question: Even if she got accepted, how would she ever foot the bill?

Two months before Susan's graduation, Dr. Martha Waldron had written a personal letter to the secretary of the college's executive committee. The letter included a straightforward request: Since Susan had no money, no means of financial support, would the Woman's Medical College of Pennsylvania grant her a full scholarship?

Now, in the wake of the college's rejection, Susan had encountered the first of many hurdles and barriers that Alice Fletcher, Dr. Waldron, and Sara Kinney, influential president of the Connecticut Indian Association, had warned her about. It wouldn't be easy, they'd told her. In those years, the mainstream medical establishment held female doctors in low esteem, referring to them derisively as "doctoring ladies." The male medical establishment considered female medical schools and their training vastly inferior, so they prevented female doctors from joining local, state, and national medical societies. Many doctors of the era also viewed female counterparts as an economic threat—there simply weren't enough patients to go around. And many male doctors firmly believed that if women got caught up in professional careers, they would soon become incompetent mothers and inferior wives, ultimately threatening the basic foundation of American family life.

Simply stated, women had been put on earth not to chase science, but "to rear the offspring and even fan the flame of piety, patriotism and love upon the sacred altar of her home," suggested Dr. W. W. Parker in a Victorian-era article entitled "Woman's Place in the Christian World: Superior Morally, Inferior Mentally to Man—Not Qualified for Medicine or Law—the Contrariety and Harmony of the Sexes."

But if Susan's cause lacked traction in the wider world, she had a remarkable and remarkably tenacious group of women in her corner. Like a growing number of her peers in the last half of the nineteenth century, Susan was the beneficiary of a sisterhood of such motivated, intelligent women, women who were bound and determined to refute the assertions of Dr. Parker and his ilk.

On the afternoon of July 9, 1848, in the village of Waterloo, New York, a Quaker preacher and an abolitionist crusader happened to be attending the same afternoon tea at the home of a mutual friend. Lucretia Mott and Elizabeth Cady Stanton were no strangers. Eight years earlier, they had met at the World Anti-Slavery Convention in London, where convention officials refused to seat them because they were women. The social gathering that day in Waterloo sparked talk among the gathered women about the recently passed—and hotly debated—New York Married Women's Property Rights Act. Stanton, the antislavery activist, took the lead. She argued the time had now come for an all-out assault designed to enhance the status of women. It was time, she told the small group of women, to establish far more political rights, to blast open the doors to higher education, and to quash morality's double standard.

By the time the socializing ended, a firm decision had emerged: The women would organize a convention "to discuss the social, civil, and religious condition and rights of woman." And it was scheduled to occur in the nearby village of Seneca Falls in a scant ten days.

It was then left to Stanton, a gifted writer, to craft a Declaration of Sentiments that would serve as the convention's backbone. Using the Declaration of Independence as a road map, the thirty-two-year-old mother of three drew up eleven resolutions—resolutions that collectively underscored the notion that men and women should be regarded equally in all respects. Her ninth resolution was a suffragette's call to arms: It was now up to women to go out and get the right to vote for themselves, a daunting challenge that startled even some of her friends.

"Why, Lizzie, thee will make us look ridiculous," said a shaken Lucretia Mott.

"But I persisted," Stanton later recalled, "for I saw clearly that the power to make the laws was the right through which all other rights could be secured."

Throughout much of the last half of the nineteenth century, however, Stanton, Mott, and their allies were often swimming against a powerful current seeking to keep things the way they were. The arguments to do so came from many different quarters, including the scientific one. For one thing, theorized a number of important Victorian-era scientists, white American women were not biologically equipped to balance intellectual and mental exertion with reproductive responsibilities. Women, they believed, jeopardized not only their own health, but the continuation of the species by pursuing mental and physical activities equal to those of men. As the respected British philosopher and scientist Herbert Spencer had said, women who insisted on the right to work and the right to vote were a threat to move society "a step backwards toward savagery."

But powerful currents or not, Stanton and Mott were undeterred. So on July 19, 1848, a crowd of about three hundred, forty of whom were men, gathered at the Wesleyan Methodist Church in Seneca Falls. By the convention's end two days later, all of the resolutions had passed unanimously, save one—a woman's right to vote. Enter Frederick Douglass. A onetime slave, the editor of the *North Star* newspaper, in nearby Rochester, New York, used his passion and eloquence to appeal to the crowd. "In this denial of the right to participate in government," Douglass told the gathering, "not merely the degradation of woman and the perpetuation of a great injustice happens, but the maiming and repudiation of one-half of the moral and intellectual power of the government of the world." Not long after Douglass finished, the resolution on women's suffrage passed.

And by dusk on July 20, the Declaration of Sentiments had one hundred signatures—sixty-eight women and thirty-two men.

Soon, word of the convention and its purpose spread far beyond the pages of the *North Star,* triggering an avalanche of derision, mockery, and ridicule in many quarters. Observed the *Oneida Whig* newspaper: "This bolt is the most shocking and unnatural incident ever recorded in the history of womanity. If our ladies will insist on voting and legislating, where, gentlemen, will be our dinner and our elbows? Where our domestic firesides and the holes in our stockings?" The outpouring of rage and rancor moved Douglass to make his own observation in his own newspaper. "A discussion of the rights of animals," he wrote, "would be regarded with far more complacency by many of what are called the wise and the good of our land, than would be a discussion of the rights of woman."

Eventually, Horace Greeley also weighed in with his thoughts in the *New-York Daily Tribune:* "When a sincere republican is asked to say in sober earnest what adequate reason he can give, for refusing the demand of women to an equal participation with men in political rights, he must answer, None at all. However unwise and mistaken the demand, it is but the assertion of a natural right, and such must be conceded."

There were no Indian women or men at Seneca Falls, but had there been, they might have pointed out that some Americans, the original ones, had long viewed men and women as equals. When Alice Fletcher first ventured out west and began her detailed studies of Indian life, of village customs, mores, and social structure, she was deeply struck by how women were regarded and treated among native people compared with how they were often treated in her own culture. As a woman, Fletcher was not allowed to vote, and women were only then gaining the right to own property. In contrast, when the federal government decreed in its 1869 allotment policy that none of the reservation lands would be given to unmarried Indian women, the Omaha were furious.

To exclude single women, the men said, was counter to traditional Omaha culture, custom, and tradition. It was the women, they forcefully pointed out, who had always owned the lodge, who owned the contents of the lodge, who owned the garden plots, who had always been a respected and stable force within the tribal unit. They had held ownership rights for as long as any of the people could remember, and they did not want the women to lose those rights in the march toward private ownership and assimilation. Single Omaha women, they insisted, must be included in the allotment process. After a time, the U.S. secretary of the interior had heard enough and he relented.

On March 11, 1850, two years after the Seneca Falls Conference, what would become the Woman's Medical College of Pennsylvania was established. Founded by a group of Quakers, abolitionists, and supporters of the women's movement, it was only the second medical college in the world for women. By the 1880s, when Martha Waldron, a graduate of the medical college, encouraged Susan to apply, it had become a respected and innovative institution.

Like the Seneca Falls Conference, the Woman's Medical College arrived at a time when women were pressing for a greater role in society. They had already become a force to be reckoned with in the most important issue of the time—by 1837, half of the members of abolitionist societies were women. Women were also actively seeking greater control over their own affairs and of their own bodies. But the efforts of the Woman's Medical College, like those of the Seneca Falls Conference, were not well received. In 1859, the Philadelphia County Medical Society issued "resolutions of excommunication" against every physician who should "teach in a medical school for women," every woman who graduated from it, and everybody else who should "consult with a woman physician or with a man teaching a woman medical student."

Despite such opposition, the college was at the forefront of medical education. Early on, it integrated microscopy and was one of the first to include bacteriology, a new science at the time. The Woman's Medical College of the 1880s and 1890s, observed a medical historian, "mounted more laboratory classes than all but a handful of American medical schools. . . ."

To those critics of women in medicine, the college—its faculty, students, and graduates—all responded with hard evidence to the contrary: Not only were women capable of doctoring, they could excel at it, push into areas long ignored by male doctors, all without being "desexed," all while engaging in and maintaining family life if they so chose. In the last half of the nineteenth century, encouraged and supported by a network of determined women, schools such as the Woman's Medical College helped transform the medical landscape. Summarizing the period, another medical historian noted: "Far from being a period when women physicians were an anomaly, the late nineteenth century witnessed a remarkable increase in their numbers. In Boston, the peak was reached in 1900 when women physicians accounted for 18.2 percent of the city's doctors."

The pressure was building. They could all feel it. There wasn't much time now between the end of one school year and the beginning of a much more complicated one. Susan's benefactors wanted some answers; most important, where would the money come from? If her dream was to be realized, they needed to set a plan in motion. Time was critical. By midspring 1886, Susan had sent a specific request for help to Alice Fletcher. And Fletcher had relayed it to the one friend in the best position to help: Sara Kinney, with her widespread connections among Indian activists on the East Coast.

Fletcher and Kinney had first met about eighteen months earlier, at the end of September 1884. It was the second annual meeting of what came to be known as the Lake Mohonk Conference, a gathering of powerful East Coast reformers and philanthropists—mostly men—at the Lake Mohonk Lodge about a hundred miles north of New York City. The conference had a twofold motive: First, to tell Americans what they believed was the most practical way to solve the Indian question; and second, to stimulate America's right-minded citizens to take the necessary steps that would result in a solution. One of the seven representatives selected for the committee that would generate specific topics for the conference was Samuel Chapman Armstrong.

In the preceding decades, America's image of Indian people had undergone a dramatic transformation: from heathen savages to conquered people to helpless children. And now it was time for the energized reformers and powerful philanthropists gathered around a table at Lake Mohonk to get to work on their behalf. "It was felt by all who took part in the work of the conference that a calm, definite, and earnest appeal made to the conscience and intelligence of the country in behalf of a poor and helpless people and for the righting of a national wrong, would not be uttered in vain," the committee noted.

The first topic the committee chose for discussion was a provocative one: Indian citizenship. It was, the committee proposed, the only real solution to the Indian problem. But that topic also begged a vital question: Was there any real proof that Indians had the capacity for citizenship? To answer that question, the group summarized, reviewed, and energetically discussed remarks they had just heard from one of the conference's keynote speakers—the only one among them who had ever lived extensively among the Indians on their own land, in their own villages.

"Under this topic an interesting and valuable address was delivered by Miss Alice C. Fletcher, of the Peabody Museum of Archaeology and Ethnology, Cambridge, Mass., regarding social conditions among the Omahas, and describing the process by which they had gained possession of their land in severalty," the summary notes stated. "Miss Fletcher's long residence among the Omahas, as a student of their customs, enabled her to present to the minds of her hearers a vivid picture of the structure of Indian society and the process of Indian thought. The facts which Miss Fletcher stated regarding Indian capacity for citizenship were of a most convincing nature. A single brief illustration may be given. Since the Omahas have (largely as a result of Miss Fletcher's efforts in their behalf) received from the Government individual titles to their land, allotments have been made to fifty-nine heads of families, seven hundred acres of land have been broken by plow, and many houses have been erected by the Indians."

Seated in the audience, Sara Thomson Kinney was fascinated by what the Harvard anthropologist had to say. The forty-two-year-old Kinney possessed a string of the bluest of blue-blood credentials: daughter of a Yale-educated doctor, granddaughter of a War of 1812 veteran, great-granddaughter of a Revolutionary War hero, member of the General Society of Mayflower Descendants, active leader in the Daughters of the American Revolution, wife of a distinguished Civil War veteran and Yale graduate, who was also the powerful editor of the *Hartford Courant* newspaper.

Established in 1881, the Connecticut Indian Association, which Kinney headed for more than thirty years, was an offshoot of the Women's National Indian Association. It shared the same social engineering goals as its parent organization and of the Victorian era in general: training, encouraging, and molding young women to become Christian homemakers devoted to, first and foremost, husband and children and a clean, secure home for the family. The organization also fought to change national Indian policy, to champion citizenship rights, and to expand vocational and educational opportunities for young Indian women. It was also not uncommon for the organization to take an interest in the special-ized educational needs of individual Indian women who showed unusual promise.

So in the early months of 1886, Susan's plight reinvigorated the friendship between Fletcher and Kinney. On February 19, Kinney wrote to Rosalie La Flesche, telling her that Alice Fletcher "has paid me a visit and we had many a pleasant talk about you and your people."

On May 21, 1886, one day after Susan gave her Hampton grad-uation speech and walked off with the gold medal, the Connecti-cut Indian Association convened in Hartford. Under the gavel of President Kinney, the members considered Alice Fletcher's request that they provide Susan's medical school expenses. As part of her strategy, Kinney had asked Hampton's principal to supply a char-acter reference for Susan. The response was not long in coming or shrouded in equivocation. "I would say that I regard her as about the finest, strongest Indian character we have had at this school," General Armstrong wrote. "She is a 'level-headed,' earnest, capa-ble Christian woman quite equal, I think, to medical studies. She deserves every chance. . . . As a doctor she can do much for her people. She is clear-headed, and independent: naturally, a deep, but not a sentimental woman. I hope your society will take her up."

By meeting's end, the group had reached an agreement: If Susan got accepted, the association would underwrite all of her expenses while she completed the three-year medical school program.

On June 16, shortly after learning of the association's decision, Susan wrote a long letter to its president. In the letter, she told Kin-ney she felt blessed to be on the verge of a career she had long dreamed of and what becoming a doctor meant to her.

"I was very glad to get your letter, and it made me very happy to think I had so many mothers, who were going to take care of and help me," Susan wrote. "I cannot tell you how thankful I feel to all of you, and how glad to think that through me you will be helping so many people. It has always been a desire of mine to study medicine ever since I was a small girl, for even then I saw the need of my people for a good physician. . . . I feel that as a physician I can do a great deal more than as a mere teacher, for the home is the foundation of all things for the Indians, and my work I hope will be chiefly in the homes of my people. I wish I could see you all face to face so that I could thank you for my people and myself."

But to convert the dream to reality, the association needed a firm plan to raise the money. So members came up with one: They decided to go public, to ask ordinary, everyday Connecticut citizens to help put an Omaha Indian woman through a Pennsylvania medical college so she could one day return to a Nebraska reservation to treat her people. To publicize that goal, they took to the pages of the *Hartford Courant*—whose editor was Kinney's husband. Now things were moving, now the association had set its plan in motion, a plan to get this young Indian woman the education she would need to do the very things she had dreamed of as a little girl. It was one of the reasons the group existed, and in the early summer of 1886 both the group's president and the newspaper's editor were using their collective power and influence to help Susan La Flesche become Dr. Susan La Flesche—a title that had never been conferred on an American Indian.

To that end, readers of the newspaper's edition of June 25, 1886—the ten-year anniversary of the Little Bighorn—could read a lengthy story about "a young woman of more than ordinary mental ability and earnestness of character, and particularly well suited to the work to which she desires to devote herself." But that woman "has no means of support, and no way by which she can pay for the professional training she desires for herself." The Connecticut Indian Association, readers were told, had opted to help Susan La Flesche achieve her goal, and now "an earnest appeal is therefore made to the Christian people of Connecticut for funds with which to assist in the support and education of this young Indian woman." In the end, the newspaper article suggested, Susan's devotion to her people was a kind of missionary work that "should appeal very powerfully to the benevolent, and particularly to the hearts of women."

One woman moved by the appeal expressed her thoughts in a testimonial letter published as part of the story. Those thoughts came from a good friend of the association's president, a woman who also had more than a passing knowledge of the aspiring doctor. She wanted to make sure the *Courant*'s readers knew they would be investing in an exemplary individual.

"She is gentle, refined, conscientious and unselfish, and seems a rare character for any walk of life," wrote Alice Fletcher. "In her sweet, quiet way, we feel she would minister not only to the physical needs of those for whom she cared, but for all their deeper wants would strive to lead them to the Great Healer."

Summer was half over. Susan had finished her Hampton education and now she was back home, back on the reservation, working the fields, tending to the family crops, taking care of her elderly father and mother—exactly what she wanted to do as a trained physician. But she had heard nothing.

Had her application to the Woman's Medical College of Pennsylvania been accepted? She didn't know. Had Sara Kinney and the Connecticut Indian Association secured the money she would need for lodging, travel, and tuition? She didn't know.

Finally, later that summer, word came that the Pennsylvania medical college had agreed to accept her into its three-year program as a "beneficiary student." So now one critical question remained: Where would the money come from to get her to Philadelphia, to pay for her room and board, to cover the costs of her books and supplies, to pay for her tuition?

August ended and still there was no word about the money. Would she have to give up the dream and stay home? Help with crops and the livestock? Stay closer to her aging parents? Maybe take another teaching job at the mission school?

Susan didn't know how desperate Sara Kinney had become in her Connecticut home some thirteen hundred miles to the east. For one thing, Kinney knew the government typically provided an annual stipend of $167 to Indian students at boarding schools. But that money had never gone to support a student in a professional school. Still, if the government would make an exception in this one case, Kinney pledged that the Connecticut Indian Association would pick up all other expenses—including tuition—for Susan's medical school. To bolster her cause, General Armstrong weighed in with a testimonial to the commissioner of Indian affairs on his former pupil. Susan, the general said, was "a young woman of unusual ability, integrity, fixedness of purpose and well worthy in every respect of such aid."

Not long afterward, in early September, the commissioner gave his answer: Yes, he informed Kinney, the government would agree to pay $167 annually for three years to support Susan's medical school education. The unprecedented contract was finalized on September 15, 1886. In exchange for government support, the contract stated, the Connecticut Indian Association would agree to "clothe, feed, lodge and care for, and educate, under this contract, at the Woman's Medical College of Pennsylvania, during the 9 months from October 1, 1886, to June 30, 1887, in a manner satisfactory to the party of the first part, one Indian pupil, by name Susan La Flesche, of the Omaha tribe, about 20 years of age."

So the major hurdle had been cleared—a mutually beneficial

marriage of public and private money that would bankroll an education to benefit a medically underserved midwest reservation. It was mid-September. Chemistry, physiology, anatomy, and obstetrics classes were but two weeks and half a continent away.

So how was she going to get to Philadelphia?

Who would pay for the long trip east?

Sara Kinney had thought all along that the U.S. Department of the Interior was going to pay the train fare. The days went by. Nothing. So Kinney frantically sent a message to the commissioner of Indian affairs. Nothing.

September came and went, classes would soon begin, and Susan was still on the reservation, in a panic.

Kinney was in Hartford, in a panic.

In the end, the Department of the Interior declined to pay the train fare.

6

∨ ∨ ∨

Dr. Sue

All in all, it wasn't the kindest of years for Philadelphia, the nation's third-largest city, one of only three in 1886 that could boast a head count of more than a million. For one thing, there was an ugly rash of fires throughout the year, commencing on January 10, when the tugboat *James Kelly* caught fire on Pennypack Creek, torching an entire block of buildings in the Thirty-first Ward. About two weeks later, another fire on Arch Street wiped out dozens of businesses, eventually racking up an estimated $500,000 in losses. Nor was it a good year for Samuel R. Shaw. On July 31, he was minding his own business in a boat on the Delaware River when a rock smacked him in the head, knocking him overboard, and he drowned. Six arrests were made.

For another thing, the local sports teams failed to provide a boost to civic spirits. That fall, the Gentlemen of Philadelphia lost a close one to the Gentlemen of England in an international cricket match. Sadly, the Philadelphia Quakers didn't fare much better in baseball, finishing fourth in the National League, fourteen games behind the first-place Chicago White Stockings. So as the year drew to a close, more than a few in the City of Brotherly Love were looking forward to ringing in a new one.

One day in the opening weeks of the new year, three dozen female medical school students gathered in a clinic room at Pennsylvania Hospital, just a few blocks south of Independence Hall. The first-year female students were joined by a group of male students from nearby Jefferson Medical College. That day, all the girls on one side of the clinic room and all the boys on the other side were focused on the same thing: an open space in the room where doctors were about to demonstrate an important part of their training. They all saw the clamps. They all saw the tourniquets. They saw the towels and bandages. They all could plainly see the saw. And moments before the surgeons began their work, they could all imagine seeing something else: a lot of blood.

But just as the surgeons were about to begin, they suddenly stopped. The room had collapsed in chaos. For weeks, the boys had taunted and teased the girls. They were not fit to see such surgical procedures. They had neither the heart nor the stomach for it. All these "doctoring ladies" would pass out, faint dead away at the first sight of such an operation. One boy in particular had led the charge, taunting and teasing the loudest. And now his prophecy had come true. Someone had fainted, blacked out, just as the surgeons were about to operate.

So all the girls from the Woman's Medical College of Pennsylvania looked around, craning their necks to see who it was. And then they saw: It was the boy who had led the taunting and teasing. He had keeled over, and now two of the other boys were pulling him up off the floor and helping him out.

The only American Indian student at the coed clinic that day recorded the moment in a letter to her family. "I think no more of seeing an amputation now than I do to see a patient drop in who has fever," she wrote her sister. The girls in the clinic room that day all took it in stride, she said. They were mostly amused and just sat back and smiled. "I wasn't even thinking of fainting," she wrote.

But three months earlier, she, too, had come close to fainting.

Susan La Flesche, age twenty-one, arrived at the Philadelphia train station in early October 1886, just a few days before her medical school classes were to begin on October 7. When she stepped off the passenger car at the Broad Street station that midautumn day, she was worn out, stressed out, and not far from passing out—from motion sickness, from what happens sometimes when you hurriedly pack up, jump on a train, and ride it halfway across the continent.

And the stress of the past few weeks didn't help. All along, the Department of the Interior had steadfastly refused to pay her train fare. And they kept their word. So at the last moment, Sara Thomson Kinney dug into her own pocket and sent the money to Francis La Flesche in Washington, D.C., who in turn wired the funds to Bancroft to pay for the ticket, giving family members strict orders to have Susan aboard an eastbound train on October 1.

With all the kinks finally worked out, her train fare resolved, and her education needs arranged, neither the medical college nor the Connecticut Indian Association wanted to leave anything to chance for a young woman both had invested a good deal in. So when Susan stepped off the train, she was immediately greeted by Mrs. Seth Talcott, chair of the Connecticut Indian Association's business committee, and Dr. Elizabeth Bundy, an anatomy professor at the Woman's Medical College. Soon, the two older women whisked the weary young woman away to her new home—a room in a boardinghouse near the college.

"I had no need whatever to dread my boarding house—I like it so much," she informed her anxious family a few weeks after settling into "such a nice, pretty, warm, cozy room." She loved the bed with a Japanese panel, walls embroidered with birds, a painting of water, rocks, and a spray of seaweed, the colorful posters, calendars, and Christmas cards, and the luxury of having all her grooming implements for nails, teeth, and hair neatly laid out by the washbasin. In fact, she found very little to complain about and much to like. She liked the food (so good and plenty of it), she liked her landlady (so kind and sweet, "like a gleam of sunshine"), she liked the other girls (so nice and sociable, they chattered away without even knowing one another's names), and she marveled at the abundance of clothing (so much that she wished she could send a lot of it back home).

And there was one other thing she quickly grew to love: She loved being neat and clean, all the time—and how easy it was to be so. No more walking a mile or two to the creek. No more lugging buckets back across stubbly patches of sandbur prairie. "I wash my feet often and always wash my neck, head and ears every morning," Susan told her family. The idea of being clean, of scrubbing often with soap and water—of basic fundamental hygiene and how important it was in heading off diseases in far-flung outposts with few doctors and no medicine—was a concept beginning to take root in the medical school's only native student. It was a root that would branch out and grow deeper and stronger in the years to come.

Throughout the early going, throughout those first few intense, complex, and hectic weeks of medical school, there was really only one cautionary note. One evening, at one of several social gatherings for the first-year students, a well-meaning woman pulled Susan aside and offered some friendly advice, more like a kindly plea: "You mustn't get homesick now," the woman told her. "We won't let you."

But now it was October 7—the first day of classes—and the thirty-six female students about to launch their medical careers had little time to think about much of anything else. Susan and her classmates (including one from India, one from Syria, and another from Japan) were under the gun from day one. All first-year students were expected to take courses in chemistry, anatomy, physiology, histology (the study of cell and tissue structures), materia medica (pharmacy), general therapeutics, and obstetrics. They also were expected to learn how to dissect cadavers, attend daily clinics at the nearby Woman's Hospital, and take weekly quizzes in chemistry, anatomy, and physiology. And at the end of their first winter term, they would all be thoroughly tested in the ins and outs of inorganic chemistry, anatomy, physiology, and histology.

All in all, it was an educational structure and teaching philosophy Susan was not used to, one that differed a great deal from what she'd experienced in Elizabeth, New Jersey, and Hampton, Virginia. She explained the difference in a letter home: "We have no visitations at all—the diff. professors lecture to us, they talk and we take notes just as fast as we can. Then we study up the subject by ourselves. We are free to go and come when we like—we may be absent if we choose and lose a lecture or a whole day. That is our own look-out but I tell you there are scarcely any absent even on Quizzes. We have to pass 90 percent so of course we want to get all we can get. We are not forced to do anything so of course we would rather do it." To make sure she passed a difficult chemistry course, Susan borrowed the lecture notes of a classmate almost every morning. And to make sure they did as well as they could, it was not unusual for Susan and several classmates to band together and pull late-night study sessions before important exams.

Early on—when the new curriculum seemed too complicated, when chemistry seemed too overwhelming, when a new social order seemed too intimidating—it was comforting for Susan to remember an incident that had occurred just a few days before classes began. Shortly after settling in, Susan and everyone else had to make their way to the dean's office to officially register. When she arrived, Dean Rachel Bodley, a chemistry professor, was seated at her desk, shaking hands with a swarm of other first-year students, telling each of them how happy she was to see them. When she saw Susan, the dean got up from her chair, walked over to greet her, then kissed her on the cheek. "We welcome you and are proud of your lineage," she said. Later that same day, at a gathering of the entire student body, the dean once again formally welcomed Susan in front of all the students and professors. "She is very nice and kind to me and always asks if I am happy here. I like her very much," Susan told her family.

Not long afterward, Dean Bodley hosted a formal reception to welcome the class of 1889. Throughout the evening, Susan observed her new classmates, who were much different from those she had known at the Presbyterian Mission School, the Elizabeth Institute for Young Ladies, and the Hampton Normal and Agricultural Institute. That evening in Philadelphia, wherever she looked in the crowded room, she saw formal evening gowns and white gloves. She saw expensive dresses adorned with beautiful flowers. She saw bustles and jewelry, gleaming leather shoes and immaculately styled hair. She saw her roommate arrive in a black silk dress with white lace and white gloves. For a while, Susan thought she, too, would show up at the reception wearing white gloves to go with a simple blue flannel dress. Her landlady said she had a pair that was too small and she wanted Susan to have them for the reception. Susan tried them on, but they were too small and she split out the thumbs, and so she couldn't wear them to the reception.

For the third time in seven years, Susan had been uprooted from her familiar prairie homeland to a spot on the crowded East Coast. But this one was different from Elizabeth and much different from

Hampton. In Philadelphia, she no longer lived in a segregated all-Indian dorm filled with girls who looked a lot like her, who mostly came from isolated and impoverished reservations scattered across the American West. Starting with the dean's reception and every day after, she was now brushing up against a group of classmates who hadn't grown up in a Village of the Make-Believe White Men. Instead, many of her new classmates had grown up in the lavish homes of white men—white men who were powerful bankers, doctors, lawyers, judges, insurance executives, board chairmen, and captains of industry. White men whose daughters arrived at the medical college from private schools and privileged backgrounds, wearing silk dresses and white gloves, beautiful flowers and stylish shoes. Throughout the early part of the winter term at the Woman's Medical College of Pennsylvania, Susan needed all of her considerable discipline and emotional strength to stay focused, to stay balanced in a complex new world in which she had not yet established a firm foothold.

And among the most valuable tools she had to maintain her equilibrium was the U.S. mail. Although the dean and her classmates had embraced her warmly, although she had been warned not to get homesick, that they wouldn't allow it, Susan was homesick, sometimes desperately so. As a cure, in the early going and throughout her three years in Philadelphia, she engaged in an intense letter-writing campaign, attempting to close the thirteen-hundred-mile gap between the Liberty Bell and the Missouri with a relentless postal assault. Sometimes, especially in the opening weeks, she'd write several letters a day—long letters covering all of the lined pages and spilling over into the margins, letters serving up a smorgasbord of gossip, weather reports, academic updates, surgical thrills, Hampton news, romantic insights, fashion commentary, social observations, and any number of other things. But before they ended, somewhere in almost every letter, she always noted how crushing the distance between school and home could be. How much she missed the Upstream People and their creeks and rivers, the woods and plains. And always how much it hurt to be so far from her family.

Throughout her life, Susan had an intense emotional relationship with Rosalie, whom she viewed as both an older sister and a mother figure. Many of her letters began "Dear Ro" and often ended, like one dated November 4, 1886, with some variation of how much she revered and missed her: "It gives me such a sense of comfort to think about you Ro—you are one of God's lovely women. One time in Washington last summer Miss Fletcher and I were talking about you and me. Both cried."

To help ward off those first early winter blues, she kept a photo of General Armstrong in her room, not far from another of Sara Thomson Kinney's Hartford home. And between classes and before bed, she would sit at her desk and write and write, then write some more—letters filled with worries about family health, regrets for acting badly, gratitude for their love of one another, thankfulness for a just and compassionate God, and longing for home:

"How I wish I was out there with you. Oh! Ro 3 years from now seems like Paradise. When I shall be at home to stay with you all the time. . . . Tell Mother I am very sorry about her hand. Of course she knows I would gladly give my life for her. . . . College closes in May, so only 7 mos. left. . . . However poor we are it is enough that we are all together. I wonder how many times a day I pray for you all. . . . You can't imagine how badly I feel when I think of how much I used to make Mother & you girls feel badly when I got mad. . . . I want to save every penny if I can so I can come home next summer. I long so for you all. . . . Sometimes when I wake up in the mornings I think to myself Well I guess poor dear Mother is up in the cold getting breakfast and Ro has dressed herself and the children and is going out to breakfast. . . . I take such pleasure in it and think you are so near to me in those times almost as if I was there with you all. I like to think at night too what you are all doing. . . . My dearest Sister-Mother: . . . don't you think we ought to feel so very, very rich with each other our dear Father, Mother and each other and our comfortable homes and land."

Throughout the fall and early winter of that first year, a one-dollar bill in Susan's possession became a recurring theme in many of her first-semester letters, alternately serving as a kind of social barometer, historical marker, and moral compass. The dollar had been a gift from Mrs. Talcott at the Connecticut Indian Association. Initially, Susan figured she'd use it to buy some white gloves, the better to blend in at social functions. But then she decided spending it on gloves was frivolous. It made more sense to save it for a few Christmas gifts to send home. Then she discovered her mother had developed sores on her arm and leg. Her mother, she thought, needed more protein. So she determined to send the dollar home to buy some food. But then she learned her mother's health had deteriorated. So she decided to send the dollar to Rosalie with specific instructions: If their mother got worse, Rosalie was to use the dollar to telegraph Susan immediately. If she got better, then the dollar was for meat, perhaps chicken, to help her mother get stronger. "I shall pray for her, tell her all the time so she will be spared to us and we will all see each other again."

As the semester unfolded, as she got a bit more comfortable, Susan, too, grew bolder and more determined. She ended one letter to her sister with a simple sentence: "I don't want to grow old and quiet before my time."

There was little danger of that. This idea, this notion of soaking it all up, of taking it all in, of packaging it into a specific set of skills that would one day help the diseased and suffering and others not yet born, was a powerful one. So it wasn't long before Susan applied the powers of concentration and determination that had been nurtured and noticed in Nebraska, New Jersey, and Virginia to her medical school classes.

One cold winter day, Susan walked into a clinic hall attached to the Woman's Hospital. The hall was a large amphitheater seating up to three hundred students in a theater-in-the-round design. Steep steps descended to a round, open space with a table where students observed patients who were laid out, examined, and operated on. Susan arrived with a surgical ticket to see several operations by Dr. William Keen, a small man with a large reputation. An esteemed surgeon, Keen would later head the team that cut out a tumor from the jaw of President Grover Cleveland. On this winter day, Keen was scheduled to perform two operations in the clinic hall. So Susan took her seat and settled in to watch.

In the first operation, Susan later wrote, Dr. Keen "took a tumor as big as a small apple from the neck or below the ear of a colored girl. He did it in about ten minutes." In the second operation, the surgeon removed a needle from the thigh of a young girl who had accidentally plunged it into her leg. After etherizing his young patient, Keen "made the incision about ½ inch deep, probed around and got the needle. He did it in 2½ minutes."

The students were stunned.

They all began to clap, but the surgeon stopped them.

Susan was thrilled. "It was wonderful."

After the operations, Dr. Keen sought her out. "Do you know I am so glad to see you?" he said. He told her how pleased the college was to have her and, personally, how proud he was that she wanted to get her medical degree, then return home to her people and help them.

Witnessing Dr. Keen's surgical skills and participating in hands-on medical experiences endeared her classes to Susan—especially anatomy and dissecting cadavers. And soon that joy and excitement, the sheer fascination with everyday medical school life, found its way into her letters home. "I like my studies very much indeed and don't mind the dissecting room at all," she gushed in a November 17, 1886, letter. "We laugh & talk up there just as we do anywhere. Six students take one body—the whole body lies there—and is divided into 6 parts. Two take the head—2 the chest—2 the abdomen and legs. Then we take off little by little. 1st the skin—then the tissue—then one muscle is lifted showing arteries—veins, nerves etc. It is interesting to get all the arteries and their branches—everything has a name from the little tiny holes in the bones. It is splendid. We have to see the surgical operations performed too in the clinic hall. I have seen operations on little tiny babies. It is wonderful. I could tell you lots of things but I don't know as you would care to hear them."

For three years, Susan was immersed in medicine from a woman's perspective: She attended a woman's medical college attached to a woman's hospital surrounded by female classmates and a good many female professors. Week in and week out, she attended many lectures, saw many clinical procedures, observed the treatment of many patients, and participated in many dissections—many of which involved women. And over time, she observed something that profoundly affected her: the horrific pain that many women and their children routinely endured, day after day.

"When I used to hear about diseases of women I never imagined what suffering there could be," she wrote. She was shaken by the sheer range of their medical problems—from serious diseases to childbirth complications—and how much pain they were often in. It was hard to even contemplate that kind of suffering, she noted, and yet there they were, still standing up, still walking around, day after day. She was thankful to be pain free, to be able to do all she routinely did each day.

As Susan got deeper into her studies, more and more letters arrived in the Village of the Make-Believe White Men, many of them eagerly dispensing a wide range of medical advice. And more than a few ended up in Rosalie's home. "Always send me as many cases as you can," she demanded of her sister. And Rosalie did. When Susan found out about sores on her mother's hand and foot, she quickly sent out carbolated Vaseline and Castile soap. When her father needed a new artificial leg, she ordered one. When her mother again fell ill, she prescribed fresh beef to boost her immune system. "That is what Dr. Sue thinks," she wrote. When Ed Farley, Rosalie's husband, was stricken, more medical advice arrived: "Tell him 'Dr. Sue' orders less quinine. And more time for meals."

But most of her advice went directly to Rosalie, who eventually gave birth to ten children and was pregnant during much of the time her younger sister was preparing to be a doctor. Dr. Sue routinely advised her on a variety of pregnancy-related topics. It is not unusual, she told Rosalie, for pregnant women to have problems with their gums and jaws. When numerous colds and toothaches got her down, she told Rosalie to eat healthier food. When she felt her pregnant sister was too stressed out, she delivered calm and soothing advice, telling Rosalie to not work too hard, avoid lifting heavy objects, exercise often with long walks in fresh air, get a good night's rest, and spend less time worrying and more time "reading, telling stories to the children."

And all the while Dr. Sue was strengthening ties with her family, giving free medical advice, and counting down the days, she was also forging stronger social bonds with her new classmates. They knew of the vast differences between her family and theirs, that Susan's family had skinned hides, built tipis, hunted buffalo, and fought off Lakota war parties while theirs shopped at Wanamaker's, built luxurious homes, hunted seaside resorts, and hosted high society tea parties. But it didn't matter. They loved her good heart and compassionate nature, so they helped her, they took good care of her.

Emily Garner was one of those classmates. She had worked with the Cherokee in North Carolina and planned to return to them as a doctor. Every now and then, she and Susan liked to walk in Philadelphia's sprawling Fairmount Park, picking up pinecones, sitting on rocks above the Schuylkill River, disappearing into the nature they both loved and missed. One day when they were there, it started snowing. So they walked back to Emily's, and when they arrived she made Susan warm her frozen feet in the oven. Susan complied, then grabbed a guitar and started strumming, and they had a boisterous sing-along while Emily whipped up a snack of bread and butter and peaches and cream—and a batch of fresh cookies for good measure.

Meanwhile, her Connecticut "mothers" never let Susan languish for long, lavishing a good deal of attention and gifts on the young Omaha woman. One evening toward the end of her first term, shortly before Christmas, an express package arrived from Hartford, from the home she kept a photo of in her room. Inside the Christmas box, Sara Kinney had packed a white comb, a hairbrush, a nailbrush, two white ties, a silk holder, an expensive pen, a book of poems, a red-and-black jacket, a large pink Christmas card, and a bottle of cologne—"the good kind."

All along, Susan had desperately wanted to return home for Christmas, had obsessed over it the whole first term, trying to save every penny she could for the train ticket west. But when the time came, she hadn't saved enough and her family had no money to send her. So she decided to do the next best thing—she decided to go back to Hampton for the holidays.

She had so many fond memories of the place, had made so many good friends there. Marguerite was still at Hampton, and Susan couldn't wait to see her. They had already shared a lot—growing up in the village, the long train rides to New Jersey and back, three years together at the Elizabeth Institute, and two more years at Hampton. During those years, the two sisters had grown close, and as soon as Susan arrived in Philadelphia, they immediately began swapping letters filled with endless gossip and family news and classroom updates and comings and goings of mutual friends and who the latest lovers were.

He, of course, was there, too. And in truth, T.I. was a major reason she was so anxious to get to Hampton for the long holiday break from the rigors of medical school. For a long time she had been dreaming about him, and she was still dreaming about him some nights in medical school, dreaming about how much he probably missed her and how glad he'd be to see her again and how much his poor English had probably improved by now, and he had said as much in his letters to her. She remembered how beautiful his face was and how good he had always looked in his smartly tailored uniform on the Hampton parade grounds, his sweet smile and gentle nature, and she remembered all the people who kept trying to talk her out of falling for the sickly boy who struggled in the classroom. Just recently, a former Hampton teacher who was now an instructor in a nursing program in Philadelphia had kept telling her how she'd be smart to start going out with another Indian boy, Charles Dixson, who was exceptional in every way—handsome, intelligent, charming, mature, sophisticated—and who would be so much better for her, so much closer to her in status, so much more her equal, intellectually, socially, professionally. But Susan didn't want to hear any of it. She was in love with Thomas Ikinicapi, a Lakota full-blood from Dakota Territory. And she couldn't wait to see him.

One of the things she loved most about him was how respectful he was to her and his devotion, his complete faithfulness, to her. She was convinced his good looks and sweet nature were too much for other girls to resist, so his loyalty and fidelity made him even more attractive. "You see he is very handsome and one of the kind girls like," she confided to Rosalie, "and he would not have to go far to get anyone so I was surprised when I found he did not go with any one but waited for me to come down."

So after Christmas, Susan took the train down from Philadelphia, and on New Year's Eve, she and T.I. and Marguerite and her boyfriend, Charles Picotte, all strolled into the Hampton gym together, arm in arm, four young American Indians in love, swept away by the rich sounds of an eighteen-piece band as 1886 began to fade away across the open waters of Chesapeake Bay.

When the band finished, she told Rosalie in a lengthy letter, they went to see the grand promenade. And when it started to sprinkle a bit, Susan put on a shawl and T.I. made sure he covered her with his umbrella. As it got closer to midnight, the foursome made their way to room 21 at Academic Hall, where it was just like old times, a room alive with a lot of boisterous black students and Indian students and Hampton teachers and everyone counting down the minutes until 1887. And when it happened, one of the teachers gathered everyone together and said a prayer, and then everyone shook hands and wished one another a Happy New Year. For Christmas, Susan had sent T.I. a nice card and a beautiful horseshoe pin, and he wore it that night. He had also been telling her how much he wanted to have a picture of her, so on New Year's Day morning, she and Marguerite walked through the campus and found a place where Susan had some small ones taken, one of which she gave to him.

Later on New Year's Day, after lunch, Susan was standing around outside a dining room, in a cluster of other students, when T.I. came up and stood beside her. Lost in thought, she looked at him and smiled but said nothing, and after a while he walked away. At four P.M. that afternoon, all the Indian boys started arriving at

Winona Lodge to socialize with all the Indian girls, and Susan got there a bit late. When she walked in, she saw T.I. playing checkers with one of the Indian girls. Soon, one of the boys asked her to play a game with him, so she did. A little later, another boy asked her to go outside and join him in a march. She did. Then shortly afterward, T.I. came out and marched with one of the Sioux girls.

After the march, Susan came back inside the lodge and stood by the door. He saw her there and came straight over, standing in silence beside her. Neither looked at the other. T.I. felt she'd been paying a little too much attention to others and not enough to him, and Susan felt he'd wasted some precious time on others at her expense. He wanted her to take the first step, to make it right again, to take the chill out of the air, and she waited and waited for him to do the same, to start the healing. But neither could do it. So they just stood there, silently, staring the other way, looking down.

Susan finally sat near a couple playing checkers. When they left, T.I. came over and sat beside her. She saw the pain and the sadness in his face, and it made her feel bad. No one spoke. After a while, he put his arm on the bench and sat there, one hand covering his face. Then he got up and grabbed the checkerboard and flung it at a nearby windowsill. The loud crash startled the room, and some of the other boys stared at the two silent figures who sat on the bench for a long time afterward.

When the supper bell rang, all of the boys began to leave, but T.I. would not leave. Finally, Marguerite came to Susan and told her it was time for them to go eat with all the other girls. T.I. stood up, but still he wouldn't go, so Susan said it was time, he must go now. "He had his handkerchief up in his face and his eyes were shining—I felt so sorry for him—I felt like crying."

She was scheduled to leave on Monday evening, and after a private dinner with one of her former teachers, she and Marguerite left for the main dining room to say good-bye. Marguerite had given her a beautiful bouquet of flowers, and when she saw T.I., she broke off a yellow tea rose and gave it to him. The dining room was crowded, and many of their friends knew how much they had loved each other, and they knew, too, that things weren't right now and they felt bad, but they didn't know what to do.

At six thirty, the carriage arrived to take Susan to the train station, and her older sister watched her walk off into the darkness, struggling with her own emotions, then turning away. After a little while, a friend told her to look up. Marguerite saw T.I. standing alone under a streetlight "with hand and handkerchief over his eyes." He looked so forlorn, she broke down and started to cry.

The long Christmas break was over now, but winter wasn't and the second half of a difficult first-year medical program was about to begin. The college's only Indian student arrived back in Philadelphia that term alone and lonely, emotionally drained, too many thoughts to sort through, too many pressures, her heart and her head struggling for control. She didn't know what to do.

Cora Folsom, her favorite Hampton teacher who was in Philadelphia with the nursing program, had a long talk with Susan after she returned. She built her case slowly, telling Susan she herself liked T.I., that his fidelity and respect for her were commendable. Boys, she said, "generally wanted to go with girls on their own level and it showed something fine in him" that he would go with someone so superior in education. "There must be something noble in him," she told Susan, "because he aspires to something higher than himself." She asked Susan about his feelings for her and said she was afraid T.I. was getting into "deep waters." The solution, Folsom told her, was obvious: They needed to have a platonic relationship. They should be friends. She should help him and he should help her—but that was it, nothing more. Susan, she said, was too good for him, too good for any of them. Susan

didn't agree, and she said so. Still, Folsom told her, it was important to keep her focus, important that she not lose sight of the
bigger picture, to remember why she had come to Philadelphia
and what it would one day mean to her people.

That winter, Susan could not escape it, the pressure that never
seemed to leave, that seemed to come from every direction at the
same time she felt so much pressure from the upcoming medical
school exams. It came right away from Miss Folsom, and it had
been there all along from all the mothers at the Connecticut
Indian Association. Long before she ever saw a dissection or an
amputation, she had agreed to their conditions: In exchange for
the association agreeing to pay for almost all of her medical school
expenses, she promised not to marry for a year or two after getting her medical degree. And now it was coming from her family,
too. Marguerite and Charles Picotte, a mixed-blood of French and
Sioux ancestry from the Yankton Agency, had met at Hampton,
fallen in love, and gotten engaged, and now it seemed certain they
would soon marry. Their father, who had always stressed the need
for education above all else, was upset with his daughter's engagement, and the news of Joseph La Flesche's displeasure didn't take
long to reach Susan. And it didn't take long for the family to make
it clear that she should not allow her feelings to go any further for
yet another Sioux boy from Dakota Territory.

But this wasn't any Sioux boy from Dakota, this was T.I. The T.I.
who was still there, still with her, still in her. The T.I. who was still
writing, still faithful, still telling her he was sorry all day long every
day since she'd left, that no matter what he did he couldn't get her
out of his mind. She'd told Rosalie before how much she, too,
would like him, how "he has been such a help to me in more ways
than one," how he'd worked so hard to polish his manners and
improve his English, how much she wanted to be a good influence
on him and become a powerful role model to push him even

further in the classroom and beyond. But wherever she turned, wherever she looked, the people she had always counted on didn't seem to understand. They seemed to have all forgotten what it was like to be young, to be listening to beautiful music on New Year's Eve and wondering all the time if the sweet, gentle, handsome boy you were holding hands with would make a good husband, a good father, someone you might want to share a life with.

In the early winter of 1887, twenty-one-year-old Susan La Flesche was perhaps the only Indian woman in America forced to thread the needle, who had to decide then and there: Career or love? Profession or family? Doctoring or mothering? There were no peers she could turn to, no other Indian women to seek wisdom from, no one like her to ask for advice. Even Alice Fletcher, the trusted mentor who helped get her into Hampton, who helped get her into medical college, had little to offer. So she wrestled with it alone, over and over. And in the end, she reached a decision on her own: She couldn't ignore the promise, she couldn't renege on her word to the Connecticut mothers. And she could never really escape the long shadow cast by the two-story wood-frame house in the Village of the Make-Believe White Men. In those first winter months of 1887, shortly before her medical exams were to begin, a resigned and weary Susan predicted her future in a letter home:

"So I will be the dear little old maid we read of in books . . . I shall . . . come and see you all and doctor and dose you all. Won't that be fine?"

She was always one of those people, the kind who genuinely loves the art of learning, who can sit for hours absorbing and collating information from a printed page, who regards the slow, steady, disciplined drip of knowledge almost as a spiritual act. It was the academic rigor of her classes then that often saved Susan, that kept her focused and satisfied, that kept the homesickness at bay and the heartache under wraps. The classes gave her emotional safety and the security of knowing that each day she was learning something that had a practical value, that would get her one step closer to the one thing that mattered more than anything else.

So while some of her childhood friends still lugged water and dug wild turnips, while some of her Connecticut mothers adjusted corsets and planned tea socials, Susan burrowed into her studies, her readings, her clinic lectures, and, perhaps most of all, her hands-on opportunities. She loved it all—learning about all the different kinds of bones, the skin, the arteries, the veins, the vital organs. And she was not the least squeamish or put off by the eight to ten P.M. dissection sessions, not at all fainthearted at the prospect of slicing up a cadaver or getting her hands a little dirty. "Tell Ed," she advised her sister with a dash of playfulness, "I am going to wield the knife tonight—not the scalping knife though."

Then, in early March 1887, the first exams came in waves: chemistry on Thursday, anatomy on Saturday, physiology on Tuesday. She made no secret that chemistry scared her the most. All term, after almost every class, she had borrowed the chemistry notebook of Sarah Lockery, a smart, older, ambitious student who was fond of Susan and generous to her. Susan readily admitted to her family that she had "some hard studying to do," so heading into exam week, she and several friends held late-night cram sessions. She also acknowledged she was leaving nothing to chance. "Pray for me dear so I can pass," she urged her sister. Apparently Rosalie did— and with good results. A week later, Susan reported the chemistry exam "was much easier than I thought it would be." And then she sailed through the anatomy exam: "It was lovely. I made a certain point to study certain bones and we were asked to describe those very bones and one or two others, so I got on swimmingly."

So Susan and her first-year female medical school classmates kept up their rigorous study habits, kept breaking into smaller groups, kept borrowing one another's notes, all the while unaware of the potentially dire consequences they faced, according to a pre-eminent Boston gynecologist of the era.

Dr. Edward H. Clarke, also a Harvard Medical School professor, believed he had ample scientific evidence to prove a theory he firmly embraced: that women who went to college risked becoming infertile. A woman in higher education, he believed, risked putting her brain and her uterus in a constant state of conflict—a conflict ultimately resulting in the potential destruction of a woman's reproductive system. Women, he noted, could educate or menstruate, but they could not do both, because a woman's "system never does two things well at the same time." And if they persisted, he said, they risked "neuralgia, uterine disease, and other derangements of the nervous system," including infertility.

Clarke's book on the subject, *Sex in Education,* was published in 1873 and became enormously popular, eventually resulting in seventeen printings. In the book, Clarke cites specific instances that he claimed underscored his point that a woman's brain and her reproductive system simply could not coexist in a college environment:

"Miss D—— went to college in good physical condition," Clarke wrote. "During the four years of her college life, her parents and the college faculty required her to get what is popularly called an education. Nature required her, during the same period, to build and put in working order a large and complicated reproductive mechanism, a matter that is popularly ignored—shoved out of sight like a disgrace. She naturally obeyed the requirements of the faculty, which she could see, rather than the requirements of the mechanism within her, that she could not see. Subjected to the college regimen, she worked four years in getting a liberal education. Her way of work was sustained and continuous, that of harmony with the rhythmical periodicity of the female organization. The stream of vital and destructive force evolved within her was turned steadily to the brain, and away from the ovaries and their accessories. The result of this sort of education was, that these last-mentioned organs, deprived of opportunity and nutriment, first began to perform their functions with pain, a warning of error that was unheeded; then, to cease to grow; . . . And so Miss D—— spent the few years next succeeding her graduation in conflict with dysmenorrhea, headache, neuralgia, and hysteria."

Nevertheless, the first-year students at the Woman's Medical College of Pennsylvania studied hard, and when physiology finally wrapped up, Susan joined two of her classmates and headed downtown, where she watched them celebrate with an intense shopping spree.

As the weeks unfolded, as she got to know them better, Susan began spending more time with her classmates and some of the city's well-to-do families, often ending up in their homes, at their dinner tables, in their guest bedrooms, at their church services and their weddings, all in a world far removed from Logan Creek. Early on, the W. W. Heritage family developed a fondness for Susan, so she sometimes spent weekends and holidays with them. At Christmas, Mrs. Heritage sent Joseph La Flesche a beloved silk handkerchief that had belonged to her father. It was a gift, she said, to express "the high regard I have for your daughter Susan." The Heritages took Susan to church and to hear celebrated temperance speakers of the day and to dinner at their luxurious home, and sometimes after tea they all gathered around the piano for exuberant sing-alongs.

Little by little, she got swept up in all the different styles around her, and after a while, she began to wear her hair in a new way, piled on top of her head, "a fold behind the hair to relieve the bareness of the back and then two coils on either side . . . the College girls said it was very becoming and asked me to wear it that way all the time." One time, she dressed up and spent the night at the home of another prominent family and marveled at the size of the big red bedroom she was given and the ivory combs and brushes all laid out and what awaited her at breakfast the next morning. The first course was oranges, served with individual finger bowls, a first for Susan. "They just dip in their fingers & wipe them on napkins," she reported to her family back on the Missouri. Then the table was cleared and a second course arrived: kidney and gravy, potatoes, and bread and butter. Next came a large silver urn with flannel beneath it. "Mrs. Ogden turned on the faucet & hot coffee came out."

Over time, the young woman from the Nebraska Plains put in place many of the pieces that helped her carve out a balanced, well-rounded life in Philadelphia. She nurtured one part of herself by staying close to her family. She nurtured another with weekly church attendance, regular student religious services in the hospital, Christian Endeavor Society meetings, and her own frequent prayer sessions. Socially, her peers elected her secretary of the Young Women's Christian Association, and she found time to attend numerous public lectures, participate in the college's many events, and keep in close contact with all of her Connecticut mothers, which included occasional speaking engagements. With a rigorous academic schedule, she had no trouble finding intellectual nourishment. And whenever she needed to escape the bricks-and-mortar and urban pressures, she took long jaunts in Fairmount Park, walking through the woods, strolling the riverbank, climbing atop rocky outcrops, and gathering baskets of wildflowers. Never one to risk the consequences of idle hands, Susan also continued her drawing lessons, played tenpins, signed up for skating sessions, and every Monday and Friday morning took a gymnastics class—and just for good measure a weight-lifting class, which the college encouraged to promote good health. "Tell Mother she ought to see us—we have to have flannel suits—blouse waists and short trousers fastened at the knee," she wrote her sister. Poised to flex a new set of muscles, she also asked Rosalie to convey a message to her husband: "Tell Ed . . . when I come home I may swing an ax or harness the horses to keep up my practice but you won't get me to go near the cows. For I am afraid of those 'critters.'"

After passing her second-year exams, Susan finally made it home, arriving on June 1, 1888, at the same Bancroft station where she'd boarded the train for Philadelphia almost two years earlier. Her family traveled the short three miles from their home for a joyous, tearful reunion. And then Susan got down to work—work far removed from chemistry notebooks, piano recitals, and silver coffee urns. With her parents sick and homebound, their youngest daughter went after everything in her path. She measured land for pasture fences, harnessed horses, raked hay, did the housework, cooked, cleaned, sewed, nursed, doctored, and explained all the different kinds of medicine—everything but the cows. "I can tell you one thing," she wrote Sara Kinney back in her East Coast home, "and that is a Western woman has to know how to do everything a man does besides her own work, for she has to be ready for any emergency that may occur when men are not around."

That summer, an emergency engulfed the Omaha Reservation, one duly noted in Agent Jesse Warner's annual report to the commissioner of Indian affairs. The year 1888, he wrote in his September 10 report, brought a "terrible scourge of measles." Before it ended, eighty-seven had died, mostly children. Susan was overwhelmed by the scope of what she saw. "Almost every family was in mourning for one, two or three little ones," she told Kinney. "It was very sad and pitiful and many were in bad want of care and food. . . .

In some places a little nursing would have been so much help, for they do not know how to give the medicine even when told, and sometimes are actually afraid to give it."

So for a while, Susan abandoned all the haying and harnessing and tended to her people, explaining the various medicinal powders and liquids and the proper way to take them, taste-testing some for skeptical patients, pulling them closer, easing their fears, gaining their trust. Then one of Rosalie's children was stricken and Susan stayed closer to home, nursing, doctoring, reading up on specific cases. Then Rosalie got sick for two weeks and Susan "had the pleasure of taking care of her." And then some friends in Easton, Pennsylvania, heard about the measles outbreak and sent out a barrel of food provisions, so Susan got in a buckboard and started fanning out across her homeland in the high, hard heat of June and July, treating the sick and dispensing the food, frustrated that some days she would be out all afternoon, ride twenty-five miles, and still see only ten families.

Throughout the long summer, Susan got an eyeful, seeing first-hand, day after day, the magnitude of the problems, seeing what it would take to elevate her people from where they were to where they needed to be. And once she saw up close how far they had to go, she was motivated by the challenge to help get them there. "So much can be done, by going to see them and while you are there tell them how to tidy up or show them *how* which is better still," Susan wrote to the woman whose organization was paying for her to learn to do exactly that. "They have so much to learn not only about cleanliness but about business, land, money and horses, what kind to buy and all. Mrs. Farley does a great deal of this work for them. So you see I told you the truth, when I said a Western woman has to know everything."

She kept going, kept visiting as many families as she could. Even if it was only a ten-minute visit, she would ask them about their troubles, try to cheer them up, convey some thoughts of Jesus—and see the gratitude on their faces. She had long envisioned how important these home visits would become and what her role would be. In a letter written a few months before starting medical school, Susan had detailed how she wanted to "help the women in their housekeeping, teach them a few practical points about cooking and nursing, and especially about cleanliness." And now she was doing it.

Throughout the long, hot summer, Susan never had to look far for the motivation to keep climbing back in the buckboard, to keep traveling across the large reservation, treating the sick, offering them hope. On the Great Plains or on the East Coast, she never forgot that her father had devoted his life to working for the Upstream People and how he, now sick and elderly, wanted so much for his children to carry on that work.

"I only can say, I *want* to do *so* much because there is so much to be done," she later told Sara Kinney. "I can only say to you, I shall try and do my best, try to aid them not only physically but mentally and morally. I may be too ambitious but I have to help My Heavenly Father, as well as the remembrance that my own father who has worked all his life long for my people last left his children expecting them to carry on his work."

In Philadelphia, she had thought about it off and on for quite some time, had mentioned it in some of her talks to various eastern missionary groups, and occasionally had even woven it into speeches to various offshoots of the Connecticut Indian Association. But what was often a somewhat vague idea back east always came into sharper focus when she returned home—when she saw firsthand how sick her people were, how far apart they lived, how difficult it was to treat them.

And in the summer of 1888, when the focus could not have been any sharper, she thought more and more about a recurring dream, the one she kept having about how best to help her people: to one day build a hospital on the Omaha Reservation.

Susan liked people. And she had a genuine hunger for new experiences, to see and do a variety of things, to meet men and women much different from her, men and women who often were just as interested to know more about her, who enjoyed showing off their city to the charming, inquisitive Indian girl from the Great Plains. So during her three years at the Woman's Medical College, Susan's social and artistic life blossomed.

It began almost immediately. A few days before Christmas 1886, the well-to-do, well-connected Mrs. Miesse took the youngest daughter of an Omaha Indian chief to see Gilbert and Sullivan's comic opera *The Mikado,* which Susan loved and couldn't wait to tell Rosalie about. And then Mrs. Miesse's friend, a theater manager, gave her three tickets to *A Wife's Peril,* starring the "Jersey Lily" herself, Lily Langtry, one of the era's most glamorous stage actresses—and of course she gave one to Susan, and soon they were transfixed watching. "I can say now I have seen a beautiful woman," Susan flatly declared afterward. Then one week it was off to see Hannah Whitall Smith, among the celebrated temperance speakers of the day, and another week Miss Haynes sent her a ticket to hear the Germania Orchestra, said to be the city's finest. And then came an invitation to journey out to Girard College to watch more than one thousand boys drill in parade formation, and Susan couldn't quite fathom the splendor of so many buildings inspired by Grecian architecture, including one modeled after the Parthenon. Then it was off to see another play, *The Little Tycoon,* and then an invitation to attend a standing-room-only Sunday service in the city's grand Catholic cathedral, with its gorgeous paintings, altars, flowers, and music—which on this day included selections from Handel's *Messiah*. Then around Thanksgiving, Mrs. Clarkman escorted Susan to the Academy of Fine Arts, where the marble staircase, the huge orchestra, and all the violins and flutes and horns and her personal favorite, the mandolin, overwhelmed her. And then they walked to the academy's galleries of paintings and sculptures, and she couldn't quite comprehend the magnificence of all the Benjamin West paintings, including *The Death of General Wolfe* and *Christ Rejected*, which was Jane Austen's favorite. They had entered the academy at four P.M. and thought they had been inside no more than ninety minutes. They were surprised to discover it was six forty-five P.M. when they finally left.

With each passing month, when Susan wasn't exploring the city's vast fine arts world or immersed in course work, she was often with her classmates, young women her own age who were quickly becoming her friends. After about five months, she finally mastered Philadelphia's complex streetcar system, and after her first-year exams were over, she and "some of the girls" set off on an extended tourist excursion through the City of Brotherly Love. Before it ended, they had visited Old Swedes' Church, the Delaware River, Philadelphia City Hall, Ben Franklin's grave, and Independence Hall.

But no matter how much art, architecture, music, and society she absorbed, Susan never lost sight of who she was or where she came from. And she always looked to maintain a bridge to her people and traditions wherever and whenever she could. The nearby Lincoln Institute, a post–Civil War orphanage, was filled with Indian children, so Susan often went to see them. The Educational Home in West Philadelphia, which she and her friends visited many times, housed a number of Indian boys who "all looked very well & happy," she was delighted to tell her family. One Sunday, one of the Dakota boys thought Susan looked particularly well, so he decided to shadow her throughout the day. "I don't care to go with any one," the exasperated medical school student later told her sister, "and I remembered someone at Hampton and wondered what he would think to see so much attention lavished on me." But the boy didn't give up easily. He followed her to morning services, then sat next to her during afternoon hymns, holding the hymnal open and turning the pages for her. "I haven't any time or patience for such things nowadays," she told Rosalie. "Doctors don't have much time *you know* and he will have to keep his place." One February day, about 130 Carlisle Indian boys and girls teamed up with some Hampton Indian students for a concert, and Susan made sure she was there to see and hear them. She was proud that so many of those students were from her tribe, and she made it a point to tell Rosalie that "the Omahas have high standing at both schools."

If Susan sought cultural sustenance and inspiration in the hallways of the local Indian orphanages and boys' homes, her attentions were reciprocated. Not long into her medical studies, her name began to crop up in Indian school publications and conversations, a name increasingly held up as a motivational tool, a role model for others to aspire to. Soon after the joint band concert, Susan described the reaction she got from some of the younger Omaha students. "I think they must have been so glad to see me and I think my graduation honors at [Hampton] must have made them feel so proud of me," she told Rosalie. The Carlisle school newspaper described her as one of Hampton's most gifted students, and most of their students knew she had received the gold medal and finished second in her graduating class.

When the younger Indian musicians arrived in Philadelphia for the concert, Susan said, "The boys were kind of glad to see me there as the Omaha girl who was studying medicine." A few years later, *Talks and Thoughts,* a newspaper edited and published by

Hampton's Indian students, ran a small reminiscence that began: "Sometimes when we are skipping around in Winona we remember one sweet-faced Hampton sister Susie, who used to help us so much with our games." The paper noted how far Susie had come since her Hampton days, how she might one day even have her own hospital, and how high she had set the bar for all the other Indian students. "There is not much use trying to be as smart as she is," the paper concluded, "but I guess it wouldn't hurt us to try and be as good."

And wherever she went, whether it was Hampton or the orphanages, to the home for boys or throughout Philadelphia, there was always the question of identity—about how people see themselves, how others see them, about who gets to decide, who gets to choose the cultural attributes that people select to create identities for themselves and for others—that kept cropping up again and again, in different places, at different times, in different ways.

An early April evening in 1887.

Susan and some of her friends walked into a missionary meeting to hear one of their classmates, a young woman from India, speak to the group. Many children were there, and after the talk, Susan noticed that one of the little white girls had arrived dressed as an American Indian. So she loaned the girl her own necklace and beads and showed the adults how to dress her properly. The adults wanted to put feathers on the little girl's head, but Susan explained that Indian women didn't wear head feathers. Then Susan told the friends she came with that the adults would probably end up putting feathers on the little girl anyway. And they did. But "how could they do it when it wasn't so?" the friends asked Susan.

New Year's Day 1888.

Francis La Flesche, the nation's first Indian ethnographer, had come up from Washington to visit his sister, soon to become the nation's first Indian doctor. That afternoon, brother and sister went to the traditional Philadelphia Mummers Parade, a raucous, festive folk festival showcasing hordes of dancers in lavish costumes pinwheeling down some of the city's main thoroughfares. Chestnut Street was so crowded, they could hardly walk. So they stopped and watched. They saw white people in blackface pretending to be black people. And then they saw something else. "They dressed up as Indians too & they looked pretty well for Indians," Susan observed mockingly. She wanted to show Francis Independence Hall, so they walked over to the cradle of American democracy, to where they could see the original Declaration of Independence and the U.S. Constitution. And then all the people there saw the two Indians dressed in white civilian clothing, and they attracted so much attention, drew so many stares, that the Omaha brother and sister fled the building, laughing most of the way.

One day that same year, in the early autumn, after Susan had finished a summer of treating and teaching her sickly people about medicine and cleanliness, about fresh air and sunshine, the old man had been out all day long, doing a long hard day's labor. Almost immediately, he came down with a severe cold. Then suddenly, on September 23, 1888, Joseph La Flesche died. He was about seventy years old. Both white and Indian people came from miles around to the cemetery just south of Bancroft. It is said that at the time, it was the largest funeral procession ever seen in that part of the state.

In the end, it was left to his oldest daughter to memorialize the man who had spent a lifetime trying to help his people, to bridge the cultural gap between red and white, to promote education as a survival tool, a man who had nurtured a village and a family perhaps unlike any other in Indian country.

"Whenever I think of my father . . . ," Bright Eyes wrote a number of years later, "Tennyson's lines come into my mind:

He prayeth best, who loveth best,
All things both great and small,
For the dear God who loveth us,
He made and loveth all."

Thursday, March 14, 1889.

Scores of people were gathered in a large room. Sara Thomson Kinney was there, along with a number of her colleagues from the Connecticut Indian Association. The faculty of the Woman's Medical College of Pennsylvania had taken their seats, and so had many others. They were all looking at thirty-six women who had endured three vigorous years of medical course work, three years of clinical studies, tutorials, formal lectures, dissections, autopsies, weekly quizzes, and demanding final exams. The women sat quietly in their caps and gowns, waiting for the formal ceremonies to begin.

Dr. James B. Walker, a professor of the principles and practices of medicine, had been chosen to deliver the graduation address to the new doctors and their many friends and relatives. He began his remarks by telling the large gathering that in at least one important way, this year's group was unique among the thirty-nine previous graduating classes. This year's class, Dr. Walker noted, included representatives from one of the oldest as well as one of the newest races within the evolutionary arc of civilization.

"Dr. Okami is, so far as I am able to learn, the first Japanese woman to attempt the study of medicine," he said of one of the new graduates. "She came to us almost a stranger to our language. She returns to her country-women loaded with the fruits of a well-earned victory."

Then Dr. Walker turned his attention to another graduate

in the class of 1889. He began by trying to provide a context, by trying to explain to the invited guests some of the challenging twists and turns on the long, winding road from the Missouri to the Schuylkill.

About two years earlier, Sara Kinney had tried to do the same thing in a letter to the commissioner of Indian affairs. "In competing with her white classmates, who have had the lifelong benefit of routine public school training, she has, of course, labored under great disadvantages," Kinney wrote. "But she has been brave—studious—conscientious—through it all, and has more than 'held her own.'"

Now it was Dr. Walker's turn. He told the group how Dr. La Flesche had learned English at her reservation school, polished her academic skills at a New Jersey boarding school, and excelled at the first-rate school for Indians in Hampton, Virginia, before heading immediately to Philadelphia to study medicine.

"The impulse to a professional career was not of recent growth nor from friendly suggestions from those who had watched her course," Walker explained. Instead, "it came as an inspiration when at home with her people and was born of a desire to see them independent, so far as she could make them, of the too frequently unskilled and oftener indifferent attention of the reservation doctor.

"What must those who oppose women physicians as impossibilities or monstrosities think of such a course?"

And then the graduation speaker brought his thoughts full circle.

"Thoughtful of a service to her people, child though she was," Walker said, "she permits not the magnitude of her task to stay the inspiration, but bravely, thoughtfully, diligently pursues the course, and to day receives her fitting reward. All this without precedent. She will stand among her people as the first woman physician."

Not only did Susan now have her medical degree, she had also achieved something else: The youngest daughter of a Plains Indian chief, a young woman born in an animal-skin tipi, graduated as the valedictorian of her class. Throughout three long, grueling years of medical school, she had, as Sara Kinney might have put it, more than held her own.

And she didn't stop there. Not long after the graduation ceremony, Susan decided to take a shot at a highly regarded appointment as a house surgeon to the Woman's Hospital in Philadelphia. The competition was stiff, but when the examination scores came in, she was one of six in a field of eleven selected for the prestigious four-month internship.

Since the internships didn't begin until early May, Susan decided to accept the invitation of her "mothers" at the Connecticut Indian Association and spend some time with them. For three years, the association and its members had nurtured, supported, and encouraged her. They had paid for much of her education, introduced her to important Philadelphia citizens, bought her gifts, sent her food, written countless letters, counseled and advised her, and stood by, ready to help in any possible way. So in early spring, Susan visited Hartford and a half dozen other Connecticut towns, speaking to various women's groups and absorbing their enthusiastic congratulations for her medical school achievements. In the eyes of the association's fervent members, and in the eyes of Indian reformers up and down the East Coast, Susan had become a powerful symbol of what could be accomplished, a powerful symbol that their vision of grounding young Indian women in white schools and grooming them in Christian ways was the right vision.

"Better fitted than Dr. La Flesche no teacher could be," exalted *Lend A Hand*, a religious periodical promoting charitable events and inspirational activities, upon learning Susan intended to return to the reservation. "In firm health of body and mind, knowing her ground thoroughly, acquainted with the nature of her pupils, and able to communicate with them in their own tongue, God-fearing, wise, and enthusiastic in her chosen work. All honor to Connecticut's first venture in Indian education!"

As Dr. Walker had noted in his commencement address, it was also the Woman's Medical College of Pennsylvania's first venture in training doctors with dramatically different racial and ethnic backgrounds.

Keiko Okami was a tiny, timid, sensitive, devout Christian who had come to the United States from Japan in 1885 to the one medical school in the world where—at the time—a woman could become a doctor. Although not the first female Japanese physician, Dr. Okami was the first of her people to earn a medical degree from a Western college.

That April, not long after the graduation ceremony, she and her husband sailed from San Francisco back to their Japanese homeland. Back home, she eventually became chief of gynecology at one of Tokyo's primary hospitals, where several years later the emperor of Japan came to visit. But the emperor refused to see her. The reason: She was a woman. Shortly afterward, shamed and dishonored, Dr. Okami resigned and went into private practice.

In the early spring of 1889, her classmate Susan La Flesche was twenty-three years old. She spoke four languages—English, French, Omaha, and Otoe. She had developed a bicultural fashion sense, was equally comfortable in leather heels and flat-soled moccasins, delicate necklaces and Indian beads. She had nurtured an appreciation for fine art and sophisticated orchestras, for harnessing horses and raking hay. She knew her way around Wanamaker's and Indian trading posts. She was revered by the Connecticut Indian Association and was a heroic role model for younger Indian students. She had graduated second in her Hampton class, receiving the gold medal for posting the highest exam scores her junior year, and then graduated first in her medical school class, winning one of six prized hospital internships along the way. She could now explain the chemical properties of medicines; write prescriptions; suture wounds; treat measles, influenza, pneumonia, and tuberculosis; insist on good hygiene, diet, exercise, and fresh air; set bones; conduct autopsies; and perform minor surgeries.

Yet that spring, there were still a few things she could not do.

All those who shared her gender—those who some believed risked infertility for a college degree—could not yet walk into a voting booth and help decide who should lead their country. That would take another thirty-one years.

And almost all those who shared a tribal heritage—those who had lived on their lands for millennia—could not yet claim citizenship in their own country. That would take another thirty-five years.

7

v v v

Going Home

He was lying alone on a blanket, an old Indian man curled up on the floor, struggling to breathe, struggling to live, a year after the dream had died in the snow and the bloody mud four hundred miles away, at a place called Wounded Knee.

On a late afternoon in December 1891, it was getting darker and colder on the Omaha Reservation.

Susan and Marguerite were in a wagon, scurrying up and over the rolling hillside, crunching through the snow, looking hard in the fading light for the old man dying alone in a small cabin on the frozen Nebraska prairie.

He had been ill for several days, and the family had said he was so sick now they didn't think he would live much longer. The medicine man could not help him, so they had sent for her.

The house was tiny but neat and clean, painted, with curtained windows. Susan and her sister climbed out of the wagon and walked inside. There was no one there, just the old man. She saw that he was very old and very poor. "With no children to care for him," she would later write, "there he lay on the hard floor, sick and in want of food. No one was there to speak a word of sympathy even, to cheer him in his pain and loneliness."

She knelt down and gently touched the old man. When he felt

her hand, he seemed so grateful that Susan was overcome and began to sob, crying hard in the corner of the dark room.

For ten years, she had traveled down a long road—a road that had taken her to Elizabeth, New Jersey, where she had seen the masses of white people and their rapidly industrialized, urban society. It had taken her to Hampton, Virginia, where she learned to juggle five A.M. floor scrubbings and drill parades, Shakespeare and the *Iliad*, harvests and heartaches, excellence in the classroom and the expectations of others. It had wound through Philadelphia, where she felt the terrible homesickness and the stress of medical school exams, where she heard the great symphonies and saw the fine paintings, where she visited wealthy families, went to the theater, made new friends, lost herself in the nature trails of Fairmount Park, and saw the healing power of medicine.

And now she was kneeling on the floor of the darkened room on a freezing December day, trying to rouse the old man, trying to get him to respond to the questions she was asking in the language of their people. After a while, she began to examine him, and when she finished, she opened her black leather bag and prepared the medicines she hoped would cure his severe influenza.

She gave him the medicines, and she looked at him and she saw again how thin he was. How weak. How hungry he must be by now. So she walked back outside, climbed in the wagon, went back across the dark, cold, snowy hills, and then back again, returning two hours later with a load of fresh beef, crackers, tea, and a light bread.

And at that moment, in the corner of the darkened room where the old man lay dying on the winter prairie, Dr. Susan La Flesche couldn't have been any happier.

She was home.

Going home had been on her mind for a long time. Home was the reason she had gone to Philadelphia in the first place, so on

June 13, 1889, about halfway through her four-month internship at the Woman's Hospital, she wrote the commissioner of Indian affairs. In her letter, she asked to be appointed government physician to the Omaha Agency boarding school in Macy, making a compelling case that in many ways she was the ideal candidate. "I feel that I have an advantage in knowing the language and customs of my people," she wrote in her application, "and as a physician can do a great deal to help them."

And those in charge of making the decision did not disagree. So by late summer, she moved into her new living quarters in the government boarding school, the same school where Marguerite was now the head teacher. It was also where the government had carved out some space for the new doctor's office, a clean and comfortable space, about twenty feet by fourteen feet, with plastered and wainscoted walls inside and out. Inside, her new office had the look of a miniature drugstore with its small counter and a weighing machine and drawers filled with bandages, absorbent cotton, and medical instruments, and behind the counter there were rows of shelves filled with a great many drugs and medicines.

Because Dr. Sue's primary patients were schoolchildren, it didn't take long for her office to fill up with books, papers, magazines, games of all kinds, and scrapbooks, some of which arrived courtesy of donations from the Women's National Indian Association. And it also didn't take long for more and more adults to find their way to the young doctor's office, a bright and comfortable place where they could find someone to talk to and picture books to look at, which they sometimes did for hours, especially on rainy days when it was dreary and they had nowhere else to go and they didn't want to be alone. In short order, the little office in a corner of the government school became a kind of social crossroads for young Omaha students and older adults, a place where the children got medical care and the older ones could meet, enjoy a good conversation and even a smoke—although there were strict rules governing the latter. The doctor intensely disliked smoking, but if an old man had walked a good distance and needed her office to rest, then she would let him smoke his pipe in peace. But if the visitor was younger, no deal. They were encouraged not to smoke at all, but if they must—it was outdoors only.

Come evening, after a long day of seeing patients both young and old, Susan often gathered up some of the students and held court conducting mini-lectures on the importance of good hygiene, playing games with them, looking at pictures, making scrapbooks, and polishing their English and arithmetic skills. She also devoted one evening each week to teaching her young students to sing "Nearer, My God, to Thee" and "My Country, 'Tis of Thee" in both English and Omaha. "When I realize all the work that God has given me to do, it almost takes my breath away to think how little justice I can do to it," she wrote in a letter to Amelia Quinton, president of the Women's National Indian Association. "But it is a comfort to turn and do the next thing to relieve some poor soul's trouble."

Initially, her assignment had been to care only for the schoolchildren while a white doctor cared for the adults. But it wasn't long before the adults began bombarding the reservation's Indian agent, requesting Dr. Susan, and within three months she had largely absorbed most of the other doctor's practice. So in January 1890, a month after the white physician abruptly left, Susan officially took his place. "I understood their language and they felt I was one of them, so I had the advantage," she wrote.

She was now twenty-four years old, the only doctor for 1,244 Omaha—adults and children with tuberculosis, influenza, cholera, conjunctivitis, malaria, dysentery, rheumatism, colds, fevers, and strep throats—scattered widely across 1,350 square miles of freezing, snowy, desolate prairie. From the beginning, getting to them was a problem. If the patient was only a mile or so away, she walked. If they were farther, she rode her big buckskin horse. But the rough terrain broke so many bottles and thermometers that she had to give it up. So sometimes she hired a team of horses, which was very expensive. Other times friends and family of desperate patients came and got her with their own team. Finally, the young doctor had to buy her own horses, buggy, harnesses, and feed, which cost her a good deal of money. And although her patient load had increased dramatically, her $500 annual government salary had not.

In those early days, not only was it hard getting to the patients, there was another problem: getting the patients to trust her, to trust what she had learned in a faraway city, to trust white medicine.

For many years afterward, she never forgot her first patient. He was an eight-year-old boy whose mother had brought him to the agency school. He had a common childhood illness, and the mother wanted to know if she could cure her son. Susan examined him, then prescribed the medicine and treatment she thought would help. When the mother and boy left, she began to worry: What if it was the wrong medicine? What if he got worse? What if word got out that the new doctor didn't really know what she was doing? If they didn't trust her?

So the next day, Susan saddled her horse and rode eight miles over the rough terrain to the boy's house, worrying all the way. When she got near the house, she stopped and saw that the boy was splashing wildly in a nearby creek with a group of friends. "This rapid recovery," she later recalled, "won for me no end of fame among the Indians. They fairly flocked in to me after that."

And as word spread, the hours began piling up, the workdays growing longer and longer. She often started out at seven A.M. and didn't return until ten P.M. Her first winter, she faced two influenza outbreaks, long trips and long days spent crisscrossing the large reservation. All along, she knew her first order of business was to spread the word about hygiene, to tell her people how to live healthier lives, that their transition to the new world order must rest squarely on a solid foundation of health, and she worked tirelessly to promote that notion. When Sara Kinney asked about her hours, Susan replied: "My office hours are any and all hours of day and night." And it wasn't long before those hours began to include far more than just tending to the sick and the injured.

As more Omaha began to crowd her small office day and night, they increasingly requested help with a variety of problems that had nothing to do with the three years she'd spent at the Woman's Medical College. One after another they arrived, asking Susan to help them with business decisions, legal questions, financial matters, land issues, political problems, personal dilemmas, translations, marital advice, and religious concerns. So the new doctor, already overwhelmed with caring for a large and diverse patient load, soon found herself wearing many different hats and fulfilling many different roles.

One of those roles included multiple religious duties, duties she had performed enthusiastically in a variety of settings for many years and was now getting more involved with among her own people on their own lands. In the early winter of 1890, the young doctor and Marguerite regularly attended Sunday morning services at the Presbyterian church, where the two sisters helped out singing hymns and interpreting the service to the Omaha. Come Sunday evenings, there were Christian Endeavor sessions for the young people. Wednesday evenings there were prayer meetings, gatherings at which the sisters often spoke on a variety of issues. They also began encouraging the Omaha to seek legal marriage licenses and to marry with the blessing of the church. And more and more, the Omaha were holding Christian burials, services unheard of but a few years earlier. The two sisters helped out with these, too.

Almost from the beginning, the young doctor was both surprised and pleased by how quickly she was able to bond with the Omaha women. They trusted her in a way they did not trust the white male doctors, and early on she began getting requests for medical help that white doctors had never before received. Soon, her patients included more women than men, and it wasn't unusual for Susan to visit them in the evenings and talk to them and help them with their sewing.

One day, in the hard, cold winter light, an Omaha woman came to visit Susan in her corner office in the government school building. She had come to tell her of the old man who just a few weeks earlier lay dying in his small, lonely cabin. She said the old man was out of danger, that he had recovered completely. But she herself was sick now, and the old man had told her to go see the new Indian doctor. She had good medicine, the old man told her, so that was why she had come. When Susan heard these stories, they affected her a great deal. She often thought about how grateful she was to the people back east who had sent her money to buy food for the hungry Omaha and warm flannels for the old and the poor.

"I am enjoying my work exceedingly, and feel more interest in, and more attached to my people than ever before," she wrote in a summary report to the Women's National Indian Association. "I have not a single thing to complain of."

By the early summer of 1890, a strange new religion had come to many of the reservations scattered between the Missouri River and the Sierra Nevadas.

A Paiute shaman had had a vision, a vision that foretold a promising new world, a world in which all the white people would soon disappear and the buffalo would return and all the dead Indian ancestors of long ago would rejoin the living in a new way of life. And it wasn't long before his powerful vision had swept through the lands of the Arapaho and the Northern Cheyenne, the Crow and the Blackfeet and the Lakota, and many of the other tribes struggling to survive on the Great Plains and throughout many of the western states.

The shaman's name was Wovoka and he was a full-blood Paiute shepherd who had been raised by white Christian ranchers in the Walker Lake region of western Nevada. On January 1, 1889, during a full eclipse of the sun, Wovoka had had a dream, a vision in which he said he had died and journeyed to heaven. He saw God there and conversed with many of the long-ago dead. And it was here that he saw a new world order, one set aside exclusively for the Indian people. Great herds of buffalo, elk, and deer were everywhere. The dead were living, and they were blessed with eternal happiness. No one suffered, no one starved. The people were without disease, strife, or material want. God spoke to him and provided a set of commandments, and if they were obeyed, they would bring about the salvation of his people. When Wovoka returned to earth, he came as the Indian messiah.

News of an Indian messiah spread quickly among the western tribes, and it also spread to the Omaha not long after Susan had been entrusted with the medical care of her tribe. Over time, like many of the other western tribes, Susan and her patients and all of the Omaha heard more and more about the strange vision. Emerging when many of the old ways and customs, traditions and beliefs, of the native people had been crushed by the relentless power of the white people and their civilization, the appeal of a messianic savior could not have been more timely among a large swath of increasingly desperate Indian people.

By that summer, the once great herds of buffalo, long the

traditional mainstay of many tribes, had been ruthlessly slaughtered, reduced to shockingly small numbers. Nineteenth-century scientists and researchers estimated that by the end of the 1880s, an animal once thought to number in the tens of millions now numbered no more than 1,091—256 in captivity, 200 under the protection of the U.S. government in Yellowstone Park, and 635 in the wild. The buffalo had grown so scarce that the Omaha had not had a traditional organized hunt in fourteen years, not since 1876, the same year a combined force of Lakota, Northern Cheyenne, and Arapaho wiped out five companies of Custer's Seventh Cavalry at the Little Bighorn.

Conversely, as the buffalo herds grew smaller and smaller, the sheer numbers of white settlers moving across the Missouri and onto the Plains grew larger and larger. In 1854, the year Joseph La Flesche and the other chiefs signed a treaty creating the Omaha Reservation, the U.S. Census had listed the official population of Nebraska, which did not include Indian people, at about 2,700. In 1880, it had grown to more than 450,000. And by 1890, just a decade later, the population had doubled to more than 900,000.

The flood that Big Elk had long ago prophesied was in full swing by the time Susan officially took over as sole physician for the Omaha people. That same year, 1890, there were 104,805 physicians in the United States—only 4.4 percent of whom were women. And only one of those women was an Indian.

Throughout that summer, the doctor and her people fared much better than many of the other Plains tribes. The Omaha, their agent noted in his 1890 report, "have good farms opened and are progressive." The tribe now occupied 210 wood-frame houses on their reservation, and the overall acreage cultivated in the last year had increased by 1,750 acres. They had also grown increasingly Christian, with two resident missionaries, two church buildings, a church organization boasting one hundred members, and regular Sunday services that were well attended. "They have always been a quiet, peace-loving people, and easy to control," observed Agent Robert Ashley.

His report differed greatly from the one filed that same year for the Oglala Lakota on the Pine Ridge Reservation, four hundred miles to the northwest. By August 1890, another summer of dry, scorching winds had decimated their food crop and white settlers began to move in, picking off their choicest lands. Faced with the prospect of another winter of starvation and disease, many Lakota increasingly turned to the one place where hope existed—to the vision of a Paiute shaman.

As summer turned to fall, the Lakota also began to mold Wovoka's largely peaceful vision into a more militaristic version. For the Lakota, ancient enemies of the Omaha, fighting had long been a way of life. They had been a warrior-based culture for generations. The Paiute shepherd had written out specific instructions, heavily cloaked in the trappings of Christianity, on how his followers should behave, with an emphasis on a certain way of dancing. The dance that would usher in the new world became known as the Ghost Dance. And, as with many of the other tribes, it wasn't long before the Lakota began shaping the Ghost Dance to conform to their own traditional rituals. Soon, hundreds of desperate ghost dancers began gathering along Pine Ridge creeks, their loaded Winchesters nearby, and Indian agent H. D. Gallagher grew increasingly alarmed. Despite repeated government threats, the Lakota refused to give up the dance. Many began dancing even longer and in greater frenzy, until their new agent, Daniel F. Royer, who knew nothing about Indians or the American West, became increasingly afraid, demanding that armed police or the military be rushed in to quell the tensions and protect the communities of scared white settlers ringing the reservation. On November 20, Lakota camped on the western edge of their lands awoke to see five companies of infantry and three cavalry troops marching onto the Pine Ridge Reservation. Bringing up the rear were the army's new Hotchkiss cannons and a Gatling gun.

During the long buildup of tensions, it did not occur to the government that restoring basic treaty rights and increasing the tribe's food and medical supplies could solve the problems on Pine Ridge. It was decided instead that military might would.

Smelling a good story, editors of many local, regional, and national newspapers began sending their reporters to a remote reservation where a desperate religious movement, sick and starving Indians, and heavily armed companies of the Seventh Cavalry, Custer's old command, had all converged as the days grew shorter and darker and colder in the winter of 1890.

While Susan doctored her people and Marguerite oversaw the school and Rosalie took care of many business matters, their oldest sister had been traveling throughout the country and beyond, speaking forcefully and eloquently on the issue of Indian rights. Bright Eyes and her husband, Thomas Tibbles, had been on a yearlong speaking tour in England and Scotland, and not long after their return, Tibbles had resumed his position on the *Omaha World-Herald*'s editorial staff.

Bright Eyes was among the first wave of outsiders to receive updates on the escalating tensions on Pine Ridge, updates that often came from her own people. As those tensions increased, more and more reporters flocked to the Lakota reservation, and in December both she and her husband were dispatched to Pine Ridge as special "war correspondents" for the *Omaha World-Herald* and the *Chicago Express*. But instead of hanging around with the mass of other reporters writing increasingly inflammatory stories, Bright Eyes and Tibbles stayed in a Lakota household, where they often spoke with the Lakota people, who told them the Ghost Dance was a dance of peace—not a prelude to an Indian uprising.

In late December, another Lakota band, the Miniconjou, left their camp on the Cheyenne River Reservation, heading for a meeting with the powerful Oglala leader Red Cloud on Pine Ridge, about 150 miles away. The Miniconjou numbered about 350— 230 women and children and 120 men—and throughout the journey, their chief, Big Foot, lay in the back of a wooden wagon, huddled beneath blankets, coughing up blood from severe pneumonia, a white flag fluttering from a pole above the old man's wagon. On the afternoon of December 28, cavalry officers intercepted Big Foot and his band and told them they would all have to go to the army camp. Big Foot agreed, and late that afternoon the Seventh Cavalry and his people all arrived at the army camp on *Cankpe Opi Wakpala,* on Wounded Knee Creek. Atop a long, flat hill overlooking the Indian encampment were two Hotchkiss guns, breech-loading cannons that weighed 337 pounds each, capable of firing fifty shells per minute.

The morning of December 29 dawned unseasonably warm and sunny. When the Miniconjou awoke, they found themselves surrounded by four Hotchkiss cannons and more than five hundred soldiers. The army officers assumed such a show of force would make disarming the Indians a simple matter. But the overwhelming display of guns and soldiers immediately triggered fear and confusion among Big Foot's people, and soon the tension escalated on both sides. About eight A.M. that morning, the ailing chief was taken from his tent and placed on the ground outside. Through an interpreter, the commanding officer then ordered the Indians to surrender all of their weapons—weapons that often were indispensable and acquired at great cost—and put them in a pile near their chief. After a while, disgusted at the meager pile, the commanding officer ordered his men to begin a tipi-by-tipi search. Then he ordered a body search, telling his soldiers to frisk the Indian men, to take their blankets. Confused, the younger men refused, backing away. Nearby, Yellow Bird, a Miniconjou medicine man painted in fantastic colors, circled the grounds in his Ghost Shirt. Singing and dancing, tossing dirt in the air, he told the warriors they had nothing to fear, that all the soldier bullets would fall harmlessly to the prairie. Soon a young, deaf Indian, Black Coyote, began to shout that he had earned his rifle, it was his, that he would not give it up without compensation. Two soldiers approached, grabbing him from behind. During the struggle, his rifle accidentally discharged and a single shot echoed through the camp.

The soldiers' guns exploded, and a withering barrage of bullets poured into the council grounds. Then a battery sergeant ordered the Hotchkiss cannons turned toward the Indian camp. Chunks of earth exploded, tipis burst into flame, and the bodies of mangled women and children fell across the village grounds. Screaming and crying, hysterical relatives joined the surviving men, running down the ravine toward Wounded Knee Creek. Mounted troops and Hotchkiss cannons pursued them. The shooting continued all morning and throughout the afternoon. When it ended, the official army report later placed the number of Indian dead at 290— 90 warriors and 200 women and children.

About eighteen miles southwest of the battlefield, Bright Eyes stood on a box in the middle of a group of terrified women and children, yelling at them to hurry and leave, to seek safety in their log homes. It was late afternoon and the women and children were all clustered among the buildings at agency headquarters in the village of Pine Ridge, buildings with thin wooden boards easily penetrated by the stray bullets flying all around. Go home, she shouted at them, go home to the log houses that will protect you from the bullets. Throughout the late afternoon and early evening, panic and chaos engulfed agency headquarters and the western edge of the reservation. No one really knew what had happened at

Wounded Knee Creek or what would happen next. Toward dusk, the edge of a severe winter storm moved in, and soon it became bitterly cold and it began to snow.

About nine thirty that night, the first wagons carrying some of the dead and some of the wounded arrived at agency headquarters. Many of the wounded were brought to the Holy Episcopal Church, where Reverend Charles Cook had hastily removed all of the pews and covered the floor with a bedding of straw and quilts. Bright Eyes had come to the church to help nurse some of the wounded. So had Dr. Charles Eastman, a Santee Sioux in charge of treating the injured. When Bright Eyes and Dr. Eastman and Reverend Cook first saw the men and women and children carried in from the wagons, they cried out in anguish.

They saw Steals a Running Horse, age five, laid out on the bed of straw. Bullets had torn apart the small boy's throat, and when doctors tried to feed him, the food and water came out the side of his neck. They saw Blue Whirlwind, wounded fourteen times. They saw Rough Feather, whose father, mother, grandmother, older brother, and younger brother had all been killed as they'd tried to run for cover. Her two-year-old son had been shot in the mouth and died in a few days. They saw a baby girl who was found three days later, covered in snow, huddled beside her dead mother. She was wrapped in a shawl, her head, hands, and feet severely frostbitten, but still alive. On her head, the eight-month-old infant wore a tiny buckskin cap with a needlepoint design in the shape of an American flag. That night, they saw all thirty-eight survivors brought in and laid out in rows on the church floor, and they saw that the church walls were still decked out in Christmas garlands and wreaths and a homemade sign—PEACE ON EARTH, GOODWILL TO MEN—still hung above the church altar.

Bright Eyes spent the rest of the night at the church, moving from one badly wounded survivor to the next, talking to them, calming them, telling them that they would soon be fed and that they were safe now. Still, an elderly woman wanted to know when the soldiers would come to the church and kill her and all the others. Bright Eyes said no one was coming to kill them, they were all safe now. But many did not believe her.

A decade later, Susan La Flesche and John Neihardt found themselves living within a block of each other in Bancroft. He respected her dignity and professionalism, and she frequently commended him on how well he understood the Indian and how well he had captured their spirit in his writing. In one of his writings, after days of talking to Black Elk, the poet had tried to capture the spirit of the Lakota holy man, had tried to capture what it was he saw when he looked back on all that had happened that long-ago day along *Cankpe Opi Wakpala:*

"I did not know then how much was ended. When I look back now from this high hill of my old age, I can still see the butchered women and children lying heaped and scattered all along the crooked gulch as plain as when I saw them with eyes still young. And I can see that something else died there in the bloody mud, and was buried in the blizzard. A people's dream died there. It was a beautiful dream."

For a long time she had wanted to make this trip, one she had dreamed of for years, so in the early autumn of 1891, Sara Thomson Kinney boarded a train in Hartford, Connecticut, and rode the rails to Omaha and then to Bancroft, Nebraska, to see the young woman her Connecticut Indian Association had been so closely involved with for the past six years. She had come not only as a friend of Susan's, but also as a special correspondent for the *Hartford Courant,* someone who would convey her personal observations and impressions of Indian life on an isolated Great

Plains reservation to a white audience clustered along the East Coast.

In two lengthy articles published that fall, Kinney gave her readers a picture of what life on a late-nineteenth-century reservation looked like to a well-meaning, well-to-do East Coast Christian woman at the height of the Victorian era. Using the standards of white civilized society as measuring sticks, Kinney provided her readers with the means to judge the Omaha people and their way of life—their housing, their schools, their religion, their food, overall health, marital status, quality of life, age-old traditions, and cultural beliefs. Among the few firsthand accounts any of her readers would ever see, Kinney's articles demolished certain stereotypes while reinforcing others. Like many other accounts of the era, they were bridges that connected how one group of people in one location came to view a much different group of people living hundreds of miles away. These kinds of stories not only created entrenched individual, racial, and ethnic perceptions, but also helped shape identities for cities and sometimes for entire regions.

"Between the dull little village of Bancroft and the surprisingly lively city of Omaha, with its asphalt pavements, its electric and cable cars and its public buildings (much more numerous and, with the possible exception of the Connecticut Mutual building, far handsomer than we have in Hartford), there is little to interest the traveler except the solid miles of waving corn and the acre upon acre of wild sun flowers through which one passes," she began her first account from Indian country on September 8, 1891.

The eastern correspondent initially stayed with Rosalie, who picked her up at the train station and brought her to the home near Logan Creek where she and her large family lived. From the beginning, Kinney wanted to make something clear to her readers: "There are several persons in Hartford, and perhaps elsewhere, who have a vicious habit of insisting that no good thing can come out of a reservation, and I would very much like to introduce them to this pretty, well-ordered, Christian Indian home."

And so she did.

"A canary swinging in its cage on the outer porch, and a hammock under the trees filled with one little, two little, three little Injuns, four little, five little, even six very jolly little Injuns, first attracted my attention as we drove into the yard," she told her readers.

Inside the home of the "six little Injuns," Kinney was pleasantly surprised to see two bookcases filled with the likes of Shakespeare, Whittier, Longfellow, and Byron, as well as a full set of Dickens— "books one would expect to find in any Hartford home of the better class."

In the composite portrait she conveyed to eastern readers, the Omaha are progressive and civilized, fighting for their rights but increasingly easy marks for scurrilous white whiskey traders who ceaselessly prowl the reservation looking for their next Indian victim. The Omaha also are a quiet, gentle, well-disposed agricultural people. "They are in many respects very like children." But they also are very new to civilization, scarcely removed from their primitive past. "A decade ago, with very few exceptions," she told her readers, "they were savages, pure and simple, with no rights a white man was bound to respect."

The path from ancient tradition to civilization, specifically when measured by a white yardstick, had been a long and complex one fraught with anger and resentment on both sides of the red and white roads. Whites frequently resented how long the process seemed to take, while Indian chiefs and their people were angry at what they saw as unrealistic timelines and impossible expectations.

Kinney told her readers how one Omaha man explained it to her. "We want to do, and to be, all that is expected of us," he said.

"We want to be men and women in the fullest sense of the words. We are trying, but it is not easy to become like the white people in a year's time." And Kinney agreed. "The man was right," she said. "We should not expect too much, at once, of the Indian. It will be a mistake, if, from abusing him, we suddenly invest him with an undue proportion of virtue. We should not expect to reverse the habits of generations in a few years."

On the one hand, many Omaha were now self-supporting, building their own homes, tilling their own fields, harvesting their own crops, asking the government for very little. On the other hand, however, she believed some unsettling vestiges of the "savage" past remained. Invited to enter a traditional medicine dance lodge, Kinney and several other whites "did so with alacrity, though one trembling paleface assured us that she felt her scalp-lock rising in the occasion, and that she was ready to perish of fright."

Susan had long admired Sara Thomson Kinney, was grateful to her "mothers" in the Connecticut Indian Association, and was glad to see her friend that fall. But she would not have agreed with many of her friend's conclusions, with many of the perceptions Kinney conveyed to her readers. They were perceptions that would spawn stereotypes in Hartford and beyond, stereotypes that would endure for decades, the same ones her father, her family, and others had fought against for so many years. Joseph stressed English and education. Bright Eyes was no one's Minnehaha. Standing Bear eventually cut his hair and dressed in civilian clothing. Francis painstakingly stitched together the richness of Omaha culture and tradition.

And now it was Susan's turn. She was proud of the Omaha, and she was becoming bolder in asserting her viewpoints, in creating an identity that belonged to her, one no longer muddled by promises or pledges or compromises made to well-meaning white "mothers" or anyone else. Increasingly, the young doctor had little patience for the stereotypes that often surrounded her, that often tried to define her people.

Weren't Indians still backward, lazy, and living off government handouts?

No, Susan would say. In fact, the Omaha were "progressing very fast in a great many things." By the early 1890s, she noted, almost every reservation family lived in a wood-frame house, clean on the inside, painted on the outside, the premises trash free. In just the last six months, between fifty and sixty new houses had sprung up on the reservation. Then, too, her tribe had recently purchased 150 cultivators, 20 corn planters, 10 corn cutters, 150 plows, 100 sets of harnesses, 40 stoves, 75 farm wagons, 40 buggies, and 185 horses and had broken three hundred acres of virgin prairie soil. And most of the men, she would say, now wore citizens' clothing, white clothing.

But do the men and women really love each other?

She heard it often—and she often could not conceal her anger. "Some ask the absurd question, 'Do the Indians really love their wives?' The Indians are *human beings* just as the white people are, and there are Indian men who are just as careful, watchful and affectionate to their wives as anyone would wish to see anymore," a frustrated Susan wrote in a June 1892 Women's National Indian Association newsletter. "One day, I had to pull a young woman's tooth, and as the husband was a strong muscular man I was in hopes he would support her head for me. He sent for his brother to do it and when he saw me take the forceps up he beat a hasty retreat. I heard him walking up and down in the other room, and when they told him I was through he appeared with such a happy relieved look on his face and thanked me earnestly."

Aren't Indian women looked down upon?

"Indian women no longer stand in the background. Few work

Susan's 1889 graduating class at the Woman's Medical College of Pennsylvania. Valedictorian of her class, Susan is in fourth row, fourth from the right. *Legacy Center Archives, Drexel University College of Medicine, Philadelphia, PA*

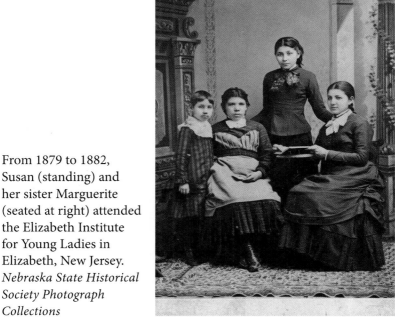

From 1879 to 1882, Susan (standing) and her sister Marguerite (seated at right) attended the Elizabeth Institute for Young Ladies in Elizabeth, New Jersey. *Nebraska State Historical Society Photograph Collections*

Joseph La Flesche, also known as Iron Eye, was the last recognized chief of the Omaha Tribe. He believed his people had to adopt many of the white customs or risk annihilation. *Nebraska State Historical Society Photograph Collections*

Susan's half-brother Francis La Flesche and her older sister Susette (Bright Eyes) on their east coast speaking tour following the 1879 trial of Chief Standing Bear. *Nebraska State Historical Society Photograph Collections*

Mother and child beside a tipi, traditionally used during the Omaha Tribe's annual summer buffalo hunts. The hunts ended in 1876—eleven years after Susan's birth.
Courtesy of the National Anthropological Archives, Smithsonian Institution

Susan La Flesche as a schoolgirl. *Courtesy of the National Anthropological Archives, Smithsonian Institution*

The only known photograph of Susan's husband, Henry Picotte (seated with puppy). Susan is at far left, next to her sister Marguerite and her husband, Walter Diddock. *Courtesy of the Hampton University Archives*

Susan's first love, Thomas Ikinacapi (T.I.), in his Hampton Institute military uniform in 1885. Susan described him as "the handsomest Indian I ever saw." *Courtesy of the Hampton University Archives*

Susan La Flesche (center) at
Hampton, when she gave the
1892 commencement address
at the institute's twenty-fourth
graduation ceremony. At far right
is Charles Picotte, later to become
Marguerite's husband. *Courtesy of
the Hampton University Archives*

Sara Thomson Kinney,
president of the
Connecticut Indian
Association, helped
Susan get into medical
school and became
one of her most ardent
advocates. *Courtesy of
NET Television*

"Class in American History," a photo taken at Hampton for the Paris Expo of 1900, showcases General Armstrong's belief in the mutually reinforcing value of educating black and Indian students together. *Courtesy of NET Television*

Harvard anthropologist Alice Fletcher, one of Susan's earliest supporters, coauthored the seminal study of the Omaha Tribe with Francis La Flesche. Fletcher also oversaw the 1882 allotment process and became a controversial figure when many Omaha artifacts ended up in east coast museums. *Courtesy of the National Anthropological Archives, Smithsonian Institution*

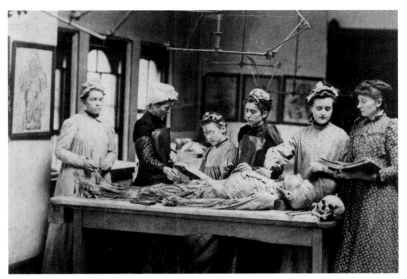

An anatomy lab at the Woman's Medical College of Pennsylvania in the early 1890s. Susan described performing an autopsy as "splendid." *Legacy Center Archives, Drexel University College of Medicine, Philadelphia, PA*

After Henry's death in 1905, Susan, her two young sons, and her elderly mother all moved into a new home Susan designed and built in Walthill, Nebraska. *Courtesy of the National Anthropological Archives, Smithsonian Institution*

Susan's sons Caryl (left) and Pierre on the porch of their new Walthill home about 1908. *Nebraska State Historical Society Photograph Collections*

The hospital that Susan had long dreamed of building opened in Walthill in 1914, serving both Indians and whites. The covered porch, facing east, provided patients with "plenty of fresh air and sunshine." *Nebraska State Historical Society Photograph Collections*

in the fields or do heavy work. Where it used to be the lot of the women to provide the wood, now the men get it in almost all cases. Even in so small a thing as walking or riding where the woman had to walk behind or ride in the back of the wagon, now she walks beside her husband."

But most of the time, Susan didn't have the luxury of debunking stereotypes. She was too busy; her work as a physician to her people, and an increasing number of whites, was all-consuming. She kept fastidious records, and those records help tell the story. In August 1891, she treated 111 patients—both in her office and in homes throughout the reservation. September: 130 patients. October: 100. November: 54. December: 114. January 1892: 120. February: 100. The diseases she encountered often were different from those among whites. On the reservation, a disease could turn into an epidemic much more quickly. Someone could have sore eyes on Monday, and then many women and children would come down with the same problem by Thursday. So she kept stressing hygiene. She visited their homes and invited them to her office, and she showed them how to use separate washbasins and separate towels, and many were spared distress, disease, or worse as a result of her insistence on simple, basic hygiene.

Then came December 1891 and a harsh winter with strong winds that whipped numbing temperatures across the sprawling reservation through January and February as well. It also brought an epidemic of colds and flu "that raged with more violence than during the two preceding years," Susan noted, and "some families were rendered helpless by it."

That winter, Susan was out in her carriage every day for three months.

The brutal winter didn't matter. She just kept going, every day. And then she began to fight back when more and more whites tried to steal more and more of the Omaha lands. She began to confront the whiskey peddlers and the swell of health problems they were creating. She forgave the debts of many patients who were too poor to pay. She overlooked the inferior medical equipment, the lack of her dream hospital, and the difficulty of getting some of her people to embrace modern medicine. She endured an expanding patient load that began to include more whites and a meager paycheck that often left her strapped. When funds were too depleted to buy more medicine, she used her own money. When the medicines didn't arrive on time, she relied on native plants and herbs. When she needed to get across the huge reservation, she bought her own team. When the temperature dropped to fifteen below, she threw a buffalo robe around her shoulders and kept going. Day after day.

"One Indian came to me and said, 'We are very grateful to you for coming to see us when we are sick, but we wish you wouldn't go out in stormy weather. It will be too much for you.' I told him I had to, for that was my duty, and he said no more."

That same year, 1891, after a fruitful relationship that included underwriting part of her medical school expenses, the Women's National Indian Association appointed Susan as their missionary to the Omaha. In exchange for agreeing to write for their newsletter and give an occasional speech, Susan would receive an additional $250 from the association, boosting her annual salary to $750.

Yet as overwhelming as the medical commitments to her people were, they still remained but a part of her overall duties. Additional educational, social, and religious obligations were never far away. By the early spring of 1891, Susan was gearing up to expand the small library she had created. She wanted to start a reading room for the children and asked the Connecticut Indian Association if they could send some more papers and scrapbooks and games. A white couple had agreed to help her out, with the husband offering night school classes twice a week and the wife hosting a sewing circle on Fridays.

Come Sunday, it was not unusual for Susan to attend two services—one in the morning as a participant, another in the evening as the conductor. Both services were held in the small Presbyterian Mission Church perched atop Blackbird Hills. The handsome church featured hardwood, stained glass, a fine parlor organ, and about one hundred Omaha Indian members. On Sunday evening, Susan oversaw a service for young people, handing out hymnals, calling upon members who had questions or comments, conducting the ceremony in the Omaha language. "But for the strange language and the dark faces all about me," observed Sara Kinney, "I could easily have fancied myself at a young people's meeting in my own church at home."

As Susan's work in the church and all of her religious-related duties deepened, so too did her Christian faith. In many ways, her faith and her profession became inextricably intertwined, and after she had spent a number of months treating the Omaha, the devotion to her people seemed to strengthen the devotion to her God. "I could not be content away from my people," she told her friends at the Women's National Indian Association. "It is a blessed work that God has given me in His goodness. Pray for us that He may send His spirit upon us to turn all unto Him."

More and more, one of the things Susan herself prayed for was some help, some relief from the increasingly serious problems alcohol was beginning to pose for life on the reservation and for all the Omaha who lived upon it.

More than thirty years had passed since her father had led the campaign to ban alcohol and severely punish anyone found drunk on the reservation. In 1856, he had formed a police unit to enforce that policy, and for more than three decades alcohol, drunkenness, and whiskey peddlers were virtually unknown among the Omaha. But all of that quickly began to change after Joseph's death in 1888.

By the fall of 1891, Sara Kinney informed her Hartford readers that many Omaha Indians "claim the right to buy and drink as much whisky as they please." And, she added, "there are plenty of white men who are more than willing to sell it to them, and the local laws are entirely inadequate to suppress the evil. Some of the Indians, including Dr. La Flesche, are taking active measures to bring the delinquents to justice, and their efforts are meeting with some success."

Susan had often seen how hard her father had worked to rid the Omaha of drink, and what she saw now was so painful, she told her "mothers" that "I cannot bear to write about it." But she did. And in a March 4, 1891, article in the *Hartford Courant* she gave a very specific example of what she and her allies were up against. There had been a recent election in which the Omaha, almost all of whom wanted to ban alcohol on the reservation, could vote for or against prohibition. A few days before the election, white men aligned with the whiskey peddlers and saloons printed up a batch of tickets that read, "Against Prohibition." One of the white men then rode among the Indians, almost all of whom were illiterate, handed out the tickets, and told them these were the tickets they should turn in on election day to stop the whiskey sales. There were two polling places, and on election day, Susan saddled her horse and rode eight miles to Omaha Creek, the farthest of the two, "just at the dawn of one of the most beautiful mornings I ever saw." No one had gotten to the voters, and Susan, who had come to ensure her people knew what they were doing, was relieved. Of the 102 votes cast on Omaha Creek, 96 were for prohibition. "It was better than I had even dared hope," she wrote.

Then she and a friend turned their horses around and headed

back to the agency polling station to monitor the results there. When they arrived late that afternoon, they encountered a much different scene. The white man who had earlier handed out the "Against Prohibition" tickets had gathered all of the Indians and marched them to a lodge about a half mile from the voting site. There, he held them for hours, offering them a dinner and explaining that their tickets would accomplish exactly what they all wanted: keep whiskey off the reservation. He then led them en masse to the voting site. When the final votes were tallied, all but nine of the Indians had voted against prohibition, had voted to keep whiskey sales legal—the opposite of what they wanted. "It seems hard that when these people are trying to save themselves from the danger of intoxicating drink, that a white man comes to put a stumbling block in the way," wrote the doctor who would have to treat the alcohol-related health problems for years to come.

As Kinney summarized in a later article to her Connecticut readers: "It is clearly evident that if these Indians fail to meet the expectations of their eastern well-wishers, as well as of the better class among their own people, it will be because of no inherent disqualification on their part for a higher civilization, but simply and solely because of—whisky, the white man's gift to the red man, a gift which carries with it a curse, and one which will surely sap all that is good and noble from any race."

Throughout her long stay that fall among the Omaha, throughout the many changes and different settings she came across, one thing remained a constant for Sara Thomson Kinney: her unwavering admiration for the young woman she had come to see—a view she was more than happy to share with her readers and colleagues at the Connecticut Indian Association.

"She is modest, and of a quiet, retiring disposition, and while lacking self-assertion, never hesitates to show her colors when a principle is involved," Kinney wrote in an October 10, 1891,

Hartford Courant article. "She is true to her ideals, and her ideals are high and worthy ones always . . . and it is very certain that the association made no mistake when it undertook the education of this young Indian woman."

On a fine spring morning in May 1892, General Samuel Chapman Armstrong sat in his wheelchair, watching the colorful pageantry unfolding on a stage along the banks of Chesapeake Bay.

When the general and the large crowd that had assembled that day all looked up at the stage, they saw a female figure, Columbia, an early symbol of American freedom and liberty, seated on a throne, flanked by famous men from America's colonial era—men such as William Penn and Miles Standish and John Smith. Then an Indian woman suddenly appeared, throwing herself at the feet of Columbia, demanding to know why no Indian people were represented on the stage. Soon, figures representing Fame and History were summoned, and they brought in Pocahontas and Samoset, who had welcomed the Pilgrims, and Taminend, who had befriended William Penn. Before long, Columbia found herself flanked by the famous sons and daughters of both white and Indian people, and then the crowd watched as scores of black students suddenly filled one side of the stage while scores of Indian students filled the other side.

When the stage finally overflowed with Columbia and all the colonial heroes and famous natives and all the students, it grew silent and a voice called out: "But what of the future?" Then the Indian students stepped forward carrying the Hampton flag and they all began to sing "Spirit of Peace." Columbia stood up with the flag and called out, "Take my banner and your place as my citizens." And then all the white figures and all the black students and all the Indian students turned to face General Armstrong and all the other guests and they began to sing "My Country, 'Tis of Thee."

Initiated several years earlier, the elaborate spectacle had been designed to celebrate the 1887 Dawes Act, federal legislation awarding private plots of land to individual Indian owners that was thought to be a key component on the road to citizenship. In that vein, the 1892 production, geared toward achieving that goal, had been designated "Indian Citizenship Day." It was all a prelude to the main event—a commencement celebration of Hampton University's twenty-fourth anniversary. As the crowd quieted, the commencement speaker took the stage to address the graduating class.

The school paper, the *Southern Workman,* captured the moment for its readers:

"Before the half circle of brilliantly costumed heroes of the past of two races stepped the dignified, erect, high-souled woman, the representative and product of the best progress of one, the best philanthropy of the other—*La Flesche,* the Arrow—Arrow of the Future from the bow of the Past strained by the cord of the Present."

So on May 19, 1892, Dr. Susan La Flesche, who had graduated from Hampton six years earlier, stepped forward and told the current graduates, their friends and relatives, faculty, and the general about "My Work as Physician Among my People."

She told them her people were civilized now, living in wood-frame homes built by themselves on excellent farmland. She told them of the many days she had her hands full, her people coming to her office for many things besides medicine, so she assumed a variety of different roles to serve their different needs. "I have to take a hand in their politics too for they need help of all kinds from any one who can give it," she told the audience. She told them of her work and the difficulties she faced—homes many miles apart filled with sick people, with only rough roads connecting them. She told them how easily reservation illnesses became epidemics. And she told them of the sheer number of hours required to take care of so many patients. The previous summer, in July, August, and September, she said, "I went out visiting them every day, starting by seven or eight in the morning, driving six miles in one direction, and a great many more before getting back at noon. Then starting out again, it would often be eight, or sometimes ten o'clock at night before I got back, with my horses tired out." In the last six months, she said, it had gotten worse. Between November 1891 and April 1892, she had treated more than 640 patients—and those didn't include the office visits, only the ones she went out to treat. "The distance being so great I cannot see all of them as often as I wish—sometimes only once in two or three days, when I would call three times a day if it were possible."

Before closing, Susan had one last thought she wanted to convey to the graduates. "General Armstrong," she began, "in the midst of our work for our people, the inspiration from your life grows most precious because then it shines out more and more in the darkness around us. My brothers and sisters, the least return we can make to our dear Principal for all his life-work for us is to live as he would like us to live."

By the spring of 1892, Susan had lived a hard life for the better part of three years. She was exhausted after her Hampton commencement address, but not tired enough to keep from giving yet another talk. So not long after finishing at Hampton, she boarded a train to Washington, D.C., to address members of the Women's National Indian Association. A year earlier, the group had appointed her their medical missionary on the Omaha Reservation, and these kinds of talks were part of the arrangement. The focus of Susan's remarks to the Washington branch of the women's association was similar to her focus when she was home: alcohol. She told the group how her father's strict policies had eliminated the problem for many years but that it had now returned in full force and become a serious health issue and a public nuisance. The solution, she told the group, was to pass a series of tough new laws that would restore order to the reservation, making it a safe haven from the increasing number of menacing drunks. Later, she would explain the situation this way: "If a drunken Indian smashes a buggy and assaults a woman and child by beating them and nothing is done, what can prevent him from doing it again?"

It was a development not lost on Omaha Indian agent Robert Ashley. "Little, if any improvement can be noted, and in some respects I am obliged to say the change has been for the worst," he wrote in his September 1, 1892, annual report on the condition of the Omaha. "Especially is this true in respect to the use of intoxicants, which has increased to an alarming extent. I am pleased to say that the better element are now awake to the extent of this evil and are making an effort among themselves to stamp it out."

In June 1892, a weary Susan finally came home, returning to her people and her reservation, picking up where she'd left off, pushing herself, pushing her team of horses across the rough roads, over the hills, along the creeks and ravines, day after day, often late into the night, treating a tubercular adult in the countryside, delivering the baby of a white mother in a nearby town, tending to an Indian child with strep throat in her office, railing against the curse of the whiskey peddlers wherever and whenever she could.

By that fall, all the seventy-five- to eighty-hour workweeks, all the rugged buggy rides in frigid temperatures, all the long treks along treacherous roads, all the translations and legal advice and financial help and church services and wedding planning and anti-alcohol crusades had begun to exact a price on the twenty-seven-year-old doctor, who had already experienced an earlier health scare. Midway through medical college, Susan had told her sister that when she lay down a certain way it was difficult to breathe, that her body went numb in places. She eventually wrote it off, telling Rosalie it likely was all in her head, that it was probably just from stress, and she never brought it up again. But in the autumn of 1892, it was not a psychological issue, it was not all in her head. The pain now was real, and it was severe: in her back and in her neck and in her ears—ears that had so often been exposed to long hours of riding in a carriage in numbing cold and wind. By early December, she was so sick and in such pain that she could not get out of bed, where she was forced to remain for a couple of weeks.

That same year, another development haunted Susan, one that took a heavy emotional toll at the same time she was fighting to regain her physical strength. Early in the winter of 1892, Charles Picotte, Marguerite's husband, became seriously ill in their home on the Omaha Reservation. They had married in late 1888, a few months after the death of Joseph La Flesche, and the young man had been sick now for a long time. The previous spring, Charles had been taken to a hospital in Detroit for treatment, but his health did not improve. When his condition worsened in January 1892, Susan arranged to have the white physician in nearby Lyons, Nebraska, come to the reservation and examine Charles. He did, and he told the family that Charles was fatally ill with tuberculosis, that he would not live much longer. Charles died shortly afterward.

Not long after his death, Susan got word that T.I.—Thomas Ikinicapi—the handsome young man she had fallen in love with, the kind and gentle Hampton classmate she had often dreamed of during her early medical school days, had also died of tuberculosis. She and Marguerite and T.I. and Charles had all gone to Hampton together, had all studied and worked and drilled and socialized together. Just five years earlier, the two young Omaha sisters and the two young Sioux men, both from the Yankton Agency, had all been sitting in the Hampton gym, enjoying the sounds of the eighteen-piece orchestra, joyfully welcoming in the new year. And now Thomas and Charles were both dead.

It was a personal trauma Susan had to deal with privately, isolated on the large reservation, alone in her bedroom with her own emotions.

By the end of the year, her family began to worry about the young doctor, about her physical health. "Susie has been sick for several weeks," Rosalie wrote Francis on January 1, 1893. "Her ears have been troubling her very much. She says she has pain in her head and the back of her neck constantly."

So Susan stayed in bed and fought the pain, resting, letting her body recover, and after a few weeks, as a new year began, she felt well enough to once again start making house calls. But she was in a much weakened state now, and the long rides across the large reservation to try to heal her people, men and women and children scattered miles apart, became more difficult. That spring, while in her buggy, she took a hard fall, injuring herself badly enough that she again had to suspend all house calls and office visits to stay at home, resting up until she got better.

And when she did, she got back up and kept going, throughout the spring and summer, treating numerous skin and eye diseases among the children, preaching over and over what she believed were the simple, basic fundamentals of good health. "Good drainage and ventilation, cleanliness, simple food excellently cooked, regular meals and regular hours for retiring, all contribute to and are the main factors in maintaining a good physical condition of our school children," she wrote in her August 20, 1893, official report to Captain William H. Beck, the reservation's acting Indian agent.

The adults that year posed a different problem. "Tuberculosis of the lungs seems to be on the increase in our tribe," she wrote. "In place of wild game, diseased meat, in many cases and pork; in place of the airy tent, close houses, where often in one room two families are found with doors and windows closed night and day." The Omaha, she also noted, "have no regular Government physician and have called upon me to attend them during the last four years I have been connected with the school." Susan closed her report by apologizing to the agent for having missed so many workdays. "On account of my health, I have not been able to attend so many cases this year as in three previous years," she told him. That summer, Alice Fletcher had also invited Susan to the Chicago World's Fair, but her health was too unstable, so she regretfully had to tell Fletcher she would be unable to attend.

By the fall of 1893, Susan's condition again worsened, the pain in her ears and neck forcing her to spend much of September and October with her mother on Logan Creek. Inside the wood-frame house, she saw how sick and lonely her mother had become since Joseph's death and, more recently, since the death of her beloved aunt, Madeline Wolfe, at age 105. Her mother's rapidly deteriorating health, her loneliness and frailty and vulnerability, scared and saddened Susan.

That fall, she told her mother she was going to resign as government physician, but her mother wouldn't hear of it. So Susan asked Marguerite several times if she would give up her teaching position to care for their mother. But Marguerite refused, afraid that if she quit, she wouldn't get her job back. Then Susan told Agent Beck she needed to stay home to regain her strength. But he refused to let her, threatening to dock her pay if she didn't get back to work.

So Susan went back to work. And then one day in November, she returned to Logan Creek after a long day of treating patients. When she opened the door of the wood-frame house, she found her mother on the floor, almost dead. And she knew she was now in a bind. She was still the only doctor on the Omaha Reservation, and she still had more than twelve hundred patients to care for. And if she didn't continue to treat them, she could lose the one job she had worked so hard to get, the only job she had ever wanted.

She quickly thought it through and came to a decision: In the late fall of 1893, the care and well-being of one patient surpassed all the others.

Susan, her mother too sick to object, sent her resignation to Agent Beck. He said he would give her two months to reconsider.

But Susan didn't care. She had made up her mind. There was nothing to reconsider, and she never looked back.

In a November 20, 1893, letter to Francis, Rosalie explained their sister's decision: "She said it was going to be hard for her as she loved her work and hated to give it up but she felt it ought to be done for mother, and she knew she would never regret it."

8

vvv

The Light in the Window

Throughout the winter of 1893 and into the early spring of 1894, Susan stayed home, stayed on the La Flesche allotment along Logan Creek, dutifully taking care of her mother, gradually nursing her back to health.

And all the while she was caring for her mother, during the many long weeks she abandoned her professional career to care for a single patient, when she was nursing herself back to health, she was also nurturing a deeply held emotion she was reluctant to share with others.

When she had been deeply in love once before, no one—her father, her Connecticut mothers, her Hampton teachers, her personal benefactors—seemed to understand. They didn't understand how difficult it had been for her to choose between professional obligations and personal happiness.

Why couldn't she have both?

Why couldn't she have a career and a family?

She didn't think they would understand now, either. They didn't understand how it felt when Charles Picotte had died two years earlier. They didn't understand the pain and the emptiness she felt when she got the news that T.I. had died shortly afterward.

She had really told only Rosalie and Marguerite about how

much she had loved T.I., so the others knew nothing about how much it hurt, how it was getting a little scarier each time she got sick, and how it felt when she lay by herself each night in the darkened bedroom on the vast prairie, alone with her mother.

So what if she told them now? What if she told them that in the spring of 1894, she was in love again? Would they be more supportive?

Would they understand that before it had always been about pleasing someone else—about pleasing a strict father, about being the good girl with the good grades, about pleasing all the well-meaning teachers, Harvard ethnographers, and Civil War generals, all the chemistry professors, government officials, and devout church leaders? About meeting the expectations of all the Connecticut mothers, about pleasing them so they could tout her as their shining light, about always agreeing to put their needs ahead of her own?

Some of those mothers did not seem to understand just how much she'd been through the past few years, riding alone in her buggy on all those bone-chilling mornings, treating the tuberculosis, influenza, measles, strep throats, and conjunctivitis in homes and schools miles apart, always putting her patients and their needs ahead of her own.

Would they understand that she was twenty-nine now? That she hadn't been in the best of health? That being a mother was highly valued within her culture? That having children and a family was a tribal expectation? Would they understand that it was time to decide not what was best for her family or her patients or government bureaucrats or Indian agents or church elders or white women living with their husbands and families in safe and comfortable homes fifteen hundred miles away?

She didn't know, but she wasn't going to put it up for a vote. She had decided the time had come to do what was best for her.

So on June 30, 1894, in a small Presbyterian church in Bancroft, Nebraska, Susan La Flesche, a highly educated, sophisticated, accomplished Omaha Indian doctor, married thirty-four-year-old Henry Picotte, a ruggedly handsome, semi-literate, mixed-blood Yankton Sioux, brother of the deceased Charles Picotte, and a former Wild West circus showman who didn't mind having a drink or two every now and then.

As soon as word got out, even before Marguerite stood as a witness for the newlyweds, the fear and concern and anger surfaced from all quarters.

On June 22, eight days before Susan and Henry became husband and wife, Marian Heritage, a close friend of the bride's from Philadelphia days, wrote Rosalie a letter fraught with anxiety and misgivings over the impending marriage. "I felt as tho' I must write to you to learn your news of the matter for I somehow feel that you cannot approve," wrote Marian, whose family had warmly embraced Susan throughout her medical school years and often invited her to their home for family dinners and social outings. "Mother has just written a reply expressing to Susan our regret at hearing the news for we cannot think her step a wise one in her condition of health." Her mother, Marian told Rosalie, "has written very plainly feeling we cannot send congratulations. . . ." And then Marian laid out her own reasons for opposing the marriage. "It is because I wish for Susie only the best things in this world with the least suffering and trouble that I wish she had decided not to take this step."

When the Connecticut mothers got wind of Susan's marriage, they published their take on the matter in the *Indian Bulletin*, the association newsletter, noting that "since her health and home restrictions do not permit of her longer engagement in actual medical practice, we must bury any regret at our loss and trust that her bright intelligent spirit will shed its light upon the new life and surroundings opening before her."

But in the early summer of 1894, she didn't care about the misgivings, regrets, and disappointments of others. She had turned her back on love once before, and she wasn't going to risk becoming an "old maid" again. Susan La Flesche Picotte loved Henry, and that was that.

Of the four sisters who had grown up together in the Village of the Make-Believe White Men, Susan was the only one who did not marry a white man. She had fallen for two Indian men, and there were a good many things Henry and T.I. had in common, things she saw in Henry that reminded her of T.I. Both were Sioux from the Yankton Agency. Both were handsome men who came from backgrounds much different from hers. Both were poorly educated and sickly and—by any objective measures—far beneath her own station. But more important to Susan, both men were also gentle, kind, considerate, and faithful.

John Neihardt, the poet, writer, and journalist who lived in Bancroft for two decades, became well acquainted with the newlyweds and had no trouble understanding the attraction. "It was easy to see how the Omaha Indian girl, Susan, could fall in love with Henry, for he was a handsome man with polite, ingratiating manners and a happy sense of humor," he later recalled.

In his earlier years, before he arrived in Nebraska and met Susan, Henry had spent some time in the Wild West exhibitions and circus sideshows that were popular in the waning decades of the nineteenth century. They began in May 1883, when William F. Cody launched Buffalo Bill's Wild West Show in Omaha, and before long the popularity of his show had spawned a number of competitors and cheap imitations. The organizers of these exhibitions, quack medicine shows, and circuses aggressively sought

Indians as their special attractions, and Sioux country quickly became their favorite hunting grounds. In the minds of many Americans, the Sioux had become the iconic Indians: fierce, stoic warriors trailing war bonnets of eagle feathers, the ones who rode painted ponies at a breakneck pace, shooting with deadly accuracy at full gallop, the ones who had taken out Custer. It was an image, an identity manipulated and imposed from the outside, which began in Omaha and would linger on in comic books, dime-store novels, and American cinema and television well into the next century and beyond.

For many young Sioux men, these exhibitions offered an opportunity to escape the boredom and monotony of reservation life. It was a chance to recapture the glory of their traditional culture by posing as romantic figures in full warrior regalia, charging hard and fast across the arena's dirt floor, taking careful aim at cavalry forces looming ahead. But it was also dangerous for many of the Wild West performers and degrading for those who wound up as "special attractions" in the circus sideshows. While some Sioux men left with permission of their agents, others were lured into the exhibitions and circuses by quasi–bounty hunters or kidnapped by middlemen who took them to a railhead and shipped them east. This "recruiting" practice peaked at the end of the 1880s, creating a great deal of ill will and hardship among the Indian participants. Families deprived of their able-bodied young men struggled to make ends meet, and the men themselves often straggled home, debilitated and demoralized.

So while Susan dissected cadavers, marveled at Benjamin West paintings, and luxuriated in plays, symphonies, and piano recitals, her future husband was engaged in vastly different activities, including a stint in one of the popular circus sideshows of the era.

Henry was likable, easy to be around, and a master storyteller, and one day he told Neihardt about how he had once lost his job in one of those sideshows. His job, he told the writer, was to play a wild man—a half-man, half-animal creature. As throngs of circus-goers passed by, a carnival barker outside the tent would yell out, pointing to Henry, who squatted near his feet. The barker told the crowds the dangerous, savage-like beast they saw had just been captured in the jungles of Borneo at great peril to the captors. Henry had been stripped to his breechcloth and chained to a stake so he couldn't lunge at the spectators. Instead, he told the writer, he stayed on the ground, tugging on the chain every now and then, gobbling up chunks of bloody meat, growling ferociously if anyone came too close.

Years later, Neihardt recounted the end of Henry's circus story in a book: "One day this had been going on for some time when a corpulent lady of obvious importance marched boldly up to him, pinched his naked arm, and said:

"'Young man, you can't fool me. You ain't no wilder than I am. How long you been civilized?'

"'I scratched my head awhile and thought hard about it,' said Henry. 'Then I said, "Oh, 'bout three weeks, ma'am!"

"'They fired me without pay, for that one!' said Henry."

In early 1892, when his brother's tuberculosis rapidly worsened, Henry left South Dakota's Yankton Agency and came to the Omaha Reservation to help Charles and Marguerite with their farmland and the mundane details of everyday life. And it was there he'd first met the doctor who was caring for his ailing brother.

For a while after their marriage, the newlyweds sometimes stayed on Susan's allotment not far from Rosalie or, more often, with her mother in the house near Logan Creek. But soon they had other plans, so they moved into a comfortable, wood-frame house in

Bancroft, across the street from the small Presbyterian church where they had been married. Then they got to work. They laid out an orchard filled with fruit trees in one part of the yard and planted a robust garden laden with all manner of fresh vegetables in another part. Before long, Susan carved out office space in their new home and quickly resumed her medical career. Now in private practice, she began treating many local whites in her Bancroft residence. Meanwhile, although now twenty-two miles from agency headquarters, she also started getting on her horse or in her buggy again and fanning out across the reservation to treat the many Omaha patients she had cared for in their homes and schools, the ones she spoke to in their own language and had formed close relationships with over the years.

And she also began doing something else: Whether at home in Bancroft or with her mother on Logan Creek, she began leaving a lighted lantern in the window each night, a beacon to guide the sick and the injured and the desperate through storms and darkness, a light to guide them to her door.

Despite her busy days and nights, Susan now was freed from the more restrictive requirements of being a government physician. So it wasn't long before she began spending less time filling out forms and filing reports and more time participating in tribal life. Soon, she and Marguerite, the sister she had spent three years with in New Jersey and another two at Hampton, grew even closer. While Bright Eyes and her husband were often occupied with their busy political agendas and travel schedules, while Rosalie was often overwhelmed raising eight children, Susan and Marguerite became active in a variety of reservation roles in which their paths frequently crossed. Come Sundays, they were fixtures at the Presbyterian church—Susan in Bancroft and Marguerite in Blackbird Hills, although occasionally they both ended up in the same church. Sometimes they would lead the service of adult worshippers, translating from English to Omaha. Sometimes it would be an evening service for the children. Other times it would be a weekday gathering of a Christian society. Or it could be a Sunday school class of Omaha youngsters, often a class of young girls, when Susan's considerable oratorical skills would light up some of the Bible's most famous stories.

As always, the two sisters also kept busy officiating every now and then at burial services, helping with wedding plans, and encouraging Omaha couples to marry within the church—something they underscored by setting personal examples. On June 29, 1895—almost a year to the day after Susan and Henry married—Marguerite wed Walter Diddock in the Blackbird Hills church. Soon, Marguerite gave birth to a baby girl, pulling the two sisters even closer together.

While Susan cared for her many Indian and white patients, Marguerite busied herself as the Omaha Reservation's first field matron. Created by the Office of Indian Affairs in 1890, the Field Matron Program had a singular mission: to transform American Indian women into women who shared the cultural values and domestic goals of the Victorian era. In other words, to assimilate Indian women into the mainstream by getting them to embrace the white establishment definition of womanhood. This, the architects of the policy believed, was the fastest way to bring Indian women under the umbrella of civilization. Being a field matron was a delicate, complex job, treading deftly between white and Indian worlds, a job that helped some Omaha and angered many others. In the end it produced mixed results, and Marguerite, who had aggressively sought a paying job, left the program after four years.

During the opening years of the 1890s, the two sisters spent more and more time together, taking care of their mother, dropping in on Rosalie and her lively brood, conducting church services and Sunday school sessions, planning weddings and funerals, and visiting the homes of their people—one to minister to their health needs, the other to nudge them down assimilation's rocky road.

Susan loved this new world. She loved her new husband and her new home and all the beautiful fruit trees and the bountiful vegetable garden. She loved her home office and treating all of her white and Indian patients, both in her home and in theirs. She loved nourishing her spiritual side with the many church services and Sunday school lessons, and more than anything, she loved having her mother nearby and her two sisters and all of her nieces and nephews so close to her.

But it didn't last.

About a year after her marriage, Susan again became seriously ill. The pain in her ears had returned, the disease slowly eating away at the bones in her inner ear, making it harder for her to hear. And then the back pain returned, making it harder to get out of bed some days. She grew weak and feeble, and her family grew more concerned until they began to lose hope, believing that this time she would not survive, that she would die.

On July 29, 1895, Rosalie wrote Francis a long letter from Bancroft. "Susie has been very sick," she told her brother. "I had given up all hopes of her when she commenced to improve. . . . Susie isn't out of bed yet but she is getting along and may get well."

Years earlier, while still in medical school, Susan had written Rosalie many times, and many times her letters focused on Rosalie's health, especially when her sister was pregnant—which was often. Susan fretted endlessly over Rosalie's every cold and headache, dispensing all kinds of advice to get her through her pregnancies. She also told Rosalie how fine a doctor she would make, offering to help her sister study chemistry and anything else if she was interested. And don't dismiss the idea of becoming a doctor simply because you have children, Susan implied in one letter. After all, one of her favorite professors, she said, was an accomplished physician who also happened to be married with children. She told Rosalie of the many women she had observed and how complicated their pregnancies often were for both mother and child, and the pain that childless women often had to endure. She and her sister were the lucky ones, Susan said.

But in the spring and early summer of 1895, Susan was not one of the lucky ones. She was pregnant and in a good deal of pain from her ears and her back. It was what some of her East Coast friends and "mothers" had feared since the marriage announcement—a frail woman with such a promising future now saddled with even more health problems, ones from which she might never recover, that might prevent her from fulfilling their dreams.

Yet, as had been the case many times before, Susan gradually recovered, her will and strong spirit pulling her through the pregnancy. Two weeks before Christmas, she gave birth to the couple's first child, Caryl Henry Picotte, a healthy eight-and-a-half-pound boy. After years of doting on Rosalie's many children, sending them drawings and candy and Christmas gifts, asking about their health and imploring her to give them all hugs and kisses from Aunt Sue, Bancroft's Indian doctor soon fell deeply in love with her own baby boy, enthusiastically conveying the joy and magic of motherhood to family and friends.

"I do wish you could see the baby, he is so sweet, and as fat, healthy and strong as can be," she wrote her Connecticut friends a few months after the birth. "He has thick black hair, and his brilliant black eyes follow us all over the room. During the two weeks after he first came, his papa staid up every night and took the entire care of him, and even now he seems to feel the care of the child at night, and once in a while I find him raising up in bed and looking to see if 'the boy' is all right. It is such a help to me, for I do not feel any too strong yet."

After regaining her strength, Susan resumed her medical practice, serving once again the many white residents of Bancroft and her many friends, relatives, and former patients throughout the reservation. But now the days and weeks were different for one of the few Indian women in the 1890s forced to strike a balance between a professional career and her family, who had to find some kind of equilibrium between the new and old worlds. Within the cultural tradition of the Omaha, mother and father had equal authority in all matters involving the welfare of their children. And in the traditional Omaha family, where children were greatly desired and loved, the baby was the mother's constant companion.

At first, Susan struggled to find the right balance. For a while, she thought of giving up her practice, of staying home with her baby boy, devoting herself to her family. But her patients refused to let her. The fathers and mothers she had cared for, former classmates who were now married and living on the Omaha Reservation with their families, the elderly Omaha who came to trust her because she spoke their language and knew their ways: They all insisted she continue to care for them, to be their doctor.

"Do not come for me," Susan would say to them. "Call in another doctor. I cannot leave my baby."

"Bring the baby with you," the patients would respond. "We will have no one but you."

So for a time, it was not unusual for Indian farmers to look up and occasionally see a buggy making its way across the land, to see a mother and her infant son, bundled up against the morning chill, making their way across the rolling Nebraska prairie. And when they arrived at their destination, there was often a willing pair of hands to care for the baby while the mother cared for the patient.

One day, Susan ended up taking baby Caryl with her on an exhausting eighteen-mile house call. It was a difficult ride, and when they returned, she decided she would never do that again to her son. So whenever Henry was tied up with farm chores, she would leave Caryl with friends or relatives, often her mother, while she went off to tend to the sick alone. But she did not like to be away from her family, especially at night.

One night, she got word that an Omaha woman was sick and needed her help. It was dark and it was late, and it was a long way across rough roads to get to her. Susan hesitated, unsure what to do. But Henry told her she had no choice, that she had to go and he would ride with her. "It won't take long, only three hours to go, and you can relieve her," he said. So he got the buggy ready and got Susan in and they set off on the long ride. But about halfway there, the buggy broke down. Henry managed to fix the problem and they set off once again, arriving in time to treat the sick woman. The woman later died, Susan told Sara Kinney, "one beautiful day in September . . . and was laid away to rest with Christian burial." One of her relatives, an elderly medicine man who had never set foot in a church, who preferred the traditional spiritual beliefs of his people, attended the burial. Before the woman was laid to rest, the medicine man folded his blanket around him and addressed the dead woman in the Omaha way.

"I stand on the borderland between this world and the next— you are through with this world and have met happiness, and you are at peace," he said. "I know not when God will send for me—I stand with one foot in the grave. When God made death for his children He was wise; we cannot pass death, we cannot avoid death, we must all meet death—be ready when it comes. We do not cry for you, for you are happy. God gave us tears for the relief of our human natures, and it is well."

Susan's days were different now, and in a letter to the Connecticut Indian Association, she tried to explain a typical day—but couldn't quite finish without a slight departure from her main topic. "I get up before daybreak, look after breakfast, bathe and dress baby, get into the buggy and drive several miles to see patients, come back to dinner, and out again," she told association members. Meanwhile, baby Caryl, she allowed, had become "quite famous around here, he is so jolly and good natured and healthy. We have been stopped several times on the road so people could take a look at 'that baby.' Mothers I know will pardon this digression from the subject."

Sometimes Susan would start off on her house calls during the day and end up having to spend the night at a patient's home. The next morning, Henry might bundle up baby Caryl and then father and son would set off to find the doctor, looking to surprise the little boy's mother with some early-morning good cheer before a new round of house calls began.

In the Victorian world of 1890s America, whether on or off the reservation, it was not the usual order of business for the woman to rise early, leave for work, and return late while the man stayed home with the children. But in the last half of the last decade of the nineteenth century, in the La Flesche–Picotte home in Bancroft, Nebraska, it was often the wife whose demanding work took her away from home for long stretches, who was able to balance career and family only with the help of a devoted stay-at-home husband.

When Caryl was about eighteen months old, his mother applied for her old job as government physician at the boarding school in Macy. The previous physician had left in the spring of 1896, and Susan figured it might mean a bit more stability, a bit less wear and tear on her family, maybe a bit more money, so she submitted her application for the job. The government had restructured Indian medical services several years earlier, and Susan heard nothing for months. Finally, she was informed that she would have to pass a competitive civil service exam to even be considered for the job. The news infuriated her, and much as her sister Bright Eyes had done years earlier to secure a government teaching position, she wrote a pointed, personal letter to Commissioner of Indian Affairs Daniel Browning, touching on all the key issues. She told the commissioner that as an Indian doctor she was exempt from the civil service rules. She told him that, unlike a few years earlier, she was now completely recovered and in good health. She noted that Bancroft's white residents relied heavily on her medical skills. And she pointed out that despite the government's current policy that forbade married women to hold such high-ranking positions, she had skillfully balanced career and family for a number of years. In resubmitting her application, she also included an Omaha Tribal Council document attesting to her medical skills and the benefits of having a school doctor who knew the Omaha language and tribal culture. The council asked that she be awarded the job. Omaha Indian agent William Beck also submitted a letter. In it, he noted that Susan was an Indian doctor with broad tribal knowledge and a strong medical track record on her own reservation. He strongly recommended she be appointed to the position.

But Susan did not get the appointment. No one really knew why. In a letter to Sara Kinney, Susan suggested it likely came down to a matter of economics: The Office of Indian Affairs simply did not have enough money to fund the job. In the end, the government never did appoint a physician for the boarding school, underscoring Susan's theory that the position had become expendable.

So she continued on, maintaining a medical office in her Bancroft home while roaming far and wide across the reservation the rest of the year and into the spring of 1897. But by that summer, she once again was desperately ill, felled by the same debilitating ear, neck, and head pain she had endured before. Susan was so sick that her family again feared for the worst, believing she would not survive the summer.

Alone in her bed that summer, she often got depressed, believing all of her hard work was in vain, that the people she had spent so much time trying to help did not understand how much she cared for them, that they did not appreciate all she had tried to do for them. But then something happened. The word got out, and then the people, white and Indian people, began streaming into her home. They came all summer, arriving at her bedside with fresh flowers, fresh vegetables from their gardens, fresh fruit from their orchards—and no small amount of encouraging words. They told her aging mother how worried they were for her daughter, their doctor and their friend, and when Susan slowly began to recover, she was overwhelmed by their encouragement and kind words. "The earnest heartfelt words of thanks" came unexpectedly, and they told Susan that she was wrong, that she had misread both the white and Indian communities she had given so much to. It was a mistake, one she would long remember and one she would not make again.

"Whenever I felt a little depressed," she later wrote Josephine Richards, one of her favorite Hampton teachers, "I would think there was not much use in trying to help people, that they did not seem to appreciate it but this summer taught me a lesson I hope I'll never forget." By letter's end, Susan told Miss Richards the experience had awakened in her a new resolve. "When I got well enough to go out, I received so many congratulations from all, I felt so encouraged to try to do right and to live a better life."

What happens when someone puts a bayonet to your back and forcibly removes you from the only homeland you've ever known, dumping you on unfamiliar lands more than five hundred miles away? What happens when someone outlaws your language and all your songs and your dances and your religious beliefs and steals some of your most sacred objects? When they try to take something that's been built up—layer by layer—over millennia, the thing that has come to define who and what you are?

"The Indians are mystical," Susan once told a visitor. "They are not understood by those who are inclined to be practical. You see that building there with the round top? Those are our dance houses. Our young people do not dance like the white people. The young men take up a subscription until they have enough money to build a big round building with a dirt floor. Here they have their dances and dance round and round a fire in the center. The women are huddled at the edge of the building and look on, often chanting a chorus.

"Our young men used to be named according to their visions. When a boy was 12 years of age he was sent along, like John the Baptist, into the wilderness to fast and pray. Here he remained, praying and fasting until he received a vision. From this vision he took his name and totem. The continued concentration and fasting and praying undoubtedly produced in them a species of coma or trance, in which they dreamed dreams and had visions. Later on, they were named again, according to their prowess in battle or hunting. And when they became old warriors they received yet a third name."

What happens when they write a name on a piece of paper and

say that is who you are now? When they try to give you a new identity based on what they want you to be, not who you are and what you've been for as long as anyone can remember? What happens when you become invisible, when they take your land and they make your culture illegal, when it all begins to disintegrate and fade away?

"It is more than ten years since we went on our last hunt," Bright Eyes once observed. "The poles of the holy tent remain. There is no one who remembers the sacred words which were said at the feast preparatory to the start. We camp no more in the great circle. The habitations of the bands are mixed in inextricable confusion. Soon we can no more tell to which band we belong than can a Jew of today tell whether he is of the tribe of Judah or the tribe of Benjamin. A few of the old men only remember our laws and customs and try to keep them. The young are passing into another life."

In many respects, the old familiar ways of life that had endured for thousands of years had been blown up, destroyed almost overnight. And there was little offered in the way of help to rebuild a new way of living.

So for many Omaha, and for many other tribes settled on remote reservations scattered throughout the western United States, the "passing into another life," a new life shorn of its cultural underpinnings, often created a treacherous psychological landscape, a landscape frequently dominated by fear and confusion, pain and isolation, desperation and hopelessness. In the last quarter of the nineteenth century, it was a landscape that gave rise to the Ghost Dance. To the Wild West shows and circus tents. To cultural and social disintegration. To unrelenting boredom and violence. To feelings of inferiority, self-loathing, depression, and suicide. And, more and more, it also gave rise to something else.

Something that had not escaped the eye of Sara Thomson Kinney when she visited the Omaha in the autumn of 1891. When Susan first began her medical practice on the reservation, Kinney told readers of the *Hartford Courant,* "she was amazed by the repeated calls for camphor. For a long time she failed to get at the root of the trouble, but finally succeeded in ferreting out the secret, which was, that camphor was being used in the place of whisky. If the Indians could get neither that nor extract of lemon (which seems to be an intoxicant), they would fall back upon camphor, and apparently regarded it as a very fair substitute for whisky."

Back then, camphor was distilled from the wood and bark of the camphor tree, and Susan quickly saw to it that the drug disappeared from her shelves. Years later, as one century faded away and a new one began, she saw something else: She saw just how far so many of her people had fallen from Article 12 in the 1854 treaty that had created the Omaha Reservation, the clause expressly banning "distilled spirits." How for more than thirty years that law and her father and his police force and the threat of a severe public flogging had kept all the whiskey peddlers and all their distilled spirits at bay. How for more than three decades the Omaha had rapidly progressed, building wooden homes, tending to their farms, sending many of their children to school, living in secure extended families. Until her father's death in 1888, distilled spirits had never been an issue.

But now it had all changed. The curse first introduced by French fur traders more than a century earlier was everywhere she looked—white whiskey peddlers invading every corner of the reservation, leaving their desperate customers littering the landscape from Blackbird Hills to Logan Creek.

"The Omaha Indians," Susan said, "had always been a very moral people . . . a fine specimen of manhood, physically and morally, of good health." But after 1888, "men and women gave themselves to drunkenness. Liquor was given to children. . . . Women who would not have dreamed of doing so while sober, committed immoralities. I will say here that there never had been any illegitimate children in the history of the Tribe until after 1888. Clothing was pawned for whiskey. Night and day were hideous with drunken brawls and people who went on the Reservation had to carry weapons for protection."

After years of alcoholic abuse, she said, her people had now become "an easy prey to tuberculosis, and the Indian child today is a weak puny specimen of humanity, many of the children being marked for tuberculosis."

Throughout the 1890s—as a wife and as a doctor, as a teacher, preacher, and public health crusader—she had seen it grow worse each passing year, more and more deaths everywhere she looked, alcohol frequently to blame. And she knew, often firsthand, about every one of them:

In 1894, Harry Edwards, unbeknownst to drunken companions, fell off a buggy and later froze to death.

In the same year, a drunken Alvin Reese spooked his horse and was dragged to death.

A year later, George Parker, an Omaha Indian, was shot and killed by a drunken Winnebago.

After a night of heavy drinking, Washington Baxter died of violent convulsions.

An elderly, drunken Philip Watson died from exposure and pneumonia.

A drunken James Walker was run over by a train.

Henry Guitar, a drunken boy, shot and killed his father and was sent to prison for seven years.

A drunken Nathan Lyon was killed by John Walker, who died in prison.

Wolf Chief, while drunk in Iowa, was hanged by vigilantes.

Sammie Fremont, who served five years in the navy, returned from service, got drunk, signed away his land rights, and, after sobering up and discovering what he had done, fatally shot himself.

On and on.

The Fremont suicide illuminated another burgeoning problem—the speed and ease with which the Omaha were now being dispossessed of their land, a problem inextricably linked to the pervasive alcohol abuse. The Dawes Act of 1887 had forbidden Indians to lease their lands until a twenty-five-year trust period had run its course. But a series of newer laws and policy shifts eventually chipped away at the act, poking enough holes in it that by the early years of the new century there were many ways for Indians to lease their lands. And lease they did—often with disastrous results.

During testimony at an inquest, Susan gave a graphic example. An Indian man sold all of his land for $6,000, she testified. Afterward, he invited a group of Indian friends to a party at his house. He laid in a good supply of liquor and gave everyone cash gifts. Then he went out and bought three new buggies for himself. Less than a year later, he was broke, the $6,000 gone.

In a letter to his nephew, Francis declared: "No one can deny that since the Omahas found it easy to get liquor they did more loafing, drunkenness and vice." And there was no doubt, he wrote, that alcohol "and the indiscriminate leasing of their lands have done them more harm than anything that happened to them in their history."

In those years, whenever his sister journeyed across their reservation to see her patients, whenever she visited any of the small Indian communities, she saw that many of the churches were empty now, the fields abandoned, the farm equipment rusted over, the houses often dilapidated. And it made her sick—sick that this out-of-control scourge could ultimately destroy her people, could destroy everything her father had worked so hard for, everything he believed in.

So she went to work, taking the curse head-on throughout the 1890s and into the next century. In 1898, she and Henry had a second child, another boy, Pierre, and because Henry frequently worked the fields, Susan had to take the new baby on her medical rounds. And although she now had two small boys, a husband, a bustling medical practice, many church-related duties, and fragile health, Susan often seemed inspired by the magnitude of the curse—a problem her father had solved and one that she, too, was now determined to solve. By launching a fierce anti-alcohol crusade, she was, in a sense, embracing the Omaha vision that had passed from Big Elk to Joseph La Flesche and now to her—an attempt to adapt, mobilize, and bolster their joint visions for the survival of their people.

To that end, she wrote endless letters and articles laying out the case against the easy sale of alcohol and its increasingly devastating effects. She discussed strategies with her allies on the Omaha Tribal Council. She implored the commissioner of Indian affairs to intervene. She actively lobbied various legislative bodies. She testified at inquests. She launched moral crusades in church and Sunday school and as head of the Omaha Christian Endeavor Society. She stocked her doctor's office with an array of picture books, magazines, and games as a deterrent to the temptations of alcohol. As early as 1891, she and several others formed a Law and Order Committee that compiled a list of bootleggers and gave them to the Indian agent for prosecution. "Their efforts are meeting with some success," Sara Kinney told her *Hartford Courant* readers, as a number of offenders "have already been brought before the courts."

Not long after, Susan helped lead an aggressive voter campaign to shut down liquor sales throughout Thurston County, to close the many saloons that had cropped up throughout the county. But the pro-liquor forces countered by hammering home their message: A clause in the Dawes Severalty Act of February 1887 had made citizens of the Omaha, so the Omaha now had the same legal rights as all other U.S. citizens—which included the right to buy and drink as much liquor as they wanted. In the end, that argument, and the overall illiteracy of the voters, victimized by the intentional mislabeling of ballots, defeated Susan's attempts to legally ban alcohol from the county. Undeterred, she then sided with the Omaha Tribal Council in its attempt to create a new tribal police force modeled after her father's, a force disbanded following his death in 1888. To bolster its cause, the council offered $500 to help pay for the force. But the offer fell on deaf ears at the Office of Indian Affairs and nothing ever came of it.

In 1897, a Nebraska congressman helped pass a law prohibiting alcohol sales to Indians falling within a wide range of reservation categories. Federal marshals were sent to the Omaha Reservation to enforce stiff penalties and crack down on the bootleggers and whiskey peddlers. The new law quickly produced results. But two years later, a cash-strapped Office of Indian Affairs eliminated the marshals, and bootleggers soon flourished, once again plunging the reservation into a deplorable state.

Soon after, a frustrated Susan eventually fired off a long letter to Commissioner of Indian Affairs William Arthur Jones. "For four years, from 1889 to 1893, I worked among the Omaha night and day attending the sick," she said. "At first I went every where alone, at any time of day or night and felt perfectly safe among my people." But intemperance had increased, she told Jones, until "men and women died from alcoholism, and little children were seen reeling on the streets of the town, drunken brawls in which men were killed occurred and no person's life was considered safe. . . . Women pawned their clothing for drink, while the men spent their rent money for liquor and the families suffered for food." The Omaha men, she wrote, traded land for liquor, and consequently "no machinery was bought, no household improvements were made, and complete demoralization, physical, mental and moral prevailed."

Motivated to explore all options, Susan remembered listening during her medical school days to Frances Willard and Hannah Whitall Smith, two of the most powerful temperance speakers of the day, and the impact they had had upon her. So it wasn't long before she began her own temperance movement, carrying that same crusade to her homeland and her people, giving impassioned speeches in the local churches and schools and communities, inspired by the words she had heard in Philadelphia and by her father's legacy.

Susan's words often went beyond the urgency of banning alcohol on the Omaha Reservation. Her speeches also focused on public health—how her people needed to ban not only booze, but also the communal drinking cup, which helped spread disease. They needed to start putting in screens to keep out flies, which helped spread disease. They needed to stop congregating in enclosed homes, which helped spread disease. The need for all of her people to focus on prevention was a message the Omaha heard over and over: If you don't get sick, she would tell them, you won't need me.

When Susan began her public health crusade in the 1890s, she was not breaking new ground. At the time, similar efforts were also under way in New York City and other metropolitan areas along the East Coast. But there was something that made her public health initiatives unique: She was doing it hundreds of miles away, largely by herself, on a remote, sprawling Indian reservation riddled with disease, alcoholism, poverty, and illiteracy—a place where the government often neglected to provide basic drugs and medical supplies, forcing the community's only doctor to rely on native herbs and plants, forcing a modern, highly educated woman to scour the prairie for ancient remedies to help keep her people alive and well.

The poet and writer John Neihardt and the local doctor were well acquainted. For a number of years, the two lived a block apart in Bancroft, where Neihardt had also come to know Henry and the two young boys and several other La Flesche relatives. Neihardt had spent many hours with some of the Omaha elders and had written extensively on Omaha Indian themes, and over time, a good deal of admiration developed between the poet and the doctor.

The doctor was so struck by one of Neihardt's books that she reviewed it in a letter to the *New York Times*. "So often I have picked up an Indian story, written by well-meaning white people, and after a few pages laid it down with a sigh of despair, for I could not find what I sought—Indian likeness, if such a term be permissible, in action, character drawing, or expressions of sentiment." That all changed, she wrote, when she picked up *The Lonesome Trail*. "Mr. Neihardt's delineation of Indian character is excellent," Susan wrote. "His Indian is not a bizarre creature of the imagination; neither does he place him on a pedestal, based on sentimentality, investing him with attributes he does not possess. The Indian is flesh and blood, with the same cardinal virtues and the same cardinal sins, and so possessed with the same amount of human nature as the rest of human kind."

After reading several of his short stories, Susan sent Neihardt a note, asking that he come see her. "I went with my heart in my mouth, for from my viewpoint at the time she seemed a most austere personage," he later recalled. "Tall, slender, black eyed, as I remember her, she bore herself with an air of dignified authority that made her seem far less gentle than she proved to be." When he arrived, Susan greeted him as *Tae-Nuga-Zhinga* ("Little Bull Buffalo"), his Omaha name, and then she began talking about his stories. "She liked them!" Neihardt wrote. "She even said that mine were the only Indians in literature from Cooper to Remington that had not been offensive to her, adding that she could not understand how a white man could represent the Indian idiom so perfectly in the English language."

Susan also left the poet with another impression: He had attended a number of her temperance talks and health crusades, and she was, he believed, the most powerful public speaker he had ever heard.

"She spoke simply, and she had a most effective way of increasing the impact of a climactic sentence by withholding it in silence overlong," Neihardt said. "During such a time, one could feel the tension building in the audience. Her face grew lighter, and she seemed to vibrate with intensity of feeling. Then, in a low voice, she said it!"

But not everyone liked what she said—or how she said it. Her frequently aggressive attempts to push Christianity and promote Western medicine often angered a number of Omaha. Her words and beliefs disgusted them, the traditional men and women who preferred their traditional culture and their traditional medicine. In her temperance talks, she also railed against how some Omaha had increasingly come to rely on the mescal bean in their traditional native religious services. Mescal, she argued, was as dangerous as alcohol, a drug that would retard their progress unless the practice was abolished. It was a difficult message for the more traditional Omaha to hear, and many resented Susan for preaching it—much as they had once resented her father when he had forcefully tried to merge Western and native cultures.

"I know that I shall be unpopular for a while with my people," Susan wrote of her anti-alcohol crusade, "because they will misconstrue my efforts, but this is nothing, just so that I can help them for their own good."

If some Omaha thought she wasn't doing enough to strengthen traditional culture, others criticized her and Bright Eyes and Marguerite for doing too much. In a *Lend A Hand* newsletter, the three sisters won high praise for their educational achievements, their courage, and their enthusiastic devotion to improving the lives of their people—specifically their efforts to rid the reservation of alcohol. But it all came at a price.

"Their lives are heroic in intention, but, in the midst of their self-abnegation," the newsletter said, "they commit the mistake of making the people too dependent upon them. It is pathetic to see how men, women and children run to them for every little thing they want, lean on them for every convenience, call upon them for counsel and aid in matters great and small, and how they never refuse a moment of their time nor an ounce of their strength, till they are absolutely in danger of sinking under the strain, while nevertheless, it is plain that 'a little wholesome neglect, my dear,' would invigorate the moral fibre of their clients, and go farther towards setting them on their feet than any amount of such petting and coddling."

To underscore its message, the newsletter quoted from a report Theodore Roosevelt had written shortly after visiting several Indian communities. At some point, he wrote, all boys must take "the inevitable plunge to learn whether they can sink or swim in the troublesome sea of life. So it is with Indians. We must protect and guard them up to a certain point; but all the while we must be fitting them as we best can for rough contact with the world; and finally, when all, humanly speaking, is done that can be done, we must turn them loose, hardening our hearts to the fact that many will sink, exactly as many will swim."

One night, Susan and Henry were alone in their Bancroft home, a night when thick black clouds began to gather above the Nebraska prairie. Soon, it began to rain. Down at the train station telegraph office, one of the young clerks was lounging around with some of his coworkers when he heard a telegram coming through. He went over to get it and saw that it was an urgent message: FIND DR. PICOTTE. BE QUICK.

It had come from the town of Lyons, a community about nine miles down the line. A woman there was in desperate shape trying to deliver her baby. Two local doctors already were there, but they were in trouble, and they said they needed Susan as soon as possible. So one of the young boys in the telegraph office ran to the livery stable, grabbed a team of horses and a covered buggy, and took off in the general direction of the small house across from the Presbyterian church.

It was dark and the rain was coming down harder now and he kept looking, but he couldn't find her house. And then he saw it in the window and he followed the light to her door. Susan quickly gathered her things and they got in the buggy and rode the nine miles to Lyons, following the section lines in the dark and the rain. They got to the hotel late that night, and one of the doctors greeted Susan and then took her with him.

The next morning, Susan and the two local doctors and the young driver all gathered for breakfast. The mother and the baby were both out of trouble. They were both doing fine. They had both pulled through, Dr. M. L. Hildreth later noted, "thanks to the skill of Dr. Susan."

Susan liked to talk, she liked dinner parties and social occasions and family gatherings, and she was a good storyteller. Many of the stories she enjoyed telling the most were drawn from her childhood. And one of those stories was how she had come to learn

English, how she had come to master it, to speak it so well at such a young age.

It was when she and Rosalie and Marguerite were all living together with their older sister, Bright Eyes, in her little log house at the agency school in Macy. Bright Eyes loved her younger sisters, but she also made all the rules and she wasn't shy about enforcing them. She wanted each of her sisters to learn how to keep house, so each of the three younger girls had very specific daily chores. One was to do the cooking, one the cleaning, and one the washing and sewing. Bright Eyes assigned her youngest sister the odd jobs—scouring knives and beating the eggs. "I beat so many," Susan recalled, "that for years I never saw an egg without instinctively reaching out for a fork to beat it." And scouring the knives after every meal, she said, "grew so irksome that I resolved that if I ever grew up and was able to earn money like my sister, I would buy silver knives that wouldn't require scouring."

Bright Eyes had gotten a teaching position at the government school, and her father wanted the three younger girls to stay with their older sister so they wouldn't have to walk all the way in each morning from the Village of the Make-Believe White Men. So all four sisters lived together, and it wasn't long before the youngest sister learned another one of the oldest sister's new house rules.

"I was much surprised the second day of our new life in the log house to hear my sister inform us that we were to speak English," Susan said. "She told us that she would not reply to Indian. It was several days before she heard a word out of me, for I could not speak a word of English. But before I knew it, I was chattering away in English and had no difficulty in learning it."

And now it was late in the spring of 1903, almost thirty years since her English lessons began, and the youngest sister was again in the home of the oldest sister. Bright Eyes lay flat on her back in a rear bedroom of the house, covered with a sheet. A damp washcloth covered her face. After she got sick, she and her husband, Thomas Tibbles, had moved from their home in Lincoln, the state capital, back to her allotment near Logan Creek, back to the land where she had grown up, closer to the river and the bluffs and the trees and animals, to the open, rolling prairie she loved and missed.

It was the early evening of May 26, and Susan was with Bright Eyes, caring for her, soothing her, trying to calm their mother, knowing that her oldest sister, the one who had helped Chief Standing Bear and nursed the injured at Wounded Knee, who had paved the way to New Jersey and campaigned tirelessly on behalf of Indian rights, had become dangerously ill and was unlikely to make it through the night.

Her husband was in a front room. The later it got, the more he heard the old mother wailing in the back, the more afraid he became, afraid the woman he loved so much would soon die and he would be sitting in the dark, all alone. He was sixty-three years old, his wife was forty-nine, and that spring, they had been married for twenty-two years.

No one, including his wife's own family, liked him much, so he sat in the front room, alone, waiting and listening. Finally, later that night, he scribbled out a message and had it delivered to John Neihardt, one of the few people in town who would agree to come and sit with him through the long night.

In the back room, Bright Eyes was fading in and out of consciousness, often bursting into incoherent mumblings, then speaking clearly and coherently, sometimes in Omaha, sometimes in English. When she would say something in Omaha to an in-law standing at her bedside, forgetting she did not understand, Susan would translate it into English.

It went on this way late into the night, and then before the new day dawned, Bright Eyes was gone. Her mother, seventy-seven years old, started to weep hysterically and then began to wail in the Indian way. Susan went over to try to calm her, but she could do nothing.

Soon, the husband heard a knock on the door and he led Neihardt, forty-one years his junior, to a chair in the front room of the darkened farmhouse near Logan Creek. For a while, the two men sat alone, not speaking, keeping a silent vigil for the dead wife. Then the husband abruptly stood up.

"I think you have never met her. Shall we go and see her now?"

He guided Neihardt to the back room, stopping at his wife's bedside. Then he bent down and slowly removed the neatly folded washcloth from her face.

"Isn't she beautiful?"

The husband began to sob loudly, and the twenty-two-year-old guest did not know what to do and soon the two men went back to the front room and sat in silence.

Each year, all of the U.S. Indian agents on the nation's reservations were required to file an annual report to the commissioner of Indian affairs, summarizing housing, health, educational, agricultural, and social conditions on their respective reservations. And each year throughout the opening years of the new century, it was clear that the Omaha agents had grown increasingly irritated, disgusted, and frustrated with the many problems the bootleggers and whiskey peddlers brought to their reservation.

Liquor traffic "is one of the greatest sources of annoyance and discouragement on this reservation, which is peculiarly situated, surrounded as it is by towns, in most of which is the ever-present saloon and the worthless whites who depend upon the 'bootlegging' profit for a livelihood," an angry Omaha agent Charles

Mathewson wrote in his 1900 report. He deplored the decision to remove deputy marshals from the reservation the previous year—marshals, he wrote, who helped arrest and prosecute bootleggers, almost eliminating the problem altogether. But practically over-night, he bemoaned, "the prosecutions ceased and in a short time the conditions were as bad, if not worse, than they had ever been in the past."

Summed up Agent John Mackey in his 1905 report: "The dif-ficulties of protecting the Indians from the harpies who ply this nefarious trade among them have been greatly increased . . . more drunkenness than ever now prevails among the Indians, chiefly due to the fact that boot leggers have encamped on the bank of the Missouri River in Iowa, and the Indians cross in boats to purchase liquor from them."

In those years, among the more than twelve hundred Omaha scattered across a 131,000-acre reservation, no one was in a better position to comprehend the stark differences between a reserva-tion of sober Indians and one awash in bootleggers than Susan La Flesche Picotte. Except for her years away at school, Susan saw firsthand what a whiskey-free reservation looked like. She saw an increasingly industrious people, people building homes and break-ing ground and harvesting crops. She saw people sending their children to school, attending church, and learning how to balance old ways and new ways. She saw virtually no crime anywhere and felt safe everywhere.

But now, making the rounds along rough roads alone in her buggy, she saw a sick and diseased people made even sicker by the flood of alcohol, a flood that further weakened already weak immune systems, leaving so many of her people—fathers and mothers, the elders and the children—even more vulnerable to a wide range of fatal diseases.

By 1905, she needn't look any further than her own family to see the ravages the curse had wrought. In earlier years, the curse had come to the home of a young brother-in-law, and for a time it had also come to Ed Farley, Rosalie's husband, who had taken to spending too much time in the many local saloons surrounding the reservation. And before 1905 had passed, the curse came to her own home, the wood-frame house in Bancroft where she had her medical office, where she and Henry were raising their two young sons, across the street from the church where they were married. Henry had been drinking for many years, and even though his wife was leading a fervent anti-alcohol crusade, he had recently taken to drinking more heavily and she could do nothing to stop him. He had also been weakened by a long battle with tuberculosis, and the heavy drinking accelerated his decline. She had fought long and hard, speaking and preaching and traveling from one end of the reservation to the other to try to save her people from the curse, but in the end, she could not save her own husband. That year, Henry Picotte died. He was forty-five.

At his death, Susan became a forty-year-old widow with a quarter section of land, an ailing mother, two young sons, and scores of white and Indian patients to care for. The pain in her ears, neck, and back had grown steadily worse, and she was deaf in one ear. And she was also desperately lonely.

In October 1905, not long after his death, Susan wrote a friend that she missed Henry so much, she longed to be able to "turn time back a little." She had such "a longing" for him "that sometimes" she felt as though she could "almost go wild."

But despite her weakened state and her many obligations, Susan became even more zealous in turning up the flame on her public health crusade. She and her allies took to the schools and the pulpits, the street corners and town halls. They lobbied politicians and got the tribal council involved, going everywhere they could, engaging everyone they could, trying to keep the pressure on the bootleggers, trying to educate their customers.

And then something happened, something no one really expected: Things suddenly got better. Conditions rapidly improved. The reservation and its people underwent a dramatic, unexpected change.

No one could quite believe it.

No one saw it coming.

Since the death of Joseph La Flesche eighteen years earlier, bootleggers and whiskey peddlers had had their way, the curse brutally unraveling the Omaha social fabric. And now, in 1906, it had abruptly stopped.

But why?

The dramatic change, Susan said, came from within the Indian himself.

"He had known what loss of self-respect was; he had tasted of disgrace; he had become thoroughly disgusted with himself," she said.

And there was something else: John M. Commons, the Omaha Reservation's new agent, came on board in 1906. Commons immediately installed a number of nonnegotiable rules. Most of the lease money flowed through his office, and he would not release any rent money to Indian landowners unless they complied with his new rules. Commons also took a personal interest in each Omaha who came to his office.

"He told them to take a little of the money that he paid out to them and spend it for garden seeds," Susan later recalled. "He visited them in their homes telling them how to farm these gardens. All over the Reservation you could see the signs of a reviving interest in industries. The Indian seemed to be anxious to take hold of anything that might assist him to climb upward again."

That fall, Susan La Flesche was heartened by the unexpected improvements she had seen among her people on their own land. She was heartened by the new agent and his commitment to her people. And she was also heartened by her dream, the dream of one day bringing her patients under one roof.

In the autumn of 1906, her dream was still alive.

9

∨∨∨

A Warrior of the People

It's still there, more than a century later.

The green clapboards are a bit faded now, washed out in the late-morning light. The three huge windows facing south. That strange trapezoidal roof. A broad porch easily lit up by a light in the window.

Still there, in the town of Walthill, the imposing two-and-a-half-story Victorian home, the one crowning three lots carved from rolling prairie, resting peacefully atop a sloping hill overlooking Omaha Creek and the old railroad depot and a reservation spreading out in all four directions, looking down on that spot where village elders had once put the communal drinking cup, the one that had caused so many problems in those early days of the town, the cup that killed too many of her people.

Even now, walk through the front door of that faded green house on the southeast corner of Taft and Main and a burst of natural light showers the expansive living room, pours across the solid oak floors, and sweeps all the way back to the sturdy brick fireplace anchoring a wall of the dining room.

Susan loved this house.

She struggled constantly with carpenters over the basic design, fretted endlessly over every architectural detail, from the foundation to the shape of the roof, from the three upstairs bedrooms to the large living room windows—the ones that firmly underscored her constant refrain: Fresh air and sunshine were nature's medicine. She supervised the layout of the kitchen and the design of the cabinets and the kind of wood she wanted for the floors. She fought for the oversize living room and for the bookcases on three sides, the ones she filled with many of the great works of literature. And then, too, it was her idea for the inscription carved into the wooden mantelpiece.

She loved this house, her house, and on any given day, at any given time, in any season of the year, who knew what a visitor might find upon walking through the front door.

Maybe a cluster of state legislators debating the wisdom of expanding legal rights for Indian women and children.

Maybe a heated discussion on land issues, about how the federal government kept treating the Omaha like ignorant children, forever incapable of managing their own affairs.

It could be a distraught Omaha man, a middle-aged man who couldn't read or write, who wanted her to help translate a complex government regulation, who wanted her to help him understand.

Or an elderly woman who had broken her ankle months earlier and didn't have any money to pay the doctor and was now offering two chickens instead.

Or maybe someone who needed her advice about how to build a new home or wanted her help to place a phone call to find out why her lease money hadn't arrived.

When you opened the door to her house in those early years of the twentieth century, you never really knew.

It could be a Sunday dinner with her family or a birthday party for her niece or a wedding ceremony for a cousin or an afternoon sewing session with some of the ladies from the Presbyterian church or a funeral for a beloved member of the community.

Maybe you'd walk through her front door on a summer evening and find a composer from Pittsburgh playing some fine music, ending with a flurry of traditional Omaha songs arranged in a way no one had ever heard before.

Soon, the tall Victorian house on the hill became a place of frequent parties and many social events, attracting white lawyers and Omaha farmers and white farmers and Omaha drummers, a place where people from two different cultures could mingle comfortably, share a little food, relax, get to know one another, get to know a bit more about Omaha traditions, about their music and songs and dances.

You never really knew.

On the morning of November 17, 1906, Dr. Susan La Flesche Picotte was the only woman, and the only Omaha Indian, waiting patiently in line to buy a lot in the newly formed railroad town of Walthill. She had received her share of proceeds from the sale of Henry's allotment in South Dakota and had also been leasing her own 640-acre allotment, so she was able to use the two incomes to buy a lot, help finance a new home, and still have enough left over to set up an education fund for Caryl and Pierre.

On that raw, chilly Saturday, Susan stood in line with her brother-in-law Walter Diddock. A local real estate man, Diddock ended up buying a corner lot that same day directly across the street from where Susan intended to build her new home. Soon, as had been the case in Bright Eyes' little log house on the reservation and again in New Jersey and then at Hampton, she and Marguerite would once again be living close together, and the two sisters, now both mothers of young children, were excited about all the traffic they imagined would flow back and forth when their new homes were built.

Until then, Susan would stay in Macy, a word that had been formed by merging "Omaha" and "Agency" into a kind of postal shorthand, and it's where she had moved after Henry's death. Not long after her move, the Presbyterian Board of Home Missions had contacted Susan with an offer: Would she be interested in becoming their missionary to the Omaha Tribe? Sixteen years earlier, she had been the first Indian to earn a medical degree. If she accepted the board's offer, she would become the first Indian ever appointed a tribal missionary.

When Susan became a widow, she also became the sole support of an elderly, ailing mother and two young sons, ages ten and eight. At the time, her application for her old position as government physician at the Macy boarding school had fallen through. And for months on end, the pain in her head had become far more intense, spreading from her ears to her neck and down into her back. By age forty, she was deaf in one ear and getting around each day had become increasingly difficult, depending on her level of pain. When the Presbyterian Board of Home Missions made its offer, Susan didn't hesitate. She said yes.

The job required her to promote Presbyterian religious doctrine, assist with a variety of church functions, and write periodic reports updating her superiors on the state of the reservation's religious well-being. The job also included furnished housing and a small stipend, so Susan soon left Bancroft, consolidating three generations of her fragmented family under one Macy roof. And then the newly minted medical missionary to the Omaha got to work.

On any given Sunday on the Omaha Reservation, at the Blackbird Hills Presbyterian Church, Susan delivered a morning sermon. She wanted to boost attendance, so she read the Bible in the language of the people she wanted to attract, the Omaha people. When they sang their hymns, she translated them into Omaha.

When the sermon ended, she convened her Sunday school class, a class that often included both children and adults, who heard Susan recount famous biblical stories in the Omaha language. "I found myself pastor, janitor, organist and clerk of the Sunday School," she would later say.

Come Sunday afternoon, she conducted Christian Endeavor meetings in her home. When she heard that an Omaha Indian couple wanted to marry, she urged them to do it in the church—and to apply for a formal license. When someone died, she performed a Christian burial. When someone arrived sick or injured, she provided medical treatment. When they needed a shoulder to lean on, someone to listen, she offered sympathy and encouragement.

Eighteen months after Susan became intimately involved in the church, three noticeable events occurred. On Sunday, December 1, 1907, twenty-one children were baptized in the Blackbird Hills Presbyterian Church—twenty of them Omaha Indians. That same day, another twenty adults were baptized and officially united with the church—all Omaha Indians. Three days later, five more children and ten more adults were baptized—all Omaha.

"This is not the result of a revival but is the culmination of the missionary work of Dr. Susan La F. Picotte," the *Walthill Times* informed its readers. Susan, the paper noted, gave "not only spiritual and medical advice but sympathy and the help of one Indian to her own people."

Throughout her adult life on the Omaha Reservation, religion and alcohol—two opposing forces, one greatly affecting the other—often became intertwined. When the bootleggers ran wild, she observed, farms grew idle, families were shattered, churches became empty, and her degraded people fell backward. But when the government and tribe combined resources to clamp down on whiskey peddlers, just the opposite occurred: productive farms, healthy families, bustling churches, an inspired people moving steadily forward.

One day in 1907, while arguing for another field matron to help maintain the tribe's momentum, Susan laid out the precarious balance between religion and alcohol in a long letter to Commissioner of Indian Affairs Francis Leupp. "The Indians are working better and so drinking much less they are beginning to get interested in the church and now is the time when they are beginning to climb up that they need the most help," she wrote. Another field matron, she said, would provide the kind of solid, steady missionary work the tribe desperately needed, "for you can't rush at the Indians with an open Bible any more than you can the white people."

Although the government declined her suggestion, Susan—despite her own precarious health, her multiple religious and medical duties, and the demands of an elderly mother and two young sons—never eased up on her anti-alcohol crusade, never let it fade into the background. For years, with the help of relatives and friends, she bombarded the Office of Indian Affairs with a specific request: Prohibit liquor sales in any town that had ever been formed within Omaha Reservation boundaries. Make this prohibition a condition for every deed on every piece of property, she urged. And eventually the U.S. secretary of the interior did, decreeing that no liquor could ever be sold on any lot in those towns that had once been a part of either the Omaha or the Winnebago Reservation—a temperance ruling that held steady until the advent of the automobile, when thirsty Indians could jump in a car and keep driving until they found a town off the reservation welcoming them with open arms and free-flowing saloons. A town such as Bancroft.

In the spring of 1907, Bancroft's village board passed an ordinance allowing saloon keepers to sell alcohol to Indians over the bar. Editors of the *Walthill Times* were not pleased. "Poor old Bancroft," the paper noted. "To pay such an ignominious price for the opportunity to harvest a few paltry dollars! . . . The possible advantage in trade to be gained is not worth half the sum of contempt the promoters of such a disgracefully clever policy will earn."

Meanwhile, Susan's job as the Presbyterian missionary began about the same time another kind of religion made its way to the Omaha Reservation. For centuries, the peyote religion had been deeply rooted in Mexico, where many tribes had come to view the short, spineless cactus as a sacred plant. Producing mescal beans that triggered hallucinations and visions, the plant became an important religious sacrament in the traditional ceremonies of those tribes. The Kiowa and Comanche visited some of the tribes of northern Mexico, eventually introducing the peyote religion to the American Southwest and then to the Great Plains. During much of the nineteenth century—faced with the annihilation of their own culture and alarmed at the loss of tribal identities— a number of native leaders came to embrace the peyote religion. And, much as they had once adapted the Ghost Dance, many began to shape the peyote religion to meet their own needs, occasionally merging it with some of the basic tenets and practices of Christianity. By the opening years of the twentieth century, the peyote religion had found its way to the Omaha Reservation.

Once the peyote religion took hold on America's Indian reservations, it almost instantly became the target of fierce opposition from government agencies and missionaries—including the Omaha Tribe's missionary. Susan had no use for peyote, for the mescaline that was extracted from the plant, or for any part of the peyote religion. In those days, she believed mescal beans were as dangerous, addictive, and culturally destructive as alcohol. Both, she stated publicly, were diseases, roadblocks on her people's path to becoming educated, productive citizens. "If we could keep them from using whisky and the mescal bean, they would progress more rapidly," she said of her people. "The mescal bean is a great evil and we are hoping to induce the government to stop its importation into this country."

Susan's position on peyote once again put her at odds with some members of her tribe, members who had quickly embraced the new religion, who were willing to give it a chance and wanted to try something new, members who said the peyote religion had already helped improve their lives. Many of those Omaha, those who saw peyote as a way to salvage and retain traditional elements of their culture, came to view Susan as a sellout, as someone who had stumbled into a white world and lost her way, someone who had become too white and could no longer relate to the cultural underpinnings that gave her people a firm identity, that made the Omaha who they were.

This issue, this dilemma—the head-on collision of two vastly different cultures, two drastically different belief systems, one old and one new—had been playing out on the Great Plains and beyond for decades. The collision created two different camps, each with very different ideas about what to do with the shattered pieces and how to put them back together.

For the Omaha, it had been playing out since 1837, when Big Elk returned from Washington, D.C., warning his people that a flood was coming, that they would have to adapt to the new world order of the white man—or they might not survive. Joseph La Flesche had embraced that vision and passed it on to his children. Others did not. And now the flood had long since arrived and the fight for cultural survival never stopped, and it had taken many forms, gone down many paths.

Following her father's advice, Susan chose one of those paths, working hard to absorb many of the hallmarks of the new world order. She learned English. She learned to read and write. She read some of the classics of modern literature. She learned about the Bible. She became a doctor. And then she went back home.

So when an expectant mother—Indian or white—needed help with her delivery, Susan could help.

When a young boy gashed his leg and needed stitches, Susan could help.

When an old Omaha man could not read the letter the government had sent him, Susan could help.

When a middle-aged Omaha woman could not understand the technicalities of the property deed, or someone needed a letter written to the reservation agent, or a young Omaha couple wanted to get married in the Blackbird Hills Presbyterian Church, or someone had died and the family wanted a Christian burial, Susan could help.

In mid-November, shortly before Thanksgiving 1907, Susan knew nothing about the recent spike in church attendance, about the twenty Omaha children and twenty Omaha adults soon to be baptized in her church. For the last few weeks, she had been lying in a bed in a room at St. Vincent's Hospital in Sioux City, Iowa, thirty miles away, the closest hospital to her home. She had collapsed from nervous exhaustion, and she was worried about being so far from home, worried about her mother, an ailing eighty-one-year-old woman she couldn't help at the moment. She was worried about her two young sons, Caryl and Pierre. She couldn't help them, either. And she worried about her people, about their precarious state of health. So on November 15, she got some stationery and a pen and composed a letter to Commissioner of Indian Affairs Leupp.

"I am an Omaha Indian and have been working as medical

missionary among the Omahas but have broken down from over-work," she wrote. "Although I have been here several weeks I have kept in touch with affairs at Macy. I know what a small figure our affairs cut with all the Department has on its hands, but I also know that if you knew the conditions and circumstances to be remedied you would do all you could to remedy them." Her words to the commissioner reflected a mixture of guilt and regret and a mounting anxiety for the condition of the Omaha. "I had intended to do so much work this fall—the Doctor tells me I cannot do any medical work for 6 mos. and I feel that something must be done for my people. . . ."

She had arrived on the reservation from Philadelphia at a time when serious, dangerous, fatal epidemics were everywhere she looked—of diphtheria, flu, smallpox, and, most ominous, tubercu-losis. Often there were no vaccines. And the reservation's remote-ness worked against her. So she began to promote a constant message, one she had first absorbed at Hampton and later at the medical college: Sanitation = Prevention. She fought for years to ban the communal drinking cup, often the carrier of tuberculo-sis. She exhorted her people to avoid crowding two and three gen-erations into single, poorly ventilated homes, homes where one person with TB could quickly infect everyone else. She forcefully urged the Omaha to use screens on doors and windows to keep out disease-carrying flies. But her message was slow to take hold.

"The spread of Tuberculosis among my people is something terrible," she told the commissioner. "So many, many of the young children are marked with it in some form. The physical degenera-tion in 20 years among my people is terrible. I have talked with them and done all I could to prevent infection and contagion. . . ." Could the government, she asked the commissioner, spare a little money to help fight the tuberculosis that was killing her people? In the end, the government could not.

As had happened many times before, Susan stayed in bed and rested. Slowly, her health improved and she was able to leave the Sioux City hospital and return to the Omaha Reservation. In early March 1908, her new home on the hill—the one with a furnace, a bathtub, indoor plumbing, and a brick fireplace anchoring the north wall of the dining room—was finished, and she and her mother and the two boys all moved in.

For years she had lived in a private house in Elizabeth, New Jersey, and shared a dorm room with other girls in Hampton, Virginia, and holed up in a Philadelphia YWCA. For years she had spent summers in a portable tipi on the annual buffalo hunt and in the Village of the Make-Believe White Men and then in the little house she shared with her three sisters. For years she had crisscrossed the vast reservation on foot and horseback and buggy, hopping from one allotment to the next, bouncing from Macy to Bancroft to Logan Creek and back to Macy again. After all those years, it felt good to be rooted, to have one place, a steady, sturdy, stable place, a home that was there at the end of every long day, a comfortable, three-bedroom house on a hill to come home to, a place to quiet her thoughts, to calm her mind, to gather her strength. After so many years, she could not imagine her life without this home, without a place to center herself, to take refuge, a place to retreat and recover and regroup.

In those days, there was a saying from the Scottish lowlands, a saying that conveyed a sense of hope to the weary traveler who had strayed too far from the hearth but whose journey was almost over. It was a saying that had become popular in the Victorian era, and the nation's only female Indian physician had it carefully inscribed on the mantelpiece of her new home in Walthill, Nebraska.

EAST, WEST—HAME'S BEST.

And she never doubted its truth. Home was best.

On March 24, the new owner hosted a lively housewarming,

inviting about forty guests to her handsome new home. "The evening was very pleasantly passed at games and social pleasantries," it was reported, "and at a late hour dainty refreshments were served."

A few days before the housewarming, a reporter for the *Omaha World-Herald* came to Walthill to see Susan, to write about what life was like for the Indian doctor, for a woman of the people in her new home in the new railroad town. Susan's mother had recently taken a bad fall and broken her hip, and she was lying on the couch in the large, sunny living room when the reporter arrived:

> It was a busy time for Dr. Picotte when I visited her. She was just moving into her new home and was occupied in arranging her furniture. Her mother was ill and unable to move without assistance. The doctor herself was recovering from a three months' siege of nervous prostration, resulting from overwork, and added to all this there was to be a wedding in the house in two days. A pretty young cousin was to be married there and all sorts of delightful preparations were in progress.
>
> Amid it all, the doctor hurried here and there, superintending and arranging in order and overlooking no detail for the comfort of her guests. She was accustomed to a house full of company . . . and there was seldom a day when the family sat down to a meal alone.
>
> The two boys, Caryl, the older, and Pierre, the younger, ran about the place, helping and hindering as all boys do. They displayed an unusual affection and respect for their mother, and deferred to her in all things. While we were in the midst of an interesting discussion of the Indians and their ways, a shrill cry came from the porch.

"Mamma," called the chubby Pierre, "come down here quick! Johnny has fallen from the porch and cut his head. Come down and tend to him."

Patiently the doctor hurried down stairs and found a little visitor suffering a cut on the forehead. Her boys stood about, watching the deft fingers wash and bind up the cut with an air of proprietary pride in her skill. The older son is resolved to follow in the footsteps of his mother, and is already preparing to take up the study of medicine. He is a studious child and spends his spare time in reading from her well-stocked and carefully-chosen library. The younger is so occupied in having a good time that he gives no thought to the future, aside from his pride in his mother and his resolve to keep near his brother.

The boys' grandmother had been on many buffalo hunts, and when the people broke camp and moved out on the great summer hunts she knew how to quickly set up a tipi and she knew all of the signals to use in case an enemy, often the Lakota Sioux, suddenly appeared on the open plains. For decades, she had done beautiful beadwork and made many moccasins and sewed all of her garments by hand, using plant and animal fibers for thread and thorns for needles. She had never agreed to learn and speak English, preferring instead the language of her people, and she had lived much of her life outdoors. And now Mary Gale was lying on a couch in a Victorian home with a furnace and an indoor toilet, her hip badly broken, desperately wanting to go outside but unable to walk.

One day, Susan contacted a close friend in Bancroft, asking her if she could come to the home in Walthill for a few days. Susan had already bought yards of beautiful black crepe and black lace. The friend arrived and she went to Mary's bedside and she carefully measured the old woman's body, and when she finished, she cut out a long black robe from the crepe, often referred to as a "dressing sack," and she began slowly stitching the pattern together as Mary watched attentively. The old woman never left her bed again, and a few months later, dressed in the beautiful crepe sack trimmed in black lace, the one she had requested, Mary was brought outside one last time and laid to rest next to Joseph La Flesche in the cemetery a mile south of Bancroft.

The two sisters now lived across the street from each other, each anchored in a modern new home, and in the opening decade of the twentieth century they both began to immerse themselves in an ever-expanding web of Walthill's cultural, social, political, and religious life. As medical missionary, Susan maintained all of her responsibilities to the Blackbird Hills church in Macy, but she also threw herself into supporting the new Presbyterian church in Walthill. She was now teaching Sunday school at both churches, and before long she and Marguerite also became charter members of the new chapter of Eastern Star, a service-based organization that stressed acts of Christian kindness and charity. They were both active members of the Missionary Society and it was not unusual for the two sisters to show up at county Sunday school conventions, agricultural meetings sponsored by the University of Nebraska Extension Service or any number of weddings and funerals where they volunteered as interpreters. They also found time to support a variety of local projects—from lectures and concerts to charity fund-raisers and the county fair, where one year Susan was put in charge of the Indian Department. Their friend Harry L. Keefe, a local attorney, gave them some space in his

Walthill law office, so the two sisters could start a library. And they routinely opened their new homes to a rotating crop of scholars dropping in from time to time to study various aspects of Omaha Indian culture and tradition.

The two sisters also opened their homes to each other. Susan's house, home to her two sons, faced west, and Marguerite's, home to her husband, Walter, two daughters, and two sons, faced east, and for years there was a constant stream of traffic flowing across Taft Street. Walter often took it upon himself to prepare Sunday breakfast for his family, and Susan often took it upon herself to drop in. There was never any doubt what was on the breakfast menu: pancakes.

"Walter, why make those doughy cakes?" Susan would say. "Can't you tell they will lie in your stomach like leather?"

Long pause.

"Fry me two or three!"

One warm summer night, a young composer arrived in Walthill. He had come all the way from Pittsburgh and he sat down that Monday evening at a piano in the large Victorian home on Taft Street and began to play. And when he finished, the fifty invited guests—the white lawyers and farmers, the Indian ranchers and musicians, all the men and women who shared the community's red and white roads—were amazed at what they had heard. The pianist, composer Charles Wakefield Cadman, had taken traditional Omaha songs—ones the Omaha had sung at their ceremonies and dances and powwows for as long as anyone could remember—and blended them in a harmonious marriage of ancient Indian songs and modern music that no one had ever heard before. Then they heard Francis La Flesche, the nation's preeminent Indian ethnographer, sing a selection of songs from the Omaha Pipe Dance Ceremony, and they heard him interpret and explain the significance of those traditional songs and of the ceremony itself, the same ceremony Chief Big Elk had used to honor Mary Gale and Joseph La Flesche in an Omaha village more than sixty years earlier. When the evening ended, the hostess had both entertained and educated a red and white swath of the local community, bringing together a cross section of Indians and whites in a comfortable setting in which they could freely exchange thoughts and ideas. In those years, the big house on the hill often became a kind of cultural center, a place for its owner to showcase Omaha traditions to a diverse audience, to expose them to a culture that she and Marguerite were increasingly embracing.

So life went on for the two sisters and their families, back and forth in their homes, throughout the town and its libraries and churches, from agricultural sessions and health board meetings to county fairs and piano concerts, from taking care of their children to birthday parties for nieces and nephews, weddings for cousins and young Omaha couples, and pancake feeds come Sunday morning.

And then one day word came to the Omaha people scattered throughout the reservation, to all the townsfolk of Walthill, and to the two sisters who lived in the facing houses on Taft Street: The government bureaucrats and the architects of Indian policy clustered in their offices thirteen hundred miles to the east had come to a number of decisions—decisions that alarmed all of the Omaha and many of the whites.

Decisions that made Walthill's Indian doctor angry and confused.

On August 7, 1882, the Omaha had become the nation's first Indian tribe awarded allotments. Under the Omaha Allotment Act, the U.S. government carved up the tribal land base into individual plots, allowing the heads of Omaha families to become sole owners of 160 acres of land. Since the government believed Indians were neither experienced nor astute enough to manage individual private property, property that had always belonged to the tribe, the act also included a controversial provision: The government would hold the privately owned parcels in trust for twenty-five years. During that time, Indian-owned land would remain off the tax rolls and could not be sold. When the trust period ended, each Omaha would then hold title to his or her lands, free and clear. It was assumed that twenty-five years was plenty of time for the Omaha—and other tribes included in the Dawes Act five years later—to learn how to become responsible, productive, self-sufficient stewards of their land, allowing the government to get out of the Big Brother business altogether. Since the last of the Omaha allotments had been made in 1884, the twenty-five-year trust period was set to expire in 1909. Then, many Omaha believed, Indian landowners finally would be liberated from the heavy hand of the government, freed of its endless red tape, its suffocating rules and regulations.

But the government changed its mind. In 1909, the government concluded that a quarter century had not been enough, that America's Indians in general remained an uninspired, uneducated, unpredictable, and untrustworthy group ill suited to become responsible landowners. So government officials, without consulting Indian leaders, isolated in the vacuum of their own offices, made a unilateral decision: They would extend the trust period for the Omaha another ten years.

Yet in its one-size-fits-all view of the nation's native people, Washington bureaucrats entrusted with formulating general Indian policy neglected to take a closer look at the Omaha specifically. The Office of Indian Affairs ignored the 1909 report from its own man on the ground, Omaha superintendent John M. Commons—a report in which he stated that 90 percent of the Omaha people under forty spoke English. That most of those between forty and sixty could speak some English. That more than 95 percent of the Omaha had acquired property and 90 percent of the children were healthy and attending one of the reservation's fourteen public schools. That the tribe now boasted two merchants, two lawyers, three or four engaged in real estate and the stock business, several more in government service, and a great many making good homes for themselves and their families as farmers. And the tribe also had its own doctor, an Indian doctor.

For more than a quarter century, most of the Omaha had done everything asked of them. They kept the peace, built wood-frame houses, and took up farming. They learned English, sent their children to school, and built Christian churches. They dressed in civilian clothing and created a network of roads. A few acquired academic degrees, and many embraced Western medicine.

But throughout the reservation era, the government had invested very little trust in the Omaha, had done little to bolster their business skills or teach them how to handle money or navigate the swamp of red tape or protect them from whiskey peddlers and unscrupulous land swindlers. So in the summer of 1909, despite their compliance with changing ways, many Omaha remained shackled to a bloated government bureaucracy that offered little opportunity for them to stand on their own feet, to become competent, self-supporting citizens free of the government's heavy yoke. Consequently, in the eyes of the government, America's Indian people, including the Omaha, remained undisciplined, unreliable wards who needed a Great White Father to oversee every aspect of their lives. And soon the Omaha discovered it would get even worse: The government also had decided to install yet another accounting system, a new way of supervising all farming operations and merging the Omaha and Winnebago agencies into one. Finally, the government announced it would create a competency commission to screen individual Omaha Indians, to determine which ones might be advanced enough to operate independently, outside the reach of the local agent.

When the word came down from Washington, all of the Omaha—the people who lived out in the country, the progressives and traditionalists, mixed-bloods and full-bloods, Christians and peyote followers, home owners in Rosalie, Macy, and Walthill— all of the Omaha people were upset, disappointed, and angry. What the Omaha wanted seemed simple enough: the right to assert control over their own lands, lands that they owned, lands they wanted to be able to lease, to rent, so they could generate an income for themselves and their families. Yet they could not get out from beneath the government's suffocating rules and regulations.

"Had some stronger race a century ago overrun this continent and resolutely sequestered the American people into little cut-off communities, bidding them 'develop' and make mental and moral bricks without straw, we would have a working analogy to our treatment of the Indians," said the *Walthill Times*. "Under these circumstances, our beef barons and our steel kings would be hard to find. Could Andrew Carnegie have added golden numbers to golden numbers on an Indian reservation? Has not the whole thing been a colossal paternalism? We have kept the Indians too long in tutelage away from all that fills out the measure of a man, substituting the rule of the agent for a man's divine right to grow by experiment and failure."

All in all, the government's decision to extend the trust period left the occupant of 100 Taft Street in a complex bind—both angered and conflicted. On the one hand, she wanted her people to have more independence, more access to their lands and the revenue they could produce. Such independence would help accelerate their growth, nudging them closer to becoming productive citizens in mainstream America. But tethering them to the government yoke for another ten years would dramatically stunt that growth.

On the other hand, she also knew—perhaps better than anyone—that too many of her people were not yet ready to be fully independent. Too many did not yet speak fluent English. Too many did not yet understand the complexities of deeds, patents in fee, land titles. Too many simply did not have the proper training and experience to stand on their own feet. These people, she worried, would become easy prey for the many land swindlers circling the reservation, deceitful grafters ready to swoop in as soon as the Omaha got legal control of their lands. Too many of her people would not know how to confront the smooth-talking thieves and their free bottles of whiskey. These Omaha were vulnerable and so they could easily end up losing all of their land. Extending the trust period would help prevent that. It would buy more time until they became more competent.

For days on end, she always had the same two competing thoughts:

If we're not freed from government's heavy hand—how will we ever learn to manage our lands? Conduct business? Become productive, independent citizens capable of standing on our own feet?

But if we're given too much freedom too soon, before we've acquired the basic skills and protection from land grabbers, how many Omaha might end up losing their allotments?

She went back and forth, week after week, confused and tormented, changing her mind, offering contradictory answers, one day indicating she wanted to see the trust period extended to protect vulnerable lands, another day saying only a more liberal policy would force the Omaha to acquire the necessary skills and business knowledge to become truly independent.

In the run-up to the July 10, 1909, trust period deadline, Susan wrote letter after letter—some angry, some bitter, some satirical—strongly urging federal officials to crack down on the entrenched ring of land thieves, to investigate charges that it was already swindling some Omaha of their property, and to stringently enforce all regulations governing land transactions. These measures, she believed, offered the best protection for her people's welfare. But she got no response from the government. And so she slowly began to embrace the notion that maybe holding the people's land in trust a while longer was the best option, that it offered the best defense against speculators, the most protection for vulnerable Omaha lands.

On July 3, 1909, a week before the deadline was set to expire, President William Howard Taft made it official: He extended the trust period on the Omaha allotments for another ten years. But Taft's trust extension did not completely close the door. A competency commission would allow some Omaha to legally acquire access to their lands. So in the months following Taft's decision, the commission sifted through the pile of applicants, evaluating which Omaha the commissioners believed were competent enough to gain legal control of their lands. They would announce those they thought were qualified the following spring.

Meanwhile, if Susan often trod a fine line on the complex trust extension issue, no such conflict existed when it came to her thoughts on the heavy hand of the federal bureaucracy and consolidating the two agencies. Her fury and frustration at both never wavered, so she did what she often did when government directives outstripped her ability to comprehend them, when government policies threatened to undo all the work it took to ban a communal drinking cup, to insist on screen doors and windows, to plead for timely shipments of lifesaving drugs, when unilateral government decisions jeopardized the physical and emotional welfare of her twelve hundred patients. She went to her upstairs bedroom, sat down at a typewriter, and wrote. At length and with passion, she laid out specific objections to the new proposals, challenging the government to give Indians the same personal and economic freedoms it had given white Americans, freedoms that had once transformed a young, backward country into a thriving economic powerhouse.

"We are fighting for the same principle for which the forefathers of this great American nation fought for and who considered human lives but a paltry offering when laid down at the shrine of liberty," Susan wrote in a column published in both the *Omaha Bee* and the *Walthill Times*. "The majority of the Omahas are as competent as the same number of white people. They are independent and self-reliant, and their wishes have always been respected by past administrations." But no more, she said. Now it had all changed. There were no freedoms for her people. Everywhere they turned, the Omaha met a bitter wall of resentment and red tape, shackled to a past that prevented them from becoming productive citizens. "We have rules and regulations to the right of us, to the left of us, behind us; do you wonder we object to continuation of them in front of us?"

She gave example after example:

An old Indian man once had driven sixteen miles to ask her to write the superintendent for permission to buy a wheelbarrow and a new stove with his own money, a request that had to be approved by agency officials. Two or three weeks later he drove another sixteen miles to ask her for the results of his request. The superintendent said he had forwarded the request to his superiors in Washington, but had heard nothing back. Three weeks later, the old Indian again drove sixteen miles to Walthill to see if he could use his money to buy the wheelbarrow and stove. But he was told that no decision had yet been made.

One fall, an Indian had to be operated on for appendicitis. He needed authorization to take him to the hospital for the emergency operation, so a request to grant that authority was telegraphed to Washington. The approval arrived the following May.

A young woman was sick with tuberculosis. A trust fund from the sale of some reservation land had been set up, and the Omaha could apply for their share from the fund—about $250. So she applied for her share, and because she was so sick, the superintendent sent it in as a "special" request. Washington officials replied that the sick woman needed to sign a document certifying that her share would be deposited in a bank under the care of the superintendent. The superintendent said there wasn't enough time, she needed the money immediately. So Washington sent a new form, requesting the sick woman sign and return it. But before anything could be signed, the woman died and was buried. Her poor and elderly mother was left to bear the expenses of her daughter's medical treatment and funeral.

Susan wanted those in Washington to know that the Omaha had had enough, that they were not to be trifled with, that they would stand up and fight for their rights. And she said so. "You can never push an Omaha down or pass a thing over his head," she warned, for "he will light on his feet facing you."

And she was one of those Omaha.

"As for myself, I shall willingly and gladly co-operate with the Indian department in anything that is for the welfare of the tribe, but I shall always fight good and hard against the department or any one else against anything that is to the tribe's detriment, even if I have to fight alone, for before my God I owe my people a responsibility."

Not long after her mother's death, Susan again became seriously ill, continuing an increasingly ominous pattern, each illness becoming a bit more serious, lasting a bit longer. By the early spring of 1909, she was so sick that she could not leave her bed for weeks on end. She was thought to be suffering from a severe case of neurasthenia, a difficult disease for doctors of the era to diagnose and one the medical community did not know a lot about. Patients with the nervous disorder often exhibited a wide range of symptoms—migraines, fatigue, a rapid heartbeat, palpitations, chest pain, clammy hands and feet, depression, and poor digestion. During the 1880s, doctors had developed a general profile of those most likely to suffer from the disease: Most often, neurasthenia seemed to surface among well-educated and cultured Americans. And extreme cases of the disorder, of nervous exhaustion, those doctors believed, could lead to an overall mental and physical collapse. Rest and withdrawal from stressful situations was the most commonly recommended cure.

Susan had many of the symptoms. She was weak and fatigued and had a difficult time digesting food, so she was forced to stay in her bedroom throughout the spring. Some weeks she was near death, and specialists were called in two or three times to examine her. For almost six weeks, a trained nurse lived with her in the large Victorian house and a local doctor often came to see her three times a day. Many did not think she would live.

And the timing didn't help. Her severe illness occurred when the people desperately needed her, when the Omaha were gearing up to fight the government's decision to extend the trust period, install a new layer of bureaucracy, and merge the Omaha and Winnebago agencies.

It wasn't until June that Susan had recovered enough to join the fight. Once she felt better, she resumed a relentless letter-writing campaign to a variety of government officials she believed were endangering the health of her tribe, whose red tape and endless regulations were bleeding the life from her people, preventing the

Omaha from leaving their own footprint on America's political and economic landscape.

For a while now, the local newspaper had been sounding the same note. "Every business action of the individual is supervised and hedged about with red tape and paternal restrictions," wrote the editor of the *Walthill Times*. The Indian "has been permitted to learn nothing . . . no comprehension of business principles . . . little incentive to prepare for citizenship."

By early fall, the letter-writing campaign had to be put on hold when a diphtheria scare overwhelmed the reservation. Schools were closed. A quarantine went into effect. The local health board examined every person with a cold, prescribed treatments, and took stringent precautions to ensure the disease did not reach the children and turn into an epidemic. "Dr. Picotte was especially active in this work and devoted practically her entire time to it," it was reported on September 17, 1909. "The community is fortunate to have her services, associated with our other two doctors on the board of health."

Later that same month, Alice Fletcher, the Harvard ethnologist who had overseen the initial Omaha allotments in 1882 and helped Susan get into both Hampton and medical college, arrived in Walthill. Almost thirty years earlier, Fletcher had come to the reservation to launch a study of the Omaha, and she and Francis La Flesche had since collaborated on a lengthy, detailed history of the Omaha Tribe that became a valuable contribution to the field of ethnography. Several tribal elders came to visit Fletcher, and one Sunday afternoon, as a guest in Susan's Victorian home on the hill overlooking Omaha Creek, she entertained about thirty local residents, regaling them with insights into Omaha religious rituals, ceremonies, and customs. "Having spent most of her life in developing this subject," the *Walthill Times* noted, "her presentation of it is fine and reveals a power and beauty in Omaha Indian character and customs. . . ."

After Fletcher's visit, Susan dove back into the volatile issue of the government imposing new layers of red tape on her people and the increasingly bitter notion of merging the Omaha and Winnebago agencies into one and locating it in Winnebago. Among the Omaha, the resentment and frustration over a single agency had reached a boiling point. It had not worked years earlier, and trying it again meant adding another ten miles from Macy to Winnebago, often in rough weather and on rough roads, an additional hardship no Omaha supported. So on December 21, a large group of angry Omaha convened a meeting to vent their frustration at the state of affairs. Before the meeting ended, they all signed a petition opposing consolidation and drafted Susan to speak on their behalf. To underscore their universal opposition to consolidation, the Omaha met again on January 4, 1910. This time, the heads of about two hundred Omaha families turned out in Macy, voting unanimously to reject the government's proposal to combine the two agencies.

But the government ignored the outcry. In early January, without fanfare or explanation, it simply declared that the two agencies representing two different tribes, with different cultures, needs, and issues, would now become one.

A few weeks later, on January 28, 1910, readers of the *Walthill Times* encountered a bold, front-page headline: OMAHA INDIAN DELEGATION GOES TO WASHINGTON, D.C. In the aftermath of their meetings, the Omaha had selected a four-person delegation to go to Washington, "empowered to secure a reversal of the plans of the Indian office in respect to the Omahas, and failing that, to take steps toward freeing the tribe from governmental supervision."

Susan was a unanimous choice to be one of four delegates

representing the Omaha in Washington. But in the early weeks of 1910, Susan wasn't feeling very well. She again suffered some of the symptoms she had come to know well—extreme fatigue and recurring problems trying to digest her food. It scared her, so she told the Omaha she didn't feel well enough to go, that she was sick and could not endure the long ride to Washington. "It makes me feel so good to know all the Omahas had so much confidence in me," she later wrote Cora Folsom, her former Hampton teacher who had become a close friend. "Their choice of me as a delegate was unanimous even the women voting and when I refused they threatened to carry me to the train and put me on." So in the end, Susan said she would go.

For the next three weeks in Washington, Susan and the other three members met off and on with Commissioner of Indian Affairs Robert Valentine, Attorney General George Wickersham, and Secretary of the Interior Richard Ballinger. Although the meetings included pointed discussions on the flawed consolidation practice and the unwieldy bureaucracy, they also began to focus more on the competency issue, on whether the Omaha were ready to assume full ownership of their own lands, on whether it was time to cut the federal apron strings and let the Omaha fend for themselves. By then, Susan had decided that time had come.

"I am fighting for the manhood of my people," she told the secretary of the interior during a face-to-face meeting on February 7. "I am fighting for those you call incompetent." Then she put the competency issue into the context of the Omaha. "Today, those most competent are those who, in spite of government restrictions, have cut loose from government supervision and managed their own affairs. Today we claim that at the end of the ten year extension the incompetents will be just as incompetent as they are today."

And if the government deemed her people incompetent, she said, it had only to look in a mirror to see why. Indian "lands are leased for him, his rents are collected for him, his bills are paid for him if the department approves them; his money is doled out to him like a pension; when he desires to purchase a horse or a blanket or a wheelbarrow or a stove, he submits his desires to the superintendent, who writes for authority to the Indian office in Washington. . . . As wards of the government we are deprived of all incentives. How can anyone grow or develop without any business experience? We are not stones—we are not driftwood. We have feelings, thoughts, hopes, ambitions, aspirations. If we lack initiative, therefore achievement, it is because we are deprived of rightful responsibilities which we are kept from assuming."

She finished by pointedly telling the interior secretary what the delegation now believed needed to be done: "We have suffered enough from your experiments—we are weary of hardships needlessly endured. . . . We have been practically robbed of our rights by the government. . . . Therefore, in the name of justice and humanity, and because we want to become a self reliant, independent, self-sustaining people, we ask for a more liberal interpretation of the law."

In the end, the Office of Indian Affairs complied, embracing a more liberal interpretation. Commissioner of Indian Affairs Robert Valentine believed the Omaha were the most advanced, the most competent, of all the tribes, and he passionately believed that forcing individual Indians to stand on their own two feet was the most expedient way to make them independent, self-sustaining citizens. So it seemed logical that Valentine created the first competency commission on the Omaha Reservation.

But there were problems. For one thing, the commission faced intense pressure from local whites clamoring for access to the Indian lands and from local governments wanting the lands released from their trust status so they could be added to the tax roll. For another, a sophisticated land syndicate had formed, waiting anxiously to snap up as much of the land as possible the instant an Indian owner was declared competent. So the commissioners got to work. By February 1, 1910, they claimed to have evaluated 605 Omaha, an astonishingly high number in such a short period. Of those, commissioners identified 294 Omaha as competent, including Susan La Flesche Picotte. And six weeks later, on March 17, 244 Omaha were all issued fee patents in a single day, patents that were rushed through, covering 20,199 acres of Indian land. "Eventually," the *Pender Times* predicted, "all this desirable farm land, as good as the best in northeastern Nebraska, will fall into the hands of whites who have awaited the move."

On April 1, 1910, the *Walthill Times* published the names of more than two hundred Omaha the commission had deemed competent, Omaha who soon would be in line to receive legal control of their allotments.

But in their haste to appease angry whites and local governments, the competency commission had conducted a deeply flawed evaluation. As a minimum competency requirement, prospective Omaha landowners had to demonstrate a solid grasp of English and be capable of self-support. And the commissioners had ended up declaring many Omaha competent who could not read, write, or speak English, who were completely incapable of managing their business affairs, and who had never been interviewed or had any of their references contacted. They had also declared more than one hundred Omaha competent who had begged the commissioners not to do so, who had said they were not yet ready and feared they would lose their land as a result.

By year's end, 60 to 70 percent of the Indian-owned land had been sold and half of the owners were destitute, having spent all of the money from the sale. By 1912, 90 percent of those the commission had declared competent two years earlier had sold their land, 8 percent had mortgaged it, and 2 percent had managed to keep it. In November of that year, an inspector with the Office of Indian Affairs filed his report on the Omaha Agency. "The work of the [1910] commission was not a success," he concluded.

In January 1908, before the owner had officially moved in, Susan's new home was now listed in the Walthill telephone exchange. In two decades of caring for her people, she had gone from making house calls on foot to horseback to buggy to automobile. And her people had gone from looking for a light in her window to calling her on the phone. For five months—from September 1910 through January 1911—Susan kept a meticulous diary noting her activities each day, a diary that reflects there often was little silence between phone calls and door knocks.

SEPT. 22 1910:

Very rainy and cloudy. Little Cook came in to ask about Willie Grant's condition. He had 3 abscesses in bowel and was operated on yesterday. Jim Wolf phoned that he was going up to Rosalie to see Mr. Kneale. Herbert Johnson came in to see about getting funds for clothes before he went back to Genoa. . . . Saw Frank Cox about Edna's baby—told him about proper feeding of it.

SEPT. 27 1910:

Cold & clear.

Mrs. Sheridan & 3 girls had breakfast with me. Wanted me to talk to Jolue and see if he wouldn't do better. Promised her I would do so. Had a long talk with R. this a.m., called on Mrs. H. and played some hymns for her. . . . Called on Mrs. P. On way back met Miss Issackson. . . . Wallace took dinner with me. Went to see him off at train. Got a telegram from Chase saying he'd be here tomorrow. . . . Gave Mr. Beith $50.00 from my work for the Board to be used toward the church building. Mary Robinson wanted me to get children's trust funds for her. Interpreted for Jan Warner. . . . Nellie Springer wants her heirship interest looked up for her. Did so.

OCT. 3 1910:

Got baby's breakfast and gave him his medicine. . . . Wrote letter about my heirship patents in fee. Mrs. R. Harlan asked me to phone for her to see about rent money. . . . Thos. P. Webster asked me to write a letter for him to Dept. & Kneale. . . . Phoned Macy for Frank Cox who wants his rent money. . . . Good Old Man wants me to see about his funeral expenses being paid out of his wife's money. . . . Teresa Blackbird spoke to me about some lots she wanted to buy. . . . Isaac Preston asked me to phone for him to Macy to get authority to buy a team.

OCT. 4 1910:

White Horse came in to see me about the plans for the new house. . . . Dan Wolf and his wife came in. He wanted me to interpret for him in his will. His wife asked me to look after her lands; that she had received no rent for 2 years. . . . Theresa B. came in to ask me to phone for her to Govt. Office about the girls' money. Wrote a letter for Nedair Walker to T.L. Sloan in Washington asking him to get her patent in fee to Jas. Walker (heirship) land. Had [Tribal] Council in P.M.

NOV. 5 1910:

Fred Grant came up before breakfast to tell me Dan wanted to see me. I went down and he asked me to help him get Fred who is 17 into school. I talked with Fred and told him an education was necessary to make the most of himself. Dan also said they wanted to get their old clothes, 3 beds and 2 chairs out of the hotel. . . . The hotel and surroundings were in fearful condition. Filthy and unsanitary. I shall serve notice on them this afternoon to clean up, or be fined. . . . Treated Noah for ear, face and neck infection.

NOV. 20 1910:

Tended to Noah who is almost well—Drafted letter for Emma H. Guitar. Dora Edwards came in for me to draft letter for her. Robt Mitchell came in for prescription for a bad cold on the lungs—gave him prescription for cough syrup as well as for external application. . . . Bertram came in later and said the baby was very bad and was sick all night. Drove over with Bertram. Found Amelia Lovejoy and Susan Lovejoy both there. They had a big tent set up and were getting ready for a mescal meeting. We attended to the baby and drove over to Macy to see Leon's wife who was a little better. The temp. was 100 and pulse 98.

NOV. 21 1910:

Chas. Robinson and wife came in to see about my renting a home for them. Called up Jos. But he wanted too much rent for no conveniences. . . . Called up Mr. Baiff about church windows. Went to Little Cooks with Emmett and June to settle dispute with their renter. . . . I did interpreting. Got back at 5:15. Sam Grant said his wife was very ill and she wanted me to come over. Took Dr. Reau with me and went in auto. Was dark. She was in bad shape—the baby was alright. I made examination and we told them they must be brought into hospital in am. . . . I was all worn out and got very sick. Went to bed as soon as I got home supperless.

DEC. 23 1910:

Stopped at hospital to see Clema—her baby had died at 1 a.m. She asked me to pray with her so I did so. She seemed comforted by it and I talked with her and asked her to take care of herself. Y.F. asked me to interpret so did Solomon Woodhull, I sent off some gifts in mail and attended to Caryl's ear. I sent over box of apples to Xmas tree at church for the Indian children and Mr. Buck took them over for nothing. I asked Jas. Grant for donation to the church and he said he would give $8.00. Clema and Parrish took their baby home. Was busy all afternoon.

JAN. 10 1911

In afternoon went to U.S. Grant's funeral. There was a large gathering there—about 50 bearers in procession. I rode with his wife and Rice & Henry so I could help them. It turned very cold up at the grave—I spoke a few words at the grave. We got very cold riding home and got home about 5:20.

Amid the phone calls and door knocks, wedged between pre-scriptions and transcriptions, juggling graveside services, ear infections, and sick babies, along with drafting letters, singing hymns, and filing health notices, Susan had plenty of other things to keep her busy. There were meetings of the Thurston County Medical Society, which she helped start, and the Walthill Health Board. She had other duties as a member of the Nebraska State Medical Society, and for three years, she served as chair of the Ne-braska Federation of Women's Clubs. She was still active as presi-dent of the Missionary Society, and she continued to preside at sermons, Sunday school, weddings, and funerals. And then, too, there were her two sons to care for. She had wanted to send both to Hampton, but they were too young. So on a September day in 1910, she, fourteen-year-old Caryl, and twelve-year-old Pierre boarded a train in Bancroft and headed to Lincoln, where the two boys entered the Nebraska Military Academy.

In March 1911, three members of the Nebraska Legislature's judiciary committee came to Walthill. One afternoon they were all gathered at the large Victorian home on Taft Street. Inside, Su-san and about sixty Omaha were waiting to tell the legislators what they thought of a controversial bill that had been proposed. After a good deal of time had been eaten up by a loud, long-winded committee chairman who vigorously opposed the bill, Susan stood up. First, speaking in the language of her people, she quietly explained the bill to all the Omaha gathered in her home. And it was an important bill, she said next, for a very specific reason: The proposal—called the Gallagher Bill—made legitimate heirs of all those born under existing marriages based on Indian customs. In other words, Susan explained, even those children born to a father with more than one wife would still be legally recognized as heirs. And with so many heirs, she continued in the Omaha language, it would be that much more difficult for land swindlers to walk away with the people's land.

Two months later, Susan turned her attention to what had long been her principal focus: elevating the importance of public health among the Omaha. As had been the case with whiskey peddlers, land swindlers, agency consolidations, bureaucratic incompetence, and trust period extensions, she now launched an impassioned campaign to educate her people on the multiple horrors of tuberculosis, the communal drinking cup, and the common housefly. On April 30, 1911, Walthill's Indian doctor offered a major address on tuberculosis. She explained what it was and stressed the importance of how to avoid getting it. She opened her talk at the Presbyterian church that chilly spring evening by saying the disease killed about two hundred thousand Americans annually. How could the deadly TB germs be destroyed? By burning all discharges, she urged. "The sick person can spit into paper cups that cost a penny apiece, or into newspapers or cheese cloth handkerchiefs," she said. "Protect yourself by having your own drinking cup that you can take wherever you go." She suggested the Omaha stay outside as much as possible and reconfigure their bedrooms to let in as much sunlight and fresh air as possible. "You won't catch cold and you'll feel like a new being in the morning," she said.

Then she went after the common housefly with a vengeance, an insect "who breeds in filth, who lives on filth and who carries it wherever he goes." To drive home her point, she created a graphically illustrated poster to underscore the importance of screens on doors and windows. And she tried to drive home both points with a series of parables. "Last summer," she began, "I saw a case of tuberculosis. It was a hot day and the room was swarming with flies. . . . On the floor sat a dear little baby eating a cookie that was covered with flies. I told the mother of the danger to the baby and to keep it out of the sic[k] room and to keep out the flies. The sick boy died in a few weeks and the baby was buried two months ago."

In the years since Henry's death, Susan had begun to look at things less and less through a white lens and more and more through a red lens. It showed in the way she increasingly relied on the language of her people, in the social gatherings in her home, in the kinds of people she invited, in the things she had said in the churches and to federal officials in Washington and to Nebraska legislators. And now it had begun to show in another way. For a number of years in the opening decade of the twentieth century, she had had many conversations with the Omaha, in their rural homes and in the larger communities, old and young, progressives and traditionalists. And she had often heard, much more than she expected, about the many improvements the peyote religion had made to their lives, to the lives of people she trusted. So she began to back off her original objections to the peyote religion, to take into account what she'd been told and what she could see with her own eyes—that they were telling the truth.

One spring the Nebraska legislators had come to her home in Walthill, so in another spring Susan decided to visit them in their home in the capital city of Lincoln. When she walked in, most of them were leaning back in their chairs, feet propped up on their desks, hats on their heads. "I have never addressed an assemblage of such barbarians in my life," Susan snapped. Soon, the men took their feet off their desks, their hats off their heads, and sat up. She had come with a specific agenda: to fight to continue the limited use of peyote in the traditional ceremonies of the Omaha—but also to adamantly ask for an outright ban on all alcohol. Unlike peyote, she told the legislators, whiskey had no cultural or religious significance to the Omaha. The legislators agreed with her on the peyote, allowing the Omaha to continue to use it in their religious ceremonies. But they said they could do nothing about the alcohol—they had no power to stop automobiles from crossing reservation boundaries.

In the September 15, 1911, issue of the *Walthill Times,* under the heading "Local News," a single sentence appeared halfway down the column of type: "Mrs. H. L. Keefe was in Omaha Sunday at the bedside of Dr. Picotte."

Many months earlier, in the midst of the long dispute on agency consolidation and extending the trust period, Susan had written a long, personal letter to Cora Folsom, her Hampton teacher and close friend.

"The Omahas depend on me so," she wrote, "and I just have to take care of myself till this fight is over."

10

▼▼▼

A Beginning and an End

So many times Susan had imagined what it could be like.

For years, she could not stop thinking about a hospital for her people, about all the possibilities, about the difference it could make.

She could see the hospital in her dream, could see what it would look like. Lots of wide-open space. Lots of windows and sunlight. Lots of fresh air. And there would be lilacs. Yes, of course. There would have to be lilacs. That much she was certain of.

Not long after Henry's death, not long after she and her mother and the boys all arrived in their new home overlooking Walthill, Susan set out to transform the dream into reality. And she soon discovered that it would require a great effort on her part to make it happen.

For a while, it seemed her old friends from the Connecticut Indian Association would make it happen. But in the end their interest in helping build a new hospital collapsed under the weight of financial and other concerns. Then it looked as though an order of sisters from the Catholic Church would come through, would finance a hospital specifically to serve the Omaha people. But that, too, eventually fell apart.

In the end, the two disappointments made Susan more

determined to achieve the dream. So she soon began to do what she had often done to focus her energy and passion on a specific target: She began an ambitious letter-writing campaign, using the U.S. mail to knit together an alliance of East Coast friends to help her bring the dream to life. She also took to the stump, spreading the word in local churches and town hall meetings and in the local paper, using every outlet to promote how valuable a local hospital would be to her people.

And then she contacted the Presbyterian Board of Home Missions, the people who in 1905 had appointed her as their missionary to the Omaha, the ones she had worked long hours for at the Blackbird Hills Presbyterian Church. In January 1911, several mission board members arrived on the Omaha Reservation and Susan made a personal appeal, telling them how the Omaha were suffering, how so many babies were dying, telling them how desperately her people needed a local hospital, that the hardscrabble roads to the nearest hospitals in Omaha and Sioux City made for a long and hazardous journey. This time, her plea for help found a receptive audience—especially Susan Pingry, an influential board member who had also taught Susan at the Elizabeth Institute for Young Ladies in New Jersey thirty years earlier.

Several months later, the Presbyterian Board committed $8,000 to build a fully equipped, modern hospital in Walthill, in the heart of the Omaha Reservation. The Religious Society of Friends in Massachusetts, the Quakers, chipped in another $500. Charles Cadman, who had earlier performed an arrangement of Omaha tribal music in Susan's home, gave a benefit concert in Pittsburgh, donating $100 in concert proceeds to the hospital effort. Soon, a Sioux City Presbyterian church offered to equip and furnish one of the new hospital rooms. Another organization in the city of Omaha agreed to do the same. Then several Sioux City firms pledged to help with the kitchen and some of the wards. A Walthill

businessman offered to furnish another of the rooms. Several local women's organizations agreed to help pay for some of the
equipment and for upkeep and maintenance. Two prominent
residents sponsored the operating and obstetrics rooms, and still
others agreed to consider building a complete bacteriologic laboratory to get a jump on serious diseases and infections. Finally,
Walter and Marguerite Diddock donated an acre of land for the
hospital site, pushing the overall package of gifts to more than
$9,000.

Originally, the idea had been to build a hospital for the exclu-
sive benefit of the Omaha people. But the gift had grown so large, it
was decided that Walthill's new hospital would serve both Indians
and whites, would welcome anyone who was sick. And once built,
the local newspaper reported, the new hospital would come under
the direction of Dr. Susan La Flesche Picotte, "whose untiring
endeavor was most largely instrumental in securing the gift."

On January 8, 1913, a throng of prominent citizens and benefactors gathered high atop a hill in the northwest corner of the village,
staring at the same thing as Walthill's Indian doctor: a white, one-
and-one-half-story building, amply supplied with large windows
and screened-in porches, built without a penny of public tax dollars, the first modern hospital in Thurston County, now open for
business to young and old, Indian and white, farmers and lawyers,
to anyone about to deliver a baby, who needed stitches, had a broken ankle, a troublesome cough, a worrisome rash, fever and
chills, red and itchy eyes, or needed any other type of medical attention, anyone who might need a personal touch, in Omaha or
English.

It had taken all of 1912 to build and now it was finished, so all
the local dignitaries, the Indians and whites, the preachers and

tribal elders who convened for the formal dedication that bitterly cold Wednesday afternoon—all marveled at the imposing structure, forty-two feet by seventy-eight feet, modeled in part after a tuberculosis sanitarium. They all saw the double-hung sash windows and the low-pitched gabled, wood-shingled roof with the wide eaves that sheltered the hospital's most distinctive feature: a spacious porch that ran along the entire east side of the building. The porch resembled a colonnade consisting of nine round-arched openings, each fully screened. In the ceiling of the porch were numerous hooks for hammocks to help ensure the recovering patients had plenty of opportunities for fresh air. Before the official hospital tour began, a Methodist Episcopal pastor opened the dedication ceremony with a prayer in English. Afterward, an Omaha elder closed the ceremony with a prayer in the language of his people.

Harry L. Keefe, the village's first attorney and a president of the Nebraska Farm Bureau, was there that day. Keefe, who would soon become an army major in the War to End All Wars, had once loaned Susan and Marguerite office space for their traveling library, and both he and his wife had since become close friends of Walthill's doctor. Keefe was impressed with the spacious thirty-nine-room hospital, with the two general wards offering six beds each and the five private wards. He and the other guests that day saw the new hospital's maternity ward, operating room, two bathrooms, full kitchen, linen closets, infants' room, and reception office. On the first floor, they could see that every room had at least one window and that the rooms on the ends of the floor had two windows each, the operating room being the only exception. That room had five windows on the north side and four more on the east side—a firm reflection of how strongly the boss believed in the healing powers of sunlight and fresh air.

For several hours that day, as the guests made their way through the hospital, they could also see that almost all of the rooms had been furnished by special gifts from private donors: On each door was a card identifying the donor. When the group made its way to the operating room, they could read the card that had been placed on the door: "Joseph La Flesche Operating Room: Furnished by Mrs. W. T. Diddock and Dr. Susan La Flesche Picotte in memory of their father who was the last of the Omaha chiefs." A little while later, the invited guests arrived at one of the two obstetrics rooms, a room "to be known as the Dr. Susan La Flesche Picotte Room." It had been furnished by Harry Keefe.

As much as she loved the new hospital, Walthill's doctor also felt strongly about teaching her people the value of not needing the hospital. "I believe in prevention of disease and hygiene care more than I do in giving or prescribing medicine," she had said, "and my constant aim is to teach those two things, particularly to young mothers." So at her urging there were now going to be several new classes at the hospital, classes that would teach the Omaha how to eat healthier foods, classes on all manner of preventive health care.

But when they were sick, the residents of Thurston County came to the new hospital on the hill in droves, Indian and white patients alike, patients who had never been to a hospital before, patients encouraged to seek treatment by Dr. William Ream and other doctors in the area. Two years after it opened, the annual report reflected the scope of the hospital's success: By then, a total of 448 patients had been treated. Of those, 168 had been hospitalized in one of the wards—and 126 of those were Indian patients. The remaining 280 had been treated and sent on their way. Over time, in the room with the nine windows, inside the Joseph La Flesche Memorial Operating Room, his youngest daughter operated on every member of the La Flesche family still living on the reservation her father helped create when he signed the treaty of 1854.

"My greatest desire in having the hospital built," Susan told the *South Sioux City Star,* "was to save the little children." For almost a quarter century, the doctor who oversaw the care of these patients had been forced to go out and find the little children and their mothers and their grandparents, forced to fan out on endless medical missions across the large reservation, covering many miles in all directions, in all seasons, in all kinds of weather. And now, she could walk out the front door of her home, go north five blocks, and the sick children and their mothers and their grandparents and all the other patients would find her—inside the beautiful new hospital high on a hill on Matthewson Street, overlooking all of Walthill.

The dream had become real.

As real as the row of lilacs she soon planted near the screened-in porch, the ones that are still there, that still bloom in the Moon in Which the People Plant, the ones that signal each May that spring is in full bloom across Thurston County, across all the Great Plains.

By the dawn of the nineteenth century, when Lewis and Clark were working their way up the Missouri River, one in every seven people who had ever lived—worldwide—had died of tuberculosis.

Throughout the nineteenth century and into the twentieth, tuberculosis had also devastated dozens of Indian tribes, tribes with no resistance to the disease and no vaccine to treat or prevent it. In 1912, of 42,645 Indians examined for tuberculosis, 6,870—or about 16 percent—had active tuberculosis. That year, according to the annual report of the commissioner of Indian affairs, the overall death rate among Indians was 160 percent of that for all other groups in the United States, and their mortality rate for tuberculosis was three and a half times greater than that for all

other Americans. Two years earlier, in his 1910 report, the superintendent of the Omaha Reservation had identified tuberculosis
as the most serious problem among the Omaha.

It was a devastating disease, and the multitude of problems it
caused was not lost on the Omaha community's Indian doctor. In
1912, while the new hospital was being built, and for several years
afterward, Susan renewed her relentless campaign to ban all communal drinking cups and crack down on the menace of houseflies
and the diseases they carried. For three years, she used her position as chairman of the State Health Committee of the Nebraska
Federation of Women's Clubs to eventually get a state law through
the legislature banning communal cups. Not long afterward, the
communal cups gave way to sanitary drinking fountains in the
local schools and disposable cups and spoons in the local stores.
To help eliminate the fly problem, she urged her people to cover
their food, screen their doors and windows, and douse fly-breeding
grounds with kerosene and lime.

But she saved most of her energy for intensifying the battle
against her people's deadliest enemy: tuberculosis, the disease that
had killed T.I. and Marguerite's husband and contributed to the
death of her husband and countless others, both Indian and white.
For years, she had waged this war—in the newspaper, at local
churches, in countless letters, in her crusade against communal
cups and common houseflies—but now she was bent on taking it
to another level. Although deaf in one ear, increasingly frail and
weak, and unable to get out of bed many days, Susan devoted endless hours while the hospital was being built and after it opened to
educating both Indians and whites on prevention and awareness.

On April 29, 1914, she wrote a lengthy letter to Commissioner
of Indian Affairs Cato Sells, laying out her detailed plan to educate every Omaha Indian on how to avoid the deadly disease. To
help out, she asked the commissioner if she could borrow the

department's comprehensive tuberculosis exhibit, which she intended to take to public gatherings of the Omaha that summer, showing them the many ways they could prevent TB. She told him she had worked among the Omaha for more than twenty-five years, knew their language and customs, and had been the Presbyterian missionary for the last nine years. She said she had given lectures on the topic in the Indian church in Macy and in the white churches of Walthill and had scattered her fly posters all over both communities. She told him she had stood out on the street one day for two hours in bitter cold, pacing back and forth, calling out to passersby, eventually convincing about eighty people—half Indian and half white—to come in and listen to her lecture on disease prevention. If she could get the department's exhibit, she said, there'd be no reason she couldn't reach many more people.

"I would like to reach every family this summer with the slides. . . . I want your office to let me have what can be used in the field. I won't keep them long," she wrote.

In her letter, she suggested that tuberculosis, communal drinking cup, and fly eradication lectures be given in all of the Indian schools. For years, she had been frustrated by the infrequent and often careless examinations of students at government boarding schools, so she also suggested to the commissioner that all Indian children in government schools be examined monthly for the disease. And then she explained why. She had recently diagnosed a young girl with tuberculosis, but the girl had come to her too late and died in six weeks. Despite all her precautions, Susan wrote, the girl had infected her mother and grandmother, and they both died. "There is no telling how many of these infected in that large school . . . could have been prevented by proper examination," she told the commissioner. "It is so terribly hard to see the people undergoing the hardships from a civilization new to them. I believe a personal visit from you in the near future would be a great encouragement to them; a word from you would go a great ways, and I hope you will come."

Despite her pleas, the exhibit never arrived, nor did the commissioner. And neither did the monthly examinations. So Susan started doing them herself, conducting the often tedious and exhausting work of screening every student in the Walthill schools for tuberculosis—for free.

Before the year ended, while foreign armies across the sea slaughtered one another along a 450-mile western front of barbed wire, snipers, machine-gun nests, mortars, and mustard gas, word had slowly begun to spread from a small railroad village in northeast Nebraska to Pittsburgh and Boston, to New Haven and Philadelphia, to Elizabeth, New Jersey, and Hampton, Virginia. And not long afterward, messages and notes and cards conveying the personal thoughts of well-wishers up and down the East Coast began to arrive at the home of Marguerite La Flesche Diddock.

Susan's first operation was in February 1915.

The bone disease that had begun in her ears many years earlier had now spread throughout much of her face, bringing with it a terrible pain. It was too far advanced, too complicated, for the local doctors at her hospital. She needed a specialist, so she was taken to Omaha's Methodist Hospital to see Dr. Harold Gifford, a former dean of the Omaha Medical College, a prominent surgeon who specialized in facial and ophthalmic surgery.

In those days, no one knew for sure what to call Susan's disease. Initially, some referred to it as "decay of the bones." Later, it was said to be bone cancer. When Dr. Gifford opened her up on that winter day, he saw how far the disease had spread and he knew she would need more operations. He removed some of the infected bones in her face and then closed the incisions, fearful of the danger additional surgeries posed for his frail patient. And fearful of what would happen if he didn't perform them. The operation seemed to relieve much of her pain, but her condition remained critical.

The second operation was in late March.

Dr. Gifford removed more of the diseased bones in her face and sewed her back up. She was listed in satisfactory condition, and not long after the second operation she sent a card to Marguerite, telling her older sister she was better, she was improving, she was getting there, but slowly.

Two months later, on June 2, 1915, Susan's youngest son, Pierre, graduated from the Nebraska Military Academy in Lincoln. The seventeen-year-old was class vice president, had excelled in several varsity sports, and, like his mother, graduated as the salutatorian.

That same month, a relative sent Francis La Flesche a letter. In it, he gave his uncle, the ethnographer back east, the latest medical news from home: Dr. Gifford said Susan was fading rapidly. He did not think she would live another month.

But June came and went, and Susan was still alive. By midsummer, she was back in her beloved Victorian home, high on the hill above her village, just a few blocks from her hospital, across the street from her sister. It was summer, and so her boys were back home, too. Pierre, a new military school grad, and nineteen-year-old Caryl, home from Bellevue College, still thinking he might follow his mother, still thinking about a medical career.

Across the street, Marguerite's daughter was also back from school.

Margie and Caryl were the oldest children in each of their families. They had spent years living across the street from each other, and now the two cousins were attending the same college in Bellevue. That summer and into the fall, Margie and Caryl stayed close by Susan's side.

By summer's end, the pain was becoming unbearable, coming in waves day and night, never letting up. She was scared and alone. She never wanted Caryl and Margie to leave the room. And they seldom did. Across the street, her sister spent long days in the kitchen, meticulously preparing the few foods Susan could keep down. Marguerite would cook them and give them to her daughter, and Margie would cross the street and take them up to her aunt's room. She needed medical attention every day now, and her oldest son was the one she trusted most; so every day it was Caryl who gave his mother the medicines and hypodermics.

"Dr. Picotte has made a decided improvement and is much stronger today than she was at the beginning of the week," the *Walthill Times* told its readers on September 3, 1915. "The prolonged pain of the past few months has reduced her strength to a degree that makes improvement slow."

And then one day that autumn a package arrived at 100 Taft Street in Walthill, Nebraska. It had come from Paris.

Born in Poland forty-eight years earlier, the young Marie Curie had been forced to study underground because women were not allowed at the University of Warsaw. So she moved to France in 1891 to continue her studies, eventually becoming the first woman to receive a Ph.D. from a French university and the first female professor at the Sorbonne. She was a pioneer in radiation research and the first woman to win a Nobel Prize. In 1911, she became the only woman ever to win the Nobel Prize twice—in two different fields, one in physics, the other in chemistry. Her long years of research had led to the discovery of radium, and by the time World War I entered its second year, Curie was actively promoting radium as a way to diminish pain and suffering and championing its therapeutic qualities as a potential cancer cure.

For so long, Susan's sister and her husband, Walter Diddock, had felt so helpless, so frustrated, that they could not do something, that they could not find a way to relieve Susan's pain and suffering. By then, Marie Curie and her pioneering work in radioactivity and radiation therapy and its potential for cancer treatment had become well-known. So finally, Walter Diddock contacted the Nobel Prize winner. He told her about Susan and asked if there was anything she could do for his sister-in-law.

On that day when the package arrived from Paris, Margie took possession of it. Inside the package was a lead-lined box, and inside the box was a radium pellet.

It was early autumn now, early evening. About seven P.M., in an upstairs bedroom in her home, Susan struggled to eat the food her sister had prepared. About three hours later, she began drifting in and out of consciousness, the pain in her face and bones, in her ears, and down her spine unrelenting. Her youngest son tried his best to care for his mother. Marguerite and her daughter Margie were at her side. Caryl was rushing home from Bellevue. They could all see how weak she was, the contortions in her face, the horrible pain. Losing consciousness, fighting to stay with them, awake for a while, then drifting off again.

In the quiet of the darkened upstairs bedroom, the family moved closer to her side, trying to comfort Susan, trying to ease her pain and suffering with their words. They told her of the remarkable life she had led, of how much she had meant to her people, how it was said there was hardly an Omaha alive she had not helped or treated, that hundreds of both whites and Indians owed their lives to her medical skills, her nursing, her kind and gentle care.

Susan didn't seem to understand. As the cancer closed in and the pain became unbearable, she struggled to respond to them in the final hours.

"I cannot see how any credit is due me," she told them. "I am only thankful that I have been called and permitted to serve. I feel blessed for that privilege beyond measure."

The agency doctor arrived about ten P.M. He examined Susan and then placed the radium pellet in her ear. But it accidentally slipped, deep down into the canal, and it took several hours to get it out.

Throughout the long ordeal to retrieve it, Susan was in terrible pain.

Saturday, September 18, 1915, the *Walthill Times*:

"Dr. Picotte passed away at 1:00 o'clock this morning, after a period of many months of suffering from an incurable malady of the bones of the head and face."

The next day, Sunday morning, there was little room to stand inside the spacious Victorian home on the corner of Taft Street.

By ten thirty A.M., they had filled the stairway leading to the bedrooms. The dining room was packed, the parlor overflowing. In the middle of the large reception room, near the fireplace mantel where she had inscribed the Scottish proverb, Susan lay in a half-open casket, surrounded by a wall of flowers and wreaths, family and friends. Nearby, a small church choir sang hymns while they waited for everyone to enter and for the service to begin.

Three Presbyterian ministers conducted the simple ceremony, filled with testimonials to the spirit and the character and the self-less sacrifices of the woman who lay before them. Reverend George Beith, pastor of the Blackbird Hills Presbyterian Church, led the service, telling all those gathered of the many years he and Susan had worked together, of her steadfast devotion to the Omaha people. Two other Presbyterian ministers followed, one from the Board of Home Missions, who praised Susan for her inspirational qualities, saying he could not bear to accept her resignation as missionary even when her failing health made it impossible for her to continue. When the three ministers finished, an elder of the Omaha Tribe offered a closing prayer for Susan in the language of their people.

Harry Keefe did not speak at the funeral. The village lawyer reserved his thoughts on his close friend for the following week, when the local paper had to add an extra page to accommodate the flood of letters and condolences. Keefe shared his feelings for Susan in a lengthy front-page memorial to his longtime friend.

"We are confronted here with a character rising to greatness and to great deeds out of conditions which seldom produce more than mediocre men and women, achieving great and beneficent ends over obstacles almost insurmountable," Keefe wrote. "In her death the Indians lose their best and truest friend; the community and the state sustains an irreparable loss; and there is ended one of the most fruitful, unselfish and useful lives."

After the Sunday morning funeral service, later that afternoon, the inner circle of Susan's closest family and friends began the journey from Walthill to Bancroft. When they arrived in the community where she and Henry and the boys had lived for many years, a large crowd swarmed around her casket, people whose babies she'd delivered, whose fevers she had cured, whose broken arms she had mended.

They continued on, a mile south of town, to the cemetery where she had been many times before. After a graveside service by the Eastern Star, she was placed beside her husband, not far from the father who had insisted on a good education, not far from the ailing mother whom she had cared for on her couch in the big home on Taft Street, not far from the oldest sister who had forced her to learn English so many years ago in the little house they all shared, the one who had been the first to go to the white man's schools in the East, who had helped at Wounded Knee, who had crusaded tirelessly for Indian citizenship, not far from the sister who had so many children and died so young, the one she had written so many letters to while studying to be a doctor in Philadelphia, the sister she had given medical advice to and considered a second mother.

By the time the grave was covered, it was late on the afternoon of September 19, 1915, and Susan was home.

Bibliography

1. BOOKS, ARTICLES, AND PERIODICALS

Books

Abram, Ruth J., ed. *"Send Us a Lady Physician": Women Doctors in America, 1835–1920.* New York: W. W. Norton & Co., 1985.

Boughter, Judith A. *Betraying the Omaha Nation, 1790–1916.* Norman: University of Oklahoma Press, 1998.

Bradford, C. J., and Laine Thom. *Dancing Colors: Paths of Native American Women.* San Francisco: Chronicle Books, 1992.

Brown, Marion Marsh. *Homeward the Arrow's Flight: The Story of Susan La Flesche [Dr. Susan La Flesche Picotte].* Grand Island, Nebr.: Field Mouse Production, 1995.

Clarke, Edward H. *Sex in Education; or, A Fair Chance for the Girls.* Boston: James R. Osgood & Co., 1873.

Clay, Mary, Bertha Wolfe, and Clifford Wolfe, Sr. *Stories from Our Elders.* Illustrated by Thurman Cook. Macy, Nebr.: Macy School Press, 1988.

Clifton, James A. *Being and Becoming Indian: Biographical Studies of North American Frontiers.* Prospect Heights, Ill.: Dorsey Press, 1989.

Cutter, Irving S. *Dr. John Gale: A Pioneer Army Surgeon.* Springfield, Ill.: Schneff & Barnes, Printers, 1931.

Dorsey, James Owen. *The Ꞓegiha Language—Myths, Stories, and Letters.* Washington, D.C.: Government Printing Office, 1890.

———. *Omaha Sociology.* New York: Johnson Reprint Corporation, 1970.

Du Bois, W. E. B. *The Souls of Black Folk.* New York: New American Library, 1969.

Ferris, Jeri. *Native American Doctor: The Story of Susan La Flesche Picotte.* Minneapolis: Carolrhoda Books, 1991.

Fletcher, Alice C., and Francis La Flesche. *The Omaha Tribe.* Vol. 1. Lincoln: University of Nebraska Press, 1972.

———. *The Omaha Tribe.* Vol. 2. Lincoln: University of Nebraska Press, 1992.

Gale, Kira. *The Story of Trading Posts in the Omaha—Council Bluffs Area.* Omaha: River Junction Press, 2011.

Giffen, Fannie Reed, and Susette La Flesche Tibbles. *Oo-Mah-Ha Ta-Wa-Tha (Omaha City).* Illustrated by Susette La Flesche Tibbles. Lincoln, Nebr.: Published by the authors, 1898.

Green, Norma Kidd. *Iron Eye's Family: The Children of Joseph La Flesche.* Lincoln, Nebr.: Johnson Publishing Company, 1969.

Hale, Edward Everett, ed. *Lend A Hand: A Journal of Organized Philanthropy.* Vol. 4: *1889.* Boston: J. Stilman Smith & Co., 1889.

———. *Lend A Hand: A Record of Progress.* Vol. 11: *July–December 1893.* Boston: J. Stilman Smith & Co., 1893.

Hoxie, Frederick E., Peter C. Mancall, and James H. Merrell, eds. *American Nations: Encounters in Indian Country, 1850 to the Present.* New York: Routledge, 2001.

Klein, Ann G. *A Forgotten Voice: A Biography of Leta Stetter Hollingsworth.* Scottsdale, Ariz.: Great Potential Press, 2002.

La Flesche, Francis. *The Middle Five: Indian Schoolboys of the Omaha Tribe.* Lincoln: University of Nebraska Press, 1978.

Laubin, Reginald and Gladys. *The Indian Tipi: Its History, Construction and Use.* Norman: University of Oklahoma Press, 1989.

Lindsey, Donal F. *Indians at Hampton Institute, 1877–1923.* Urbana and Chicago: University of Illinois Press, 1995.

Mark, Joan. *A Stranger in Her Native Land: Alice Fletcher and the American Indians.* Lincoln: University of Nebraska Press, 1988.

More, Ellen S. *Restoring the Balance: Women Physicians and the Profession of Medicine, 1850–1995.* Cambridge, Mass.: Harvard University Press, 1999.

Morgan, Lewis H. *Houses and House-Life of the American Aborigines.* Chicago: University of Chicago Press, 1965.

Moses, L. G., and Raymond Wilson, eds. *Indian Lives: Essays on Nineteenth- and Twentieth-Century Native American Leaders.* Albuquerque: University of New Mexico Press, 1985.

Neihardt, John G. *Black Elk Speaks: Being the Life Story of a Holy Man of the Oglala Sioux.* New York: William Morrow & Co., 1932.

———. *Patterns and Coincidences: A Sequel to All Is but a Beginning.* Columbia: University of Missouri Press, 1978.

Pascoe, Peggy. *Relations of Rescue: The Search for Female Moral Authority in the American West, 1874–1939.* New York: Oxford University Press, 1990.

Peitzman, Steven J. *A New and Untried Course: Woman's Medical College and Medical College of Pennsylvania, 1850–1998*. New Brunswick, N.J.: Rutgers University Press, 2000.

Prucha, Francis Paul, ed. *Americanizing the American Indians: Writings by the "Friends of the Indian," 1880–1900*. Lincoln: University of Nebraska Press, 1978.

Russett, Cynthia Eagle. *Sexual Science: The Victorian Construction of Womanhood*. Cambridge, Mass.: Harvard University Press, 1989.

Schlereth, Thomas J. *Victorian America: Transformations in Everyday Life, 1876–1915*. New York: HarperPerennial, 1992.

Starita, Joe. *"I Am a Man": Chief Standing Bear's Journey for Justice*. New York: St. Martin's Press, 2008.

———. *The Dull Knifes of Pine Ridge: A Lakota Odyssey*. New York: G. P. Putnam's Sons, 1995.

Tibbles, Thomas Henry. *Buckskin and Blanket Days*. Lincoln: University of Nebraska Press, 1969.

Tong, Benson. *Susan La Flesche Picotte, M.D.: Omaha Indian Leader and Reformer*. Norman: University of Oklahoma Press, 1999.

Waggoner, Josephine. *Witness: A Hunkpapha Historian's Strong-Heart Song of the Lakotas*. Lincoln: University of Nebraska Press, 2013.

Walsh, Mary Roth. *Doctors Wanted, No Women Need Apply: Sexual Barriers in the Medical Profession, 1835–1975*. New Haven, Conn.: Yale University Press, 1977.

Wanken, Helen M. *"Woman's Sphere" and Indian Reform: The Women's National Indian Association, 1879–1901*. Ann Arbor, Mich.: University Microfilms International, 1981.

Washburn, Wilcomb E. *The Assault on Indian Tribalism: The General Allotment Law (Dawes Act) of 1887*. Philadelphia: J. B. Lippincott Co., 1975.

Washington, Booker T. *Booker T. Washington's Own Story of His Life and Work*. Atlanta: J. L. Nichols & Co., 1915.

———. *Up from Slavery: An Autobiography*. Garden City, N.Y.: Doubleday & Co., 1963.

Weisner, Stephen G., and William F. Hartford, eds. *American Portraits: Biographies in United States History*. Vol. 2. Boston: McGraw-Hill, 1998.

Welsch, Roger L. *Omaha Tribal Myths and Trickster Tales*. Chicago: Swallow Press, 1981.

Wilkerson, J. L. *A Doctor to Her People: Dr. Susan LaFlesche Picotte*. Kansas City, Mo.: Acorn Books, 1999.

Williams, Neville. *Chronology of the Modern World, 1763–1965.* Harmonds-worth, UK: Penguin Books, 1975.

Wilson, Dorothy Clarke. *Bright Eyes: The Story of Susette La Flesche, an Omaha Indian.* New York: McGraw-Hill, 1974.

Wishart, David J. *An Unspeakable Sadness: The Dispossession of the Nebraska Indians.* Lincoln: University of Nebraska Press, 1994.

———. *The Fur Trade of the American West, 1807–1840: A Geographical Synthesis.* Lincoln: University of Nebraska Press, 1992.

Articles and Periodicals

Allan, James McGrigor. "On the Real Differences in the Minds of Men and Women," *Journal of the Anthropological Society of London,* 1864.

Armstrong, Samuel Chapman. "Indian School," *Southern Workman,* June 1885.

———. "Normal School," *Southern Workman,* June 1886.

———. "Of Graduates," *Southern Workman,* June 1886.

Awakuni-Swetland, Mark J. " 'Make-Believe White-Men' and the Omaha Land Allotments of 1871–1900," *Great Plains Research: A Journal of Natural and Social Sciences,* August 1, 1994.

Chilton, Richard, and Margery Coffey. *Grandfather Remembers: Dr. Susan La Flesche Picotte,* Omaha Tribal Historical Research Project, Inc., Walthill and Rosalie, Nebraska.

Cutcheon, Byron M. As quoted in *Southern Workman,* June 1886, 73.

Emmerich, Lisa E. "Margaret Laflesche Diddock: Office of Indian Affairs Field Matron," *Great Plains Quarterly* Vol. 13, no. 3 (Summer 1993).

Green, Norma Kidd. "Four Sisters: Daughters of Joseph La Flesche," *Nebraska History,* June 1964.

Hale, Edward E., D. D. "Training of Indians," *Lend A Hand* Vol. 11 (1893): 166. J. Stilman Smith & Co, Boston, Massachusetts.

Hamilton, Robert H. "Girls Tailoring Department," *Southern Workman,* June 1885.

Hauptman, Laurence M. "Medicine Woman: Susan La Flesche, 1865–1915," *New York State Journal of Medicine* 78, no. 11 (September 1978).

Indian Bulletin 6 (December 1894). Newsletter of the Connecticut Indian Association.

——— 11 (February 1897). Newsletter of the Connecticut Indian Association.

Indian's Friend. Monthly newsletter published by the Women's National Indian Association.

La Flesche, Francis. "The Past Life of the Plains Indians," *Southern Workman,* 1905.

La Flesche, Marguerite. Letter in *St. Nicholas Magazine,* September 1880.

Mathes, Valerie Sherer. "Susan Laflesche Picotte, M.D.: Nineteenth-Century Physician and Reformer," *Great Plains Quarterly* Vol. 13, no. 3 (Summer 1993).

———. "Susan LaFlesche Picotte: The First Indian Woman Physician," City College of San Francisco: Undated typescript.

McDonnell, Janet A. "Land Policy on the Omaha Reservation: Competency Commissions and Forced Fee Patents," *Nebraska History* 63 (1982).

McKee, Jim. "The Rise and Fall of Trading Posts Along the Missouri River," *Lincoln Journal Star,* July 31, 2011.

Parker, W. W. "Woman's Place in the Christian World: Superior Morally, Inferior Mentally to Man—Not Qualified for Medicine or Law—the Contrariety and Harmony of the Sexes," *Transactions of the Medical Society of the State of Virginia,* 1892.

Popular Science Monthly, December 1878.

Richards, Josephine E. "Report on Indian School," *Southern Workman,* June 1885.

Sears, Elizabeth. "Glimpses of a Woman's Work Among the Omahas," *Omaha World-Herald,* March 22, 1908.

Southern Workman. Hampton Normal and Agricultural Institute, issues of 1882–1894.

Spencer, Herbert. "Psychology of the Sexes," *Popular Science Monthly,* 1873–1874.

Stowe, Harriet Beecher. "The Woman Question," *Hearth and Home,* September 1869.

Talks and Thoughts. Hampton Normal and Agricultural Institute, issues of 1882–1886 and March 1889.

2. NEWSPAPERS

Fremont Tribune (Nebraska)
Hartford Courant (Connecticut)
New-York Daily Tribune
New York Times
Omaha Bee (Nebraska)
Omaha World-Herald (Nebraska)
Oneida Whig (New York)
Pender Times (Nebraska)

Rochester North Star (New York)
Seneca County Courier (New York)
Sioux City Journal (Nebraska)
Sioux City Star (Nebraska)
Walthill Times (Nebraska)

3. GOVERNMENT DOCUMENTS

"Address to the Lake Mohonk Conference." *Sixteenth Annual Report of the Board of Indian Commissioners, 1884.* Washington, D.C.: Government Printing Office, 1885.

Armstrong, Samuel Chapman. "Report of the Hampton School: Girls Work." *Annual Report of the Commissioner of Indian Affairs for 1884.* Washington, D.C.: Government Printing Office, 1884.

Ashley, Robert H. *Annual Report of the Commissioner of Indian Affairs for 1890.* Washington, D.C.: Government Printing Office, 1890.

———. *Annual Report of the Commissioner of Indian Affairs for 1892.* Washington, D.C.: Government Printing Office, 1892.

Department of the Interior, Office of Indian Affairs. Contract Between the Office of Indian Affairs and the Connecticut Indian Association, September 15, 1886.

"Dr. Susan LaFlesche Picote [*sic*] Memorial Hospital." National Historic Landmark Nomination. Submitted to the National Park Service on November 2, 1992.

Inquest testimony of Susan La Flesche, May 22, 1914, into the death of Harry Warner. La Flesche Family Papers. Nebraska State Historical Society, Lincoln.

Kent, M. B. *Annual Report of the Commissioner of Indian Affairs for 1876.* Washington, D.C.: Government Printing Office, 1876.

Mackey, John. *Annual Report of the Commissioner of Indian Affairs for 1905.* Washington, D.C.: Government Printing Office, 1905.

Mathewson, Charles. *Annual Report of the Commissioner of Indian Affairs for 1900.* Washington, D.C.: Government Printing Office, 1900.

"Susan La Flesche Picotte House." National Register of Historic Places, Registration Form, September 23, 2009. Nebraska State Historical Society, Lincoln, Nebraska.

Warner, Jesse. *Annual Report of the Commissioner of Indian Affairs for 1888.* Washington, D.C.: Government Printing Office, 1888.

Wilkinson, George W. *Annual Report of the Commissioner of Indian Affairs for 1884.* Washington, D.C.: Government Printing Office, 1884.

4. LETTERS AND DIARIES

Connecticut State Library, Hartford. Thomson-Kinney Collection, 1728–1923. Archives RG 69:3, descriptive report.

Fletcher, Alice C. Letter of May 21, 1886, to Rosalie La Flesche Farley. La Flesche Family Papers. Nebraska State Historical Society, Lincoln.

Heritage, Marian. Letter of June 22, 1894, to Rosalie La Flesche Farley. La Flesche Family Papers. Nebraska State Historical Society, Lincoln.

Heritage, Mrs. W. W. Letter of December 23, 1887, to Joseph La Flesche. La Flesche Family Papers. Nebraska State Historical Society, Lincoln.

Kinney, Sara Thomson. Letter of October 10, 1886, to Ed Farley. La Flesche Family Papers. Nebraska State Historical Society, Lincoln.

La Flesche Farley, Rosalie. Letter of August 24, 1882, to Alice Fletcher. La Flesche Family Papers. Nebraska State Historical Society, Lincoln.

———. Letter of January 1, 1893, to Francis La Flesche. La Flesche Family Papers. Nebraska State Historical Society, Lincoln.

———. Letter of July 29, 1895, to Francis La Flesche. La Flesche Family Papers. Nebraska State Historical Society, Lincoln.

———. Letter of November 20, 1893, to Francis La Flesche. La Flesche Family Papers. Nebraska State Historical Society, Lincoln.

La Flesche, Francis. Letter of February 4, 1901, to nephew Caryl Farley. La Flesche Family Papers. Nebraska State Historical Society, Lincoln.

———. Letter of September 27, 1886, to Ed Farley. La Flesche Family Papers. Nebraska State Historical Society, Lincoln.

La Flesche, Susan. Letter of January 12, 1887, to Rosalie La Flesche Farley. La Flesche Family Papers. Nebraska State Historical Society, Lincoln.

———. Letter of October 24, 1886, to Rosalie La Flesche Farley. La Flesche Family Papers. Nebraska State Historical Society, Lincoln.

———. Undated letter fragment c. January 1888 to Rosalie La Flesche Farley. La Flesche Family Papers. Nebraska State Historical Society, Lincoln.

Susan La Flesche Picotte diary, 1910–1911. La Flesche Family Papers. Nebraska State Historical Society, Lincoln.

5. SELECTED LETTERS FROM SUSAN LA FLESCHE

Unless otherwise noted, all letters following can be found in the La Flesche Family Papers at the Nebraska State Historical Society in Lincoln, Nebraska; the Hampton University Archives in Hampton, Virginia; or the Connecticut State Library in Hartford, Connecticut.

To Rosalie La Flesche Farley:
October 24, 1886
October 27, 1886
October 29, 1886
November 4, 1886
November 5, 1886
November 17, 1886
November 20, 1886
December 1, 1886
December 15, 1886
January 1, 1887
January 12, 1887
January 19, 1887
January 26, 1887
February 2, 1887
February 9, 1887
March 2, 1887
March 9, 1887
April 4, 1887
April 5, 1887
December 24, 1887
January 4, 1888
March 9, 1889

To Others:
August 7, 1885, Josephine Richards
April 2, 1888, Sara Thomson Kinney
November 19, 1888, Sara Thomson Kinney
December 1889, Amelia S. Quinton, President, Women's National Indian Association; reprinted in the *Indian's Friend,* December 1889
October 24, 1891, Women's National Indian Association
March 1896, Marguerite La Flesche
November 14, 1896, Sara Thomson Kinney
December 9, 1897, Josephine Richards
January 27, 1900, Thomas W. Jones [sic], Commissioner of Indian Affairs
June 24, 1909, Miss Andrews
June 27, 1909, Robert Ogden
July 2, 1909, Robert G. Valentine, Commissioner of Indian Affairs

July 13, 1909, Robert G. Valentine, Commissioner of Indian Affairs
February 15, 1910, Cora Folsom
April 29, 1914, Cato Sells, Commissioner of Indian Affairs

6. SELECTED ESSAYS AND SPEECHES BY SUSAN LA FLESCHE

"My Childhood and Womanhood." Salutatorian's Address to the Graduating
Class of 1886, Hampton Normal and Agricultural Institute, May 20, 1886.
Southern Workman, July 1886.

"My Work as Physician Among my People." Address to the Graduating Class
of 1892, Hampton Normal and Agricultural Institute, May 19, 1892. *Southern Workman,* August 1892.

"Sketches of Delightful Work." Report to the Women's National Indian Association. Women's National Institute, 1893.

7. WEB RESOURCES

Armstrong, Samuel Chapman. *History: The Hampton Normal School.* Hampton University Web site. http://www.hamptonu.edu/about/history.cfm.

Seneca Falls Convention, Web document. http://tag.rutgers.edu/wp-content
/uploads/2014/05/Seneca-Falls-Convention.pdf

Woolf, Christopher. "Historical Photos Depict Women Medical Pioneers."
Public Radio International, July 12, 2013. http://www.pri.org/stories/2013
-07-12/historical-photos-depict-women-medical-pioneers.

8. INTERVIEWS

By author unless otherwise indicated.

Don Blackbird, April 2010.

Winona Caramony, July 2015.

Chris Conn, December 2013.

Lisa Drum, September 2014.

Caroline Johnson and Meg Johnson, 2010–2015.

Jane Johnson, April 2010.

Taylor Keen, September 2014.

Tita Merrick, July 2010.

Vida Stabler, August 2010.

Wehnona Stabler, interviewed by Christine Lesiak. Nebraska Educational Television, August 8, 2014.

Mike Wolfe, July 2010.

Notes

CHAPTER 1

2 "In the beginning": Fletcher, Alice C., and Francis La Flesche, *The Omaha Tribe* 1, 70.

5 "The position of a married woman": Stowe, Harriet Beecher, "The Woman Question," *Hearth and Home*, September 1869.

6 "I cannot go": Fletcher and La Flesche, *Omaha Tribe* 1, 117.

6 "Venerable man!": Ibid., 118.

6 "I speak to you": Ibid., 119.

8 "The white people speak": La Flesche, Francis, *The Middle Five*, xx.

9 "I am like": Boughter, Judith A., *Betraying the Omaha Nation*, 33.

10 "My chiefs, braves": Fletcher and La Flesche, *Omaha Tribe* 1, 84.

14 "'My son,' Big Elk said": Giffen, Fannie Reed, *Oo-Mah-Ha Ta-Wa-Tha*, 29.

14 "My son, I give you": Ibid.

14 "The white man looks": Fletcher and La Flesche, *Omaha Tribe* 2, 638.

16 "I was always sure": Ibid., 634.

18 "In the evolutionary": Russett, Cynthia Eagle, *Sexual Science: The Victorian Construction of Womanhood*, 11.

19 "Just, therefore": *Popular Science Monthly*, December 1878.

20 "suffer under a languor": Allan, James McGrigor, *Journal of the Anthropological Society of London*, 1864.

CHAPTER 2

32 "The progress of advancement": Kent, M. B., *Annual Report of the Commissioner of Indian Affairs for 1876*, 97.

33 "Sometimes I am sorry": La Flesche, Marguerite, letter in *St. Nicholas Magazine*.

35 "We are strangers": Fletcher and La Flesche, *Omaha Tribe* 2, 638.

37 "It is either": Giffen, *Oo-Mah-Ha Ta-Wa-Tha*, 31.

38 "The officers are in charge": La Flesche, Francis, *Southern Workman*, 1905, 590.

40 "You all believe": Giffen, *Oo-Mah-Ha Ta-Wa-Tha*, 31.

45 "My kingdom is": Ibid., 36–37.

45 "I will speak": Dorsey, J. Owen, *The Œegiha Language,* 488.

46 "Take it carefully": Giffen, *Oo-Mah-Ha Ta-Wa-Tha,* 39.

46 "When you see": Ferris, Jeri, *Native American Doctor: The Story of Susan La Flesche Picotte,* 18.

50 "Once there was": Welsch, Roger L., *Omaha Tribal Myths and Trickster Tales,* 23.

56 "That hand is": Starita, Joe, *"I Am a Man,"* 151.

58 "My dear young daughters": *Walthill Times,* September 18, 1915.

CHAPTER 3

63 "I come to you": Starita, *"I Am a Man,"* 185.

64 "*This* is Minnehaha!": Ibid., 189.

64 "Take away the accident": Ibid., 192.

64 "an athletic savage": Ibid.

68 "The doctors": Tibbles, Thomas Henry, *Buckskin and Blanket Days,* 238.

70 "there is no selfishness": Starita, Joe, *The Dull Knifes of Pine Ridge,* 91.

73 "They made us many promises": Ibid., 92.

78 "those two faculties": Spencer, Herbert, *Popular Science Monthly,* 1873–1874.

80 "a determined and progressive people": Wilkinson, George W., *Annual Report of the Commissioner of Indian Affairs for 1884,* 118.

80 "No one": La Flesche Farley, Rosalie, letter to Alice Fletcher, August 24, 1882, La Flesche Family Papers.

82 "My life dwindled away": Mark, Joan, *A Stranger in Her Native Land,* 90.

CHAPTER 4

84 "I venture": Armstrong, Samuel Chapman, *Southern Workman,* June 1886, 65.

85 "160 uniform coats": Hamilton, Robert H., *Southern Workman,* June 1885, 65.

88 "felt his poverty": Du Bois, W. E. B., *The Souls of Black Folk,* 49–50.

88 "The thing to be done": Armstrong, Samuel Chapman, Hampton University Web site.

89 "I guess": Washington, Booker T., *Up from Slavery: An Autobiography,* 38.

89 "the most perfect specimen": Washington, Booker T., *Booker T. Washington's Own Story of His Life and Work,* 37.

92 "each room": Richards, Josephine E., *Southern Workman,* June 1885, 69–70.

95   "Most of us studied": Waggoner, Josephine, *Witness*, 187–88.

96   "This mingling": Armstrong, *Southern Workman*, June 1885, 64.

98   "On the Indian girl": Armstrong, Samuel Chapman, *Annual Report of the Commissioner of Indian Affairs for 1884*, 192.

100 "her legs drawn round": Fletcher and La Flesche, *Omaha Tribe* 1, 329.

101 "The intermarriage of graduates": Armstrong, *Southern Workman*, June 1886, 64.

106 "It is a great thing": Cutcheon, Byron M., *Southern Workman*, June 1886, 73.

107 "was very lovely": Fletcher, Alice, letter to Rosalie La Flesche, May 21, 1886, La Flesche Family Papers.

CHAPTER 5

109 "to rear the offspring": Abram, Ruth J., ed., *"Send Us a Lady Physician,"* 64.

110 "to discuss the": Announcement in the *Seneca County Courier*, July 14, 1848.

110 "Why, Lizzie": Seneca Falls Convention, Web document.

111 "a step backwards": Russett, *Sexual Science*, 149.

111 "In this denial": Douglass, Frederick, speech to Seneca Falls Convention, 1848.

112 "This bolt": *Oneida Whig*, August 1, 1848.

112 "A discussion": Douglass, Frederick, *North Star* (Rochester, N.Y.), July 28, 1848.

112 "When a sincere republican": Greeley, Horace, *New-York Daily Tribune*, 1848.

113 "resolutions of excommunication": Walsh, Mary Roth, *Doctors Wanted*, 72.

114 "mounted more laboratory classes": Peitzman, Steven J., *A New and Untried Course*, 77.

114 "Far from being a period": Walsh, *Doctors Wanted*, xvi.

115 "It was felt by all who took part": "Address of the Lake Mohonk Conference," *Sixteenth Annual Report of the Board of Indian Commissioners*, 1884, 37.

115 "Under this topic": Ibid.

117 "has paid me a visit": Kinney, Sara, letter to Rosalie La Flesche Farley, February 19, 1886, La Flesche Family Papers.

117 "I would say that I regard her": Armstrong, Samuel Chapman, *Hartford Courant*, June 25, 1886.

118 "a young woman": Ibid.

119   "She is gentle": Fletcher, Alice C., *Hartford Courant*, June 25, 1886.

120   "a young woman of unusual ability": Mathes, Valerie Sherer, letter from General Armstrong to the Commissioner of Indian Affairs, *Great Plains Quarterly*, August 20, 1886, 175.

120   "clothe, feed": Department of the Interior, Contract Between the Office of Indian Affairs and the Connecticut Indian Association, September 15, 1886.

CHAPTER 6

125   "You mustn't get homesick": La Flesche, Susan, letter to Rosalie La Flesche Farley, October 24, 1886.

127   "We welcome you": Ibid.

131   "Do you know": Ibid., c. January 1888.

138   "generally wanted to go": Ibid., January 12, 1887.

142   "system never does two things well": Clarke, Edward H., *Sex in Education*, 40.

142   "Miss D—— went to college": Ibid., 83.

143   "the high regard": Heritage, Mrs. W. W., letter to Joseph La Flesche, December 23, 1887.

145   "terrible scourge of measles": Warner, Jesse, *Annual Report of the Commissioner of Indian Affairs for 1888*, 170.

151   "Sometimes when": *Talks and Thoughts*, March 1889.

152   "Whenever I think": Giffen, *Oo-Mah-Ha Ta-Wa-Tha*, 40.

153   "Dr. Okami is": Walker, Dr. James B., Graduation Speech, Woman's College of Medicine, *Hartford Courant*, March 16, 1889.

154   "In competing": Wanken, Helen M., *"Woman's Sphere,"* 69; letter of Sara Kinney to Commissioner of Indian Affairs, June 29, 1887.

154   "The impulse": Walker, Graduation Speech, Woman's College of Medicine, *Hartford Courant*, March 16, 1889.

155   "Better fitted": Hale, Edward Everett, ed., *Lend A Hand*, vol. 4, 878.

CHAPTER 7

166   "have good farms": Ashley, Robert H., *Annual Report of the Commissioner of Indian Affairs for 1890*, 139.

172   "I did not know": Neihardt, John G., *Black Elk Speaks*, 276.

173   "Between the dull little village": Kinney, "In the Indian Country: Old Impressions Knocked Almost Out of Memory," *Hartford Courant*, September 22, 1891.

175 "did so with alacrity": Kinney, "In the Indian Country: Mrs. Kinney Tells of the Medicine Dance," *Hartford Courant*, October 10, 1891.

179 "But for the strange language": Ibid.

180 "claim the right": Kinney, "In the Indian Country: Old Impressions Knocked Almost Out of Memory."

181 "It is clearly evident": Ibid.

182 "But what of the future?": *Southern Workman*, June 1892, 82.

185 "Little, if any": Ashley, *Annual Report of the Commissioner of Indian Affairs for 1892*, 306.

187 "Susie has been sick": La Flesche Farley, Rosalie, letter to Francis La Flesche, January 1, 1893.

189 "She said": Ibid., November 20, 1893.

CHAPTER 8

192 "I felt as tho' ": Heritage, Marian, letter to Rosalie La Flesche Farley, June 22, 1894.

192 "since her health": *Indian Bulletin* 6 (December 1894).

193 "It was easy": Neihardt, John G., *Patterns and Coincidences*, 40.

195 "One day": Ibid., 41.

198 "Susie has been very sick": La Flesche Farley, Rosalie, letter to Francis La Flesche, July 29, 1895.

200 "Do not come": Sears, Elizabeth, "Glimpses of a Woman's Work Among the Omahas," *Omaha World-Herald*, March 22, 1908.

201 "It won't take long": *Indian Bulletin* 11 (February 1897); letter from Susan La Flesche Picotte to Sara Kinney.

201 "I stand on the borderland": Ibid.

206 "It is more than ten years": Tibbles, *Buckskin and Blanket Days*, epigraph.

207 "she was amazed": Kinney, "In the Indian Country: Mrs. Kinney Tells of the Medicine Dance."

208 "In 1894, Harry Edwards": Inquest testimony of Susan La Flesche, May 22, 1914, into the death of Harry Warner.

209 "No one can deny": La Flesche, Francis, letter to nephew Caryl Farley, February 4, 1901.

210 "Their efforts": Kinney, "In the Indian Country: Old Impressions Knocked Almost Out of Memory."

213 "So often": *New York Times*, letter from Susan La Flesche, June 8, 1907.

213 "I went": Neihardt, *Patterns and Coincidences*, 39–40.

215 "Their lives": Hale, Edward Everett, ed., *Lend A Hand* 11, July–December 1893, 166.

216 "thanks to the skill": Green, Norma Kidd, *Iron Eye's Family: The Children of Joseph La Flesche,* 148.

219 "I think you have never met her": Neihardt, *Patterns and Coincidences,* 44.

219 "is one of the greatest sources": Mathewson, Charles, *Annual Report of the Commissioner of Indian Affairs for 1900,* 277.

220 "The difficulties": Mackey, John, *Annual Report of the Commissioner of Indian Affairs for 1905,* 249.

CHAPTER 9

228 "This is not": "Omaha Indians Unite with Church," *Walthill Times,* December 6, 1907.

230 "Poor old Bancroft": "Bancroft Bids for Trade," *Walthill Times,* May 17, 1907.

235 "The evening was very pleasantly passed": "Dr. Picotte Entertains," *Walthill Times,* March 27, 1908.

235 "It was a": Sears, "Glimpses of a Woman's Work Among the Omahas," *Omaha World-Herald,* March 22, 1908.

242 "Had some stronger race": "Citizen Lo! Red Tape and Red Indian," *Walthill Times,* August 13, 1909.

248 "Every business action": Green, *Iron Eye's Family,* 156.

248 "Dr. Picotte": "Diptheria [sic] Scare Is Over," *Walthill Times,* September 17, 1909.

248 "Having spent most of her life": "Miss Fletcher Visits Walthill," *Walthill Times,* September 24, 1909.

249 OMAHA INDIAN: OMAHA INDIAN DELEGATION GOES TO WASHINGTON, D.C., *Walthill Times,* January 28, 1910.

252 "Eventually": McDonnell, Janet A., "Land Policy on the Omaha Reservation: Competency Commissions and Forced Fee Patents," *Nebraska History* 63 (1982): 401.

253 "The work": Ibid., 407.

253 "a meticulous diary": Susan La Flesche Picotte diary, 1910–1911.

258 "The sick person": "How to Protect Yourself Against Tuberculosis," *Walthill Times,* May 12, 1911.

CHAPTER 10

263 "whose untiring endeavor": "$8,500 for a Hospital in Walthill: Walthill Secures an Appropriation for Hospital," *Walthill Times,* July 21, 1911.

265 "Joseph La Flesche Operating Room": "Presbyterian Hospital Opened with Appropriate Services: Many Flattering Comments Heard on the Design and Completeness of Hospital, Now Ready for Services," *Walthill Times,* January 10, 1913.

266 "My greatest desire": *Sioux City Star,* March 30, 1989, B11.

271 "Dr. Picotte has": *Walthill Times,* September 3, 1915.

271 "And then one day": "First female Indian doctor's struggles, victories recalled," *Sioux City Journal,* undated article by Rebecca Schossow, c. 1989.

272 "On that day": Clifton, James, *Being and Becoming Indian,* 63.

273 "Dr. Picotte passed away": "Special: Dr. Susan LaF. Picotte Passes Away, Relief Comes After a Long Period of Intense Suffering," *Walthill Times,* September 18, 1915.

274 "We are confronted here": "The Mystery of Her Genius: Born in a Tipi, the Child of the Wilds Rises to Leadership in Civilization," *Walthill Times,* September 24, 1915.

Index